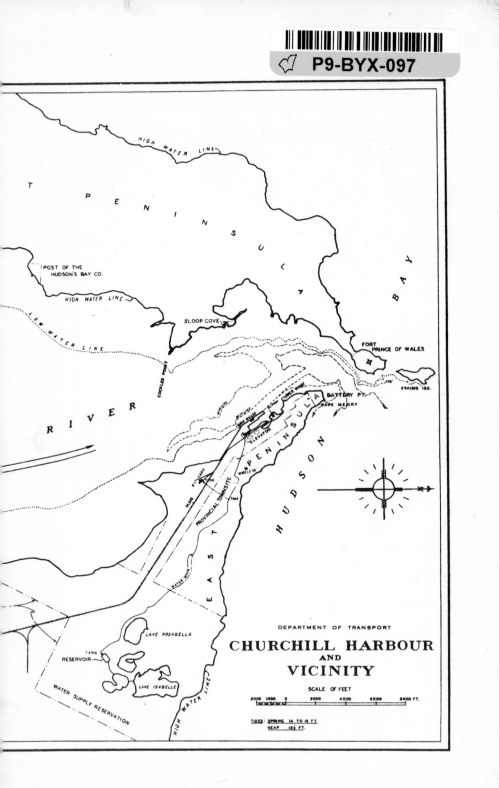

HIGH WATER LINE

T   P   E   N   I   N   S   U   L   A

B A Y

POST OF THE
HUDSON'S BAY CO.

HIGH WATER LINE

LOW WATER LINE

SLOOP COVE

FORT
PRINCE OF WALES

COCKLES POINT

ESKIMO ISO.

R I V E R

BATTERY PT.

CAPE MERRY

PIPE LINE

MILE POINT

ELEVATOR

WIRELESS

PENINSULA

HUDSON

Nº YARD
TANK

PROVINCIAL TOWNSITE

TANK

MAIN

WATER MAIN

E   A   S   T

LAKE ROSABELLA

TANK
RESERVOIR

LAKE ISABELLE

WATER SUPPLY RESERVATION

HIGH WATER LINE

DEPARTMENT OF TRANSPORT

CHURCHILL HARBOUR
AND
VICINITY

SCALE OF FEET

2000 1000 0   2000   4000   6000   8000 FT.

TIDES: SPRING 14 TO 16 FT.
NEAP 12½ FT.

THE BATTLE FOR THE BAY

The "Durham Trader" loading grain at Churchill, Manitoba. — Saskatchewan Archives.

The Battle for the Bay

By

Grant MacEwan

WESTERN PRODUCER BOOK SERVICE
SASKATOON, SASKATCHEWAN
1975

Copyright © by Grant MacEwan, 1975
Western Producer Book Service
Saskatoon, Saskatchewan
Printed and Bound in Canada
by Modern Press, Saskatoon
ISBN 0-919306-51-9

DEDICATION

To the On-To-The-Bay Association and to the Hudson Bay Route Association whose dedication contributed greatly to the realization of the northern route.
Their faith never wavered.

PREFACE

Back of it all was the conviction held by many Western people that Hudson Bay — The Great Canadian Sea — would someday play a big role in the life of the nation. To men of the early fur trade, the Bay was of more importance than the St. Lawrence, by far, and they breathed gratitude for a gift of geography which allowed ocean-going vessels to penetrate close to the heart of the continent. It could be expected that members of the homestead generation would see the Bay as a possible solution to their transportation handicaps, a chance to move grain to Liverpool with a saving of a thousand miles in shipping distance. What an advantage that could be!

Over the pioneer years, Westerners begged for a railway to the Bay and finally resolved to build it by their own efforts if the Government of Canada would not do it. But federal governments were caught between Western demands for the railway and Eastern indifference and outright opposition. The resulting delays were long and exasperating. Even after the road to the Bay was started, work advanced indifferently and it took longer to finish the job than to construct the first transcontinental railway.

Finally, the West had its Hudson Bay Railway. It was like the fulfillment of a dream and grain was actually being exported over the Route. But there was the lingering obstacle of indifference in other parts of Canada and the use of shipping facilities increased slowly. Two hundred and eighty-three years after the first export shipment from Churchill — twenty-eight casks of whale oil — sixty years after the railway to the Bay was started, and forty years after the first wheat was loaded for export aboard the S.S. *Farnworth,* the full potential of Bay shipping was still rather remote. Loyal Westerners, speaking through the Hudson Bay Route Association, had reason for impatience but they continued to declare faith and to plead with Canadians elsewhere to cast their eyes, their enthusiasm, and their investments northward.

The explorers and early traders were extremely conscious of the Canadian North and made Hudson Bay the focal point of Western history. Then, with the coming of the Canadian Pacific Railway, the North lost much of its former attraction and modern Canadians were slow in rediscovering it; slow, also, in trying to obtain a full return from their investment in a transportation facility to the Bay and more distant points. The Hudson Bay Railway and terminal were bought at a high price in money, time, and effort and should have been put to broader use. It is not difficult to imagine numerous products from Western resources and industry moving to Old World markets that way, perhaps 50 million bushels of wheat per year, rapeseed oil from a processing plant at the port, potash, pulp, paper, minerals, liquified natural gas, and even goods from prairie factories. It is not difficult to envision Churchill as a major transshipping metropolis, employing its air, water, and rail facilities to help bind southern Canada and the Canadian Arctic together.

There has been discussion about another Hudson Bay seaport farther north and perhaps a second will be needed. But Canadians should insist upon fuller use of what they have already bought before making another and bigger investment. At a small fraction of the cost of a second port, there could be an investment in bigger icebreakers, more grain storage at Churchill, improved port facilities, some changes in the harbor, and a better program of promotion. Indeed, there could be and should be a new rallying of interest in the North.

For one who witnessed much of the long struggle to obtain the northern railway and then to make it effective, there was the urge to capture the story and relate it to the new need. And, of course, the preparation of such a treatise could not be completed without the help of others, among whom should be mentioned the officers of the Hudson Bay Route Association, Arthur Mauro, author of the Mauro Commission Report on Northern Transportation, staff members at the Alberta Legislative Library, Peter Dalgliesh, Newcastle-On-Tyne, and the congenial people at Modern Press.

Edmonton, 1974
Grant MacEwan

CONTENTS

ILLUSTRATIONS

LAND OF THE BIG SILENCE

According to North American Indian legend, the Great Spirit's workshop was located in the Far North — Land of the Big Silence — and all living things originated there. It explained why birds by the billions continued to return northward at the call of the nesting season and why the earliest human migrations were from north to south. Scholars agreed that the first human immigrants to the continent arrived in the North, having crossed from Asia by way of Bering Strait. Some of the newcomers followed the Mackenzie River valley to more southerly regions; some, like the Eskimo people, never left the North.

The north-south axis was obviously of extreme importance in Nature's scheme of things. Seasonal changes followed it and birds and animals in migration did the same. Western Canada's recorded history began in the North, began with Henry Hudson and others exploring for the Northwest Passage and a short route to China.

Nevertheless, the Canadian North became a land of mystery and misunderstanding. For too many years, too many people thought of it only as a "land of ice and snow." It could be chilly, to be sure, but it could be fascinating and inspiring. The land of permafrost, pingos, igloos, polar bears, and midnight sun had its own attractive personality. Having Canada's highest mountain, longest river, biggest island, most numerous lakes, best fishing, most daylight in summer, most darkness in winter, richest wealth in minerals, hardiest people, biggest challenges, and damndest mosquitoes, it had to be the land with the best claim to superlatives.

It was the land of charm and tall tales. Visitors at Whitehorse heard about the local farmer who drove to town with team and wagon on a Saturday night and, after tying the horses to a tree, made the customary rounds to purchase grocery supplies. Returning at the end of an hour to deposit the groceries in his wagon, he found to his surprise and horror that only the harness and horseshoes remained where he had left his horses; the two animals had been consumed completely by the ravenous mosquitoes. And at Yellowknife, travelers heard about a big mosquito which landed on the local runway and had a hundred gallons of high-test gasoline pumped into it before the dutiful attendants realized that it was not one of the many light aircraft constantly coming and going.

Many parts of the Canadian North were short of good agricultural soil but they had waterpower, oil, gas, gold, silver, iron, copper, nickel, zinc, and numerous other minerals. It was gold that brought the new North to public attention. The strike made at Bonanza Creek, a tributary of the Klondike River, started the gold rush of 1898, the most famous in history. Miners and would-be miners by the thousands landed at Alaskan ports and traveled over mountain passes and dangerous watercourses to Dawson City. Many of the miners enriched themselves with nothing more than experience, but nevertheless, a hundred million dollars worth of gold was taken from the Klondike gravel bars in seven years.

That rush to the Klondike passed as most stampedes do and was followed by years of quiescense. But again and again, with increasing frequency, the "big silence" was being broken. The Imperial Oil Company made an important strike at Norman Wells on the Mackenzie River in 1920 and this was followed by a dramatic penetration of the North by aircraft. With the years of World War II came the construction of the costly Alaska Highway and the Canol Pipeline from Norman Wells to Pacific tidewater. Rather suddenly, the North was losing its former isolation and prospectors began fanning out to stake claims and lead the way for bigger mining operations than the North had known.

In succeeding years Northern travelers could see development at Fort McMurray where the Athabasca sands were known to hold as much oil as in all the proven reserves of the Middle East lumped together. They could see huge hydroelectric projects at such places as Churchill Falls in Labrador and the Peace River in British Columbia; silver mines with major Canadian output at Keno in the Yukon and Great Bear Lake in the Territories; renewed mining interest around

Whitehorse; areas of unbelievable iron ore riches in Ungava and northern Yukon; gold mining at Yellowknife; flourishing activity at Pine Point; the Port Radium mine which furnished uranium for the first atomic bombs and triggered the atomic age. They could see mining activity in scores of places and new oil production and drilling operations in remote parts. A sleeping giant was stirring.

The North had all the resources needed to captivate Canadians everywhere, and in addition to all other attractions, it had fabulous Hudson Bay, the huge, chilly inland sea with a very special place of importance in Canadian history and the possibility of growing importance in Canada's future.

Midwestern people chose to believe that Hudson Bay belonged to them, a providential provision to meet a special Western need. For almost 200 years it had been an essential in the fur trade and when the settlers came, they gazed northward — almost instinctively — breathing prayers of hope and gratitude for a natural seaway reaching inland far enough to relieve their problems of costly transportation. As seen on the map, the outline of the Bay and Hudson Strait resembled a plump farmer seated on a bale of straw, facing the markets of Europe and pointing an outstretched arm at Liverpool, Antwerp, and Amsterdam.

Feeling for Hudson Bay as a shipping route, neither uniform across the nation nor steady anywhere, ranged from eager enthusiasm in the prairie wheat country to indifference and even hostility in Montreal. It was quite understandable. The particular attraction for Western wheat growers was explained by the simple fact of the Port of Churchill on the shore of the Bay being as near to Liverpool and many other overseas port cities as Montreal, yet a thousand miles nearer the wheat fields and shipping points like Saskatoon, Regina, and Edmonton. Growers had no trouble in translating the substantial savings in freight mileage into needed dollars.

At the same time, the great landlocked sea shared by the Northwest Territories, Manitoba, Ontario and Quebec, possessed enough of strictly geographical wonder to command widespread Canadian interest and attention. With James Bay — a Bay within a Bay — it had an area of about 400,000 square miles, making it roughly four times the size of the Great Lakes, one and a half times as big as the province of Alberta and about seven times the size of England.

Ranking close to the Gulf of Mexico in size, the Great Bay of the North is almost a thousand miles in its north-south dimension and roughly 600 miles at its maximum width. Again considering Hudson Bay and James Bay as one body of water, its total shoreline is about as long as the boundary separating Canada and United States. It is a shoreline to account for a big part of Canada's 10,000 miles of northern coast. With very few inhabitants and extremely little to attract agriculturally minded settlers, the land contiguous to the long Bay shore would appear barren but not without interest. Except in the southern regions, it is not tree country, and except at a few trading posts, there is scarcely any evidence of the advance of civilization.

The coast on the eastern side of the Bay is higher and more rocky than on the Churchill side where the tundra country levels off to meet the tides. At the James Bay end, still different conditions obtain, relatively flat and marshy shores making striking contrast with the high and craggy coasts of Hudson Strait.

Although the surroundings appear wild — and are wild — the Bay waters remain surprisingly calm. Contrary to what many people expect, the Bay remains relatively free from ice. Winter ice forms close to the shoreline and ice conditions can become overpowering in Hudson Strait, but the great body of Hudson Bay remains clear and calm. Conditions in Bay and Strait differ widely; the Strait has a high tide and because of ocean currents carrying floes and bergs from the Far North, it is periodically choked with ice. The Bay, on the other hand, is subject to neither high tide nor the ocean currents. Captains of cargo ships have often wished for better shipping conditions in the Strait but have been commonly high in their praise for the Bay.

How was the existence of this huge indentation on the northern coast to be explained? Was it the result of a supersized heavenly body striking the earth and gouging out a monster basin, or was it from the enormous weight of glacial ice at some point in time which caused the earth's crust to sag? In support of the latter suggestion there is evidence of a continuing earthy recoil, causing the basin to become progressively smaller. Nobody can be very sure about the contributing forces but apparently the Bay of modern times is measurably smaller than it was a hundred years ago.

One question suggests another. Is Hudson Bay to be seen as an arm of the Atlantic reaching far inland by way of Hudson Strait, or is it an extension of the Arctic penetrating through Foxe Channel? Having regard to ice from the north passing at the top of the Bay and the character of native vegetation and animal life found in and around its water, the Bay is probably more Arctic than Atlantic. Eskimos living nearby would agree. But the point is of minor consequence. Instead of wasting time on debate, it might be better to recognize the Bay's characteristics, which make it the most distinctive feature on the Canadian map, and accept it as a great inland sea, neither Arctic nor Atlantic. Most of all it deserves to be considered as one of Geography's special gifts to the Canadian West, not something to be ignored as if Northern remoteness condemns it to oblivion.

Moreover, is it really so far north? Be it noted that Saskatoon, Prince Albert, Grande Prairie, and London, England, are in the general latitude of James Bay. Glasgow, Moscow, and Copenhagen are in line with Hudson Bay, and Leningrad and Stockholm are farther north than the Port of Churchill. Fur traders, Selkirk settlers, and men in the initial waves of Western homesteaders certainly did not think of the Bay as being too far north to be useful. It was only after they began to enjoy the relatively costly convenience of transcontinental railways that many Canadians grew indifferent or skeptical about alleged benefits from northern shipping connections with Europe.

A study exercise on and about Hudson Bay would seem quite new to many Canadians — even many Western Canadians — but it should not go unnoticed that the Bay was the starting point in recorded Western Canadian history. Explorers saw Hudson Strait before they saw the St. Lawrence and they saw Hudson Bay before they saw Lake Superior or the Western ₁nterior. Furnishing what seemed like an unbelievable salt water penetration far into the heartland of a continent, the newly discovered Bay beckoned cordially. It was the logical approach, traders said again and again, surely created for those who would live or work far inland.

It was what gave the Hudson's Bay Company its biggest advantage over the rival North West Company. The Montreal-based North-westers were well aware of their handicap in having to ship by way of the St. Lawrence. With such a business advantage, Hudson's Bay Company men knew they had to be ready to defend their monopoly right — with force if necessary. They resolved to build a mighty fort at some strategic location. But where? With all of Rupert's Land to choose from, the site selected for the defense of a fur empire was at the mouth of the Churchill River, on the west side of the Bay.

For almost 200 years the value of Hudson Bay for fur trade shipping was unquestioned. The season for navigation might be for only a few months each year but even at the time of sailing vessels, cargoes were moved as required and with extremely few losses.

The earliest Western farm settlers inherited the fur traders' confidence in the importance of Hudson Bay shipping. Some said they would build a railroad to Hudson Bay themselves if the government would not do it for them. They could see no reason why they should be denied the advantages of the ocean outlet on their north side, big enough and deep enough to accommodate the biggest ocean-going ships and bring communities like Yorkton and Melfort and North Battleford and Vegreville a thousand miles closer to Liverpool and Glasgow than would be possible on the Montreal route.

A prairie resident, writing in 1891, expressed the sentiment sounded by a thousand others: "By this route, Saskatchewan and Assiniboia are as near tidewater as Ontario. . . . The people of Manitoba and the Territories are becoming impatient."[1]

Politicians promised a railroad to the Bay and charters were granted but there were repeated delays and frustrations for those who worked and argued for the fulfillment of a dream. Opposition generated in the East was proving effective, and

[1]Mair, Charles, *Western World*, Winnipeg, Dec. 1891

impatient prairie farmers waiting for a rail connection with the Bay continued to calculate the amount of money they were losing annually by being forced to export their grain by the longer haul.

Finally, the railroad to Hudson Bay was started but there was another long delay occasioned by World War I and it was not until 1929 that the rails were laid all the way to Churchill, at the mouth of the river by the same name. But by this time, many things had changed. Some of the pioneer enthusiasm for the northern shipping route had evaporated. Many of the older people were still eager and loyal promoters but some others seemed to have yielded to the view — perhaps from propaganda — that the North was really a land of ice and snow and Westerners might have lived very well without the Hudson Bay Railway. With about 90 per cent of Canadians choosing to live on a 200-mile-wide ribbon of land extending along the International Boundary, there was an apparent tendency to relate the North with frigidity and unfriendliness.

The Hudson Bay supporters had their problems. The acceptance of the new route was not measuring up to expectations. The use of the Northern Port increased with annoying slowness. The loyal friends who labored tirelessly to obtain the railroad facility were faced with the task of winning enough public interest to make it work successfully. Fortunately, those dedicated supporters — not numerous but unfailing — did not lose their confidence or surrender their determination to see the northern route to world markets used to something near its capacity.

HENRY HUDSON AND OTHER PIONEERS ON THE BAY

The Old Man of the Sea for whom the Bay was named was unaware of rich resources in furs and saw the Americas mainly as obstacles to shorter shipping routes between Europe and the Orient. Trade with the great Cathay — land of gold, perfumes, silks, spices, and jewels on the eastern coast of Asia — offered opportunities for wealth and every merchant and mariner wished it was not so far away. Ever since seamen accepted the idea of the world being round instead of flat, they knew there must be alternative routes to the goal.

Columbus was the first man to sail westward across the Atlantic in the hope of reaching the Far East. His voyage brought important discoveries but did not achieve the main purpose, that of taking him to the East Indies and China.

Columbus, however, was not the first European to make footprints on North American soil. Almost 500 years earlier, the northeastern coast was visited by the robust tramps of the sea, the Vikings or Norsemen, and nobody knows how far they penetrated inland or into northern waters. As courageous as they were hardy, those tall, blonde and scrappy people occupied part or all of what is now Norway, Sweden, Denmark, Iceland, Belgium, and France — plus the Orkney and Hebrides Islands — and sailed far for trade or plunder. They were the most adventuresome and most inquisitive people of their time.

Toward the end of the tenth century, Eric the Red, one of the most notorious of the seagoing breed, was finding it difficult to conform to accepted standards of behavior among his own people in Iceland and was outlawed for three years. A man should always try to make the most of circumstances and the penalty simply meant spending more time at sea. The Terrible Eric sailed west and came to a land which looked attractive to him. He called it Greenland and proposed colonization.

A ship carrying settlers for the new land set sail a very short time later but was carried off course in a storm and swept to the coast of another land, no less inviting. The mariners recovered their course and brought their ship to Greenland where they related their adventure and discovery. On hearing of what might be another pleasant land, Leif Ericsson, son of Eric the Red, resolved to find out. With the same hundred-foot-long boat used by the settlers, he sailed away with a crew of thirty-five men and came to what was known later as Newfoundland, Nova Scotia, and the coast of the state of Maine. To the Norsemen it was Vinland and they are believed to have wintered at the northern point of Newfoundland where archeologists have uncovered evidence of brief Viking occupation. These sea rovers may have been there for several years and then, for reasons never very clear, they left for good. Did they bring their long boats equipped with both sails and oars, as far as Hudson Bay? Nobody knows.

By the time of Columbus, westward exploration from Europe had a fresh purpose; the great goal was a short route to the trading opportunities and wealth of the Far East. The hope was to reach the East by sailing west. When a continental obstacle was encountered, those who followed Columbus desired to sail through it or around it. The Spaniard, Balboa, in 1513, crossed the Isthmus of Panama to find the Pacific only a short distance from the Atlantic. That was encouraging. The challenge then was to discover a water connection between the two oceans, thereby bringing Oriental fortune within a more convenient reach of every European trader.

Jacques Cartier believed the St. Lawrence River might hold the answer and furnish a water course to the Pacific, and Henry Hudson, in sailing up the Hudson River in 1609, entertained similar thoughts. Hudson was already a seasoned navigator and his exploits in northern waters were extensive. In the interest of English trade with Russia, as pursued by the Muscovy Company, he made two expeditions northeasterly into the Arctic Ocean and White Sea. The latter of these ended in mutiny by the crew.

Temporarily breaking his English connection, Hudson accepted the backing of the Dutch East India Company and crossed the Atlantic to ascertain if the desired course to the Far East might be found by penetrating the new continent where the city of New York was to arise and sailing westward on the river now bearing his name. But failing to get through on the river, he returned the next year, 1610 — this time with English backing — to make the more northerly thrust at the obstacle to shorter shipping.

With his good ship, the fifty-five-ton *Discovery,* Hudson sailed from Gravesend on April 17, 1610. Entering the northern strait which was to take his name, he continued hopefully and turned southward into the "Great Bay" on August 3. He followed the coast and then the south shore which he thought might minimize the distance to his Asian destination.

It has been told that Hudson was carrying letters of introduction from British officials to those Oriental princes and potentates he hoped to meet. But Hudson did not use the credentials; the opportunity never came. He wintered at the extreme southerly point in the Bay, probably at the mouth of Rupert River, and experienced great hardship. Encountering very few natives, Hudson's men had to rustle for food, and being unaccustomed to the conditions, they had trouble in obtaining enough to eat. Nor was food shortage the only serious problem for the master of the ship; early in the voyage he quarreled with members of the crew and replaced his mate for reasons of alleged insubordination. It was the beginning of dissension and winter hardships caused the men to become irritable. They wanted to return to England as soon as they had open water in the spring and criticized their captain for desiring to explore further. Why would he want to probe into every inlet on the south coast? Why would he consider going further from home?

When the coast was free of ice in June, the *Discovery* weighed anchor and sailed away from winter quarters, carrying such limited food provisions as the men were able to obtain. Hudson distributed the supply, hoping that each man would conserve it to his own advantage. But after three days the ship was caught in ice and the unhappy men became rebellious. Criticism of the captain's policies mounted, especially of an alleged unfair distribution of the food supplies. The climax came when the mutinous crew seized the leader and placed him along with his son John, and seven others, including the ship's loyal carpenter and some sick men, in a small open boat tied to the main ship with a towline.

Those in the small boat were given a gun, an iron pot, and some food and told that they would have to make their own way. After much effort, the *Discovery* was brought clear of the ice, and as soon as it was in open water, the towline to the shallop bearing Hudson and his friends was cut and the two vessels parted — forever.

The crew of the parent ship encountered bigger troubles than ever. Food shortages became more acute and the men found themselves relying almost entirely upon sea gulls. Stopping at Digges Islands for the purpose of varying their rations, the Englishmen met Eskimos who appeared friendly at first and then turned hostile. The natives attacked with bows and arrows and one of the wounded seamen died before he could be carried back to the ship. Several others died of wounds later and at least one man was said to have died from starvation on the return journey.

After a difficult voyage the *Discovery* arrived back at port in the Thames River but troubles for the members of the crew were not over. They were charged with criminal misconduct and all but four were sent to prison. Two of the four, Robert Bylot and Habbakuk Pricket, were cleared sufficiently to be allowed to accompany Thomas Button when he sailed in the next year to look for Hudson and continue the search for the Northwest Passage. As for Hudson, he was never seen again.

Although the expedition ended in disaster, the English backers were convinced that Henry Hudson had been close to finding the answer to the biggest geographical puzzle of the time and were ready to send another exploratory party to pursue the search from the point at which Hudson had been obliged to stop. Obtaining a charter for what was known as the Governor and Company of Merchants of London, Discoverers of the North-West Passage[1], they fitted two ships, the *Resolution* and Henry Hudson's *Discovery,* for departure from Gravesend on April 15, 1612. Captain Thomas Button who was in command

[1]Morton, Arthur S., *A History of the Canadian West to 1870-71,* p. 29, Thos. Nelson and Sons Ltd., Toronto, 1939

was to study carefully the direction of the tide or current after passing Hudson Strait and then move against it in the hope of finding the channel connection with the western sea. The ships made their way to Digges Islands where they halted to explore for some trace of the lost Hudson but finding nothing of importance, Captain Button took a westerly course and came to the west side of the Bay to enter the mouth of the river to which he later gave the name Nelson in honor of the skipper of the *Resolution,* Francis Nelson, who died while there.

In view of the lateness of the season, Button's decision was to spend the winter at that point on the coast. His first impressions of the country were favorable and he would call it New Wales, honoring the land of his birth. But again there was food shortage — not much of anything except wild fowl — and scurvy became serious before the end of winter. Button tried to keep his men contented by keeping them busy and they spent their spare time studying mathematics and geography. But men were being weakened by malnutrition, and when the river and Bay were sufficiently open for navigation in the spring, Button was obliged to abandon one of the ships, the *Resolution,* and attempt to man the other.

Again it was not a rewarding expedition and Button returned to his home port, forced to admit failure in finding either an outlet to the Pacific or a trace of Henry Hudson and his friends. But the stubborn Englishmen were not ready to quit and in 1615, Hudson's old ship, the *Discovery,* sailed again, this time with Robert Bylot as the captain and William Baffin as the pilot. The result was no better; the Northwest Passage continued to elude its searchers.

The next expedition of importance to students of Hudson Bay history was that of the Danish explorer, Jens Munck. The Danes had been seagoing people for generations and they could not ignore the challenge of the northwestern route to China. Munck was an experienced navigator and with him were two Englishmen who were supposed to know something about the previous expeditions. Two ships, the *Unicorn* and the *Lamprey,* were fitted out for the undertaking but the navigators made some miscalculations about conditions in and about the Bay. Noting that the bottom of Hudson Bay was more to the south than Copenhagen, they supposed it would be warmer and the sailors were allowed to depart from the home port without adequate clothing. Moreover, the planners made the same mistake as predecessors made, of provisioning without those foods most likely to prevent scurvy.

Munck sailed for the west coast of the Bay and came to the mouth of the Churchill River. He noted the big and splendid natural harbor at the river's mouth and after exploring thereabout, he decided to winter at an inlet which became known as Munck's Cove on the north shore of the harbor. One ship, the *Unicorn,* was drawn onto the beach to be above the reach of outgoing ice in the spring, and men set themselves to gathering driftwood for winter fuel and for the building of a shelter to accommodate their supplies. As for their own accommodation, they elected to make winter home on the ship.

Seeing no Indians from whom they might obtain fresh food supplies, Munck and his crew were wholly dependent upon their own hunting successes. But shooting on the tundra was not like birding on the English moors and they were hard pressed to meet all needs. Their shooting brought mainly rabbits and ptarmigan, and as their skill improved, they believed they could escape starvation.

But about the beginning of January, the awful scourge of scurvy made its appearance. The role of vitamins was completely unknown and nobody knew the exact cause of scurvy. Every seafaring man knew the symptoms, however, and knew it was something to be expected after a prolonged absence of fresh foods. It was known as the "mariner's particular disease." In the few weeks following the appearance of the disease, deaths began to occur. By February 25, the dead numbered twenty-two and by June 4, the toll had reached sixty-one.

Of the sixty-four men who sailed away from the home port a few months before, only three remained alive. Munck, one of the miserable trio of survivors, gave up all hope of escaping death and prepared a written request that any person finding his body would be so kind as to bury it in the earth.

But with the coming of spring and the growth of wild vegetation, fresh foods rich in vitamin C became available and Munck and his two companions regained sufficient strength to lighten the *Lamprey* and get it afloat on a high tide. Hopefully, they started for Denmark, wondering if a crew of three could take the ship across the Atlantic. To their credit, they succeeded.

In finding no clue to the fate of Henry Hudson and his friends, and no further indication of a northern passage to China and India, Munck was no more successful than those who preceded him in the searches. He was, however, the first European of record to see the Churchill River and the first to winter within sight of the spot where an imposing terminal grain elevator would one day be built to serve the prairie country a few hundred miles inland.

The cost in human lives was mounting but still men came, men for whom the lure of the unknown was irresistible. And much about the North remained unknown. The motives for coming were unchanged. The dangers were scarcely reduced. That many had lost their lives did not seem to deter others.

After Munck came Captain Thomas James and Captain Luke Foxe whose names are inscribed in Northern geography and who, working independently, found the Bay to be a "dead end" for travelers hoping to reach the Pacific. Both sailed from England in the same year, 1831, and both went with the same motives which drove Button and Munck to the Great Bay. And although their missions were no more successful than those of the men who went before, they added something to the story of the Bay and both men were honored appropriately by the perpetuation of their names in James Bay and Foxe Channel.

Of course there was rivalry between the two courageous fellows sailing simultaneously, a sort of professional jealousy. They met when the James ship, *Henrietta Marie,* and the Foxe ship, *Charles,* came together in the Bay, and the captains exchanged perfunctory courtesies without compromising their animosities.

Foxe returned to England before the winter set in. James, after penetrating to the bottom of the Bay and getting a taste of winter conditions, resolved to remain at Charlton Island until spring. Preparing the *Henrietta Marie* for winter in the uncertain northern waters presented problems. James did not trust the tides and gales and resolved to sink the ship in shallow water and thus allow it to rest in the sand until spring. It required only an auger to make holes to admit the sea water and drop the keel to rest on the mud and sand.

It was a trying winter and four of the James crew died. Others were sick, probably with scurvy. But with the coming of spring, James plugged the auger holes in the boat's bottom and pumped out the water until the *Henrietta Marie* rode freely again to allow the sailors to set a course for home.

Back in England, both James and Foxe wrote about their adventures and observations. James was the better writer but he was accused of exaggeration. Perhaps he was guilty on that count but he was convinced that the coveted Northwest Passage to China did not exist — and said so.

TRADERS ON THE BAY

More fearless men with passion to explore the unknown sailed into northern waters and some did not return. Hope of finding the short and economical sea lane to China and India was fading and more people were satisfied to think of the northern shores of the new continent as inhospitable, dangerous, and useless. English business leaders lost interest in financing expeditions which returned nothing better than maps and charts of an unproductive polar region.

Such North American interest as did survive was directed at the Atlantic side of the continent, especially at the St. Lawrence and Hudson rivers where a growing trade in furs was proving profitable. Beavers and other furbearers were abundant and these North American pelts were the finest seen by European merchants. The Indians, ever the experts in hunting and trapping, were ready to exchange skins for anything the white men offered, anything from good beads to bad whisky. As the years passed, ambitious traders penetrated farther and farther inland and returned to Montreal with great bales of the most valuable furs.

With no thought for conservation and no feeling for the beavers, hunters were quick to deplete the areas close to the St. Lawrence. But the continent was vast, and for those men who would accept the increased costs and hardships imposed by greater distances, there were always more beavers farther back. It was helpful, too, to have the Huron Indians bringing furs from their tribal neighbors on the west to the French on the St. Lawrence, and the Iroquois doing the same for the Dutch dealers on the Hudson River. But when the powerful Iroquois, in 1650, dealt a series of defeats to the Huron and forced them to retreat to the region of Lake Michigan, French trading fortunes suffered disastrously. Leaders in French Canada were anxious to bring the Huron back and restore their standing as fur trade "middlemen." This was a service which two hardy young

Frenchmen, Médard Chouart Groseilliers and Pierre Esprit Radisson, believed they could render. Clearly, they would have achieved something equally helpful for their community had not the French leaders been so obstinate and dogmatic.

These inimitable fellows — brothers-in-law — were born in France but seemed to be created for adventure in the New World. Partly because of his writings and partly because he never failed to give himself a hero's role when he had opportunity, Radisson became the more familiar name in history. It was the view of Prof. Arthur S. Morton[1] that Groseilliers was the "master mind," the planner and strategist, while Radisson had the more varied experiences with Indians. He (Radisson) could tell of taking to the warpath with the Huron, against the Iroquois, and being captured by the latter. Because of his courage and manner, however, he was not put to death by his captors and was later adopted by an Iroquois family. After living, hunting, and fighting as an Iroquois brave and taking his full share of scalps, he resolved to escape and return to the St. Lawrence. Now he saw himself as the Man of the Hour in restoring a movement of furs from the West.

The first Groseilliers-Radisson achievement of note was in penetrating overland as far as James Bay in 1661 and recognizing it as the same body of salt water which Henry Hudson had discovered about half a century before. Leaving Quebec without the Governor's approval earlier in that year, their fourteen canoes moved up the Ottawa River, on to Sault Ste. Marie and along the south shore of Lake Superior. Their exact course remained in doubt but the essential point was their arrival at James Bay, probably at the mouth of the Rupert River where the remains of huts built by Henry Hudson's men fifty years earlier would still be visible. They wintered there and spent the following summer in that area — to which they directed English traders six years later.

The obvious lesson was that if this was indeed Henry Hudson's Great Bay, the nearby fur country could be reached more easily by sea than by land. Enthusiastic about their dis-

[1]Morton, Arthur S., *Under Western Skies*, p. 48, Thomas Nelson and Sons, Ltd., Toronto, 1937

covery, the two Frenchmen sensed great business possibilities and with all the formality the wilderness circumstances would allow, claimed the Great Bay in the name of the King of France. That the same shore had been claimed by others for the King of England would be unknown and unimportant to those robust fellows.

Returning in 1663 to the St. Lawrence, they had 300 canoes loaded with the finest north-country furs ever displayed. Quite fairly, they believed they were doing something useful for New France and should have been accorded some recognition or thanks. But the Governor did not see it that way and instead of being acclaimed for their enterprise and success, the two adventurers were charged with the felony of absence without permission from the Governor and trafficking in furs without a license. Arrested like common criminals, they were convicted, fined, and deprived of their valuable furs. Their proposal to transport Far Western furs through Hudson Bay instead of the St. Lawrence was interpreted as a scheme to destroy the trade for New France. It was unfortunate for the French community which, by rejecting the proposal, lost the chance of a monopoly in trading in north-country furs, and may indeed have changed the entire course of Western history and Canadian destiny.

Groseilliers and Radisson were not ready to abandon the prospect of trading fortune and while still smarting from what they saw as injustice in the Governor's treatment, Groseilliers turned to France, hoping to find approval and support for a bold venture in trading by way of the Bay. There, however, the reception was little better and he returned to Quebec.

The brother-in-law pair would try elsewhere. They went to Boston and met George Cartwright, a special representative of the English King, who showed interest and persuaded them to take their proposal to England. Such a suggestion would, no doubt, come as a surprise and they would have to consider their position. Sure, their first loyalty was to their native France but when both Old and New France had rejected their offer, they were ready to work with imaginative people in some other country. Cartwright, recognizing merit in the idea of trade through Hudson Bay, accompanied the two Frenchmen to England and there introduced them to Sir George Carteret who arranged an audience with the King. In the sovereign's presence they related their proposal for a great new undertaking in trade.

Englishmen of that time were eager for overseas trade, ready to venture into any part of the world. King Charles II, having occupied the throne for eight difficult years, was indeed interested and directed the two Frenchmen — now nicknamed "Gooseberry and Radish" — to interview his cousin, Prince Rupert. The Prince was a man of many parts, a good soldier, a recognized scientist, an engraver, and a daring entrepreneur. Like Groseilliers and Radisson, he was not one to turn his back on a challenge and he received the pair with the encouragement they so much wanted. He set about to find backing for an experimental venture to the shores of Hudson Bay.

English leaders who remembered the unrewarding investments in earlier expeditions to Hudson Bay welcomed the possibility of obtaining a return. If the proposition proved to be as good as Radisson and Groseilliers said it would be, the efforts of Hudson and Button and Munck and others would not have been totally in vain.

Radisson became the vociferous salesman. Groseilliers was the quiet and reasonable salesman. Between them, they proved convincing. The Londoners would band together in financing an experimental voyage to the northern fur country and if the result was favorable, they would request a Royal Charter with monopoly trading privileges. Such charters were not unknown or even uncommon, as the pages of British history reveal by telling of the Muscovy Company set up to conduct trade with Russia, the Virginia Company, and the East India Company.

It was handy and reassuring to have the King's cousin as a charter member of the group, also to have such men as the Duke of Albemarle, who was known to have strong influence with the King, the Earl of Craven, Lord Arlington, Lord Ashley, and Sir Robert Vynor, who later became Lord Mayor of London. It was a most distinguished list and the new company did well in winning royal favors. With the King's approval, a ship from the Royal Navy, the *Eaglet,* was borrowed for the expedition and a second vessel, the *Nonsuch,* was provided and outfitted by the Gentlemen Adventurers.

With Captain William Stannard commanding the *Eaglet* and Radisson on board, and Captain Zachariah Gillam from Boston in charge of the *Nonsuch* and Groseilliers on board, the two ships sailed out of the Thames on June 3, 1668, and headed out on the Atlantic, in the general direction of Hudson Strait.

All went well until the *Eaglet* suffered damage in a storm in Hudson Strait and was forced to return to England. The *Nonsuch,* however, continued and although the journey was not a fast one, the ship reached the bottom of James Bay on September 29, 1668, 118 days after leaving the home port. The season was far advanced and the days and nights were becoming cool. It was not too soon to be thinking about winter quarters and there, near the mouth of Rupert River, the men constructed a humble log house with a sturdy stockade. It was the beginning of Fort Charles, named to honor the English King who had given so much assistance, and there Captain Gillam along with Groseilliers and the ship's crew spent a rather dull winter. Their only frivolous pastime appears to have been in brewing ale. Most of their time, no doubt, was occupied at hunting wild meat, gathering wood for fuel, and trading with those Indians who happened to come that way. The natives were willing and thanks to the experience and understanding of Groseilliers, they remained peaceful.

Meanwhile, back in England, the Adventurers had turned the damaged navy ship, *Eaglet,* back to its base, and had taken in its place one called *Wivenhoe.* With Captain Stannard as master and Radisson going along as a sort of consultant, the replacement ship sailed about the time the *Nonsuch* started on the return journey from the bottom of the Bay.

As soon as the river and the Bay were free of ice the *Nonsuch* was loaded with a big and splendid stock of furs and made ready for sailing. It was a cargo which, when delivered at London, would be sufficient to excite the fur merchants and the Governor and seventeen Adventurers who backed the expedition.

The two ships passed somewhere in the Atlantic and the men of the *Nonsuch* came home to a rousing welcome. The

London backers were happy, sensing continuing trade and profit. Almost at once, they made application for a Royal Charter which would insure exclusive trading rights at the top of the new continent. The King who had been watching with more than passing interest, was ready to accommodate the application and on May 2, 1670, the Royal Charter was granted to "The Governor and Company of Adventurers of England, Trading into Hudson's Bay." It was the birth of a Company which was to play a vigorous and vital part in the history and development of Western Canada and to make a longevity record in Canadian business.

Prince Rupert, as the first Governor of the Company, no doubt looked with satisfaction upon a Charter making the distinguished members of his group "the true and absolute Lordes and Proprietors" of almost half a continent. They would have trading and jurisdictional rights from the entrance of Hudson Strait to points farther west than any members of the white race had seen. The territory over which they would hold authority was technically all those parts of the North American continent from which waters drained to Hudson Bay, whether the European newcomers had seen them or not. The area included all of what was to become the provinces of Manitoba and Saskatchewan, much of southern Alberta, a corner of the Northwest Territories, northern portions of Ontario and Quebec, and parts of Minnesota and North Dakota. It was enormous, and Hudson Bay, to which the two intrepid Frenchmen had led the Englishmen, would be like the beating heart of a new trading giant.

The Governor and Company of Adventurers acknowledged their debt to the two French transients but not to the extent of giving them permanent positions of responsibility. The bosses preferred to pay them well for doing menial work like sorting furs and interpreting, and hope for their contentment. The treatment was not flattering, and French pride was slightly wounded. Before long, Groseilliers and Radisson, having already demonstrated the ease with which they could change loyalties, returned to France.

In 1682, they led a party from Quebec to Hudson Bay where Radisson blithely told the Englishmen he met at York Factory that the country thereabout belonged to the King of

France. The British, he added, were interlopers and should go home. At an opportune moment, Radisson and his followers seized the Company post at Nelson River and invited the occupants to leave. To the English, it was an act of piracy and the chief pirate should be hanged, regardless of his usefulness in other years.

Shortly thereafter, the fort was restored to the Company but the Radisson hostility — warranted or not — was the beginning of a long period of intermittent warfare for possession of the Bay. The French won most of the local skirmishes and battles but the British won the Bay.

BATTLING FOR THE BAY

One of the few naval battles on Canadian waters was fought, oddly enough, in Hudson Bay, August 26, 1697. The combatants were British and French and the victor in the four-hour engagement was the French commander, Pierre Lemoyne D'Iberville, proving that Britannia did not always "rule the waves." One British ship was sunk and at least 313 British and French lives were lost from drowning and gunfire.

It was a dramatic battle. But for what were the naval ships of two nations fighting? They were fighting for possession of chilly Hudson Bay. Both sides considered it very important.

The Gentlemen Adventurers of England were happy with their Charter and had every intention to expand operations in their recently acquired territory, known as Rupert's Land. To increase the volume of incoming furs they would build additional forts, choosing sites at the mouths of rivers flowing into the Bay where they would be the greatest inducements to back-country Indians. Fifteen years after the Charter was granted, there were Company posts at Rupert River, Moose and Albany on James Bay, and the one later known as York Factory at the mouth of the Nelson and Hayes on Hudson Bay.

The Company men knew they would have to be prepared to defend their installations against Indian and Eskimo attack and constructed sturdy stockades. But as time was to show, the greater danger was from guns and ships in the hands of the French who were infuriated by the English presence on the Bay.

France and England were periodically at war over North American possessions though the outbreaks on the Bay did not necessarily wait for declarations of war or fighting elsewhere. In French eyes the British entry into the fur trade on the Bay was an act of aggression and there was no attempt to hide the hope of driving the intruders out. On several occasions when war came to the Bay, it seemed that the French hope was about to be fulfilled.

The first major assault was a surprise attack from the southern landside in 1686 when Chevalier de Troyes came out of the forest with a hundred men — French soldiers and volunteers — and captured Moose, then Rupert and Albany. Having tramped and canoed 600 miles from Quebec, the French force meant business. Company servants and goods were seized and what was not wanted was burned. Only the post at Nelson River — York Factory — remained in Company hands.

England and France were not actually at war at that moment and Company men had no warning of an attack. They were quite unprepared for it. But the attackers cared nothing about London-Paris diplomacy; their single purpose was to rid the Bay of these intruders. They attacked undefended Moose at midnight and took Albany under similar circumstances. Their policy was to fire the captured forts and hope they would never rise from the ashes.

Not only did the Company lose the forts on the Bay but later in the year King James II of England and Louis XIV of France signed an agreement of peace based on the mutual acceptance of land and chattel ownership as held at that time. Apparently the French King knew about the seizures of James Bay posts and the English King did not. The pact threatened to confirm the Company losses and the Governor made protest. King James listened dutifully and transmitted a request to the French King for reconsideration of the status of the lost forts. The matter was passed to a commission and both sides in the dispute recited their claims. The English noted the discoveries and explorations by Henry Hudson, Button, James, and Foxe, then explained how treaties had been made with Indians in the area and occupation had been maintained since 1668.

The French advocates, on the other hand, contended that the territory in question, by virtue of contiguity, belonged to French Canada even before the earliest English explorers saw it. There was no boundary to set James Bay and Hudson Bay apart from French Canada and were they not Frenchmen who were the first white men to reach the Bay from the south? And as an offset to the British point about a territorial grant to the Company of Adventurers, the French could report that the land extending from Florida to the Great Bay of the North had been given earlier by Louis XIII to the Company of One Hundred Associates.

The Commission hearing the case, obviously puzzled, recommended a division of the forts on the Bay. Such an arrangement, which would mean a division of trade, was quite unacceptable to men of the English Company.

With the James Bay posts in enemy hands, the Company people knew they would have to make other provisions in order to maintain a reasonable flow of furs to overseas markets. They resolved upon post expansion on the west side of the Great Bay, particularly at the mouth of the Severn River and on the big river which carried the name of Lord Churchill, Governor of the Company since the former Governor had inherited the English throne in 1685. Work on the Churchill site — close to the place where Jens Munck had wintered disastrously — began on the first day of August, 1689, but the builders were unenthusiastic about the location, calling it a "miserable place," and whether by accident or evil design, the new fort burned to the ground before it was completed.

Simultaneously, the Company's hope to stimulate the flow of furs from far inland on the rivers led its leaders to propose sending an emissary to visit with the natives and win their interest. He would have to be a man who thoroughly understood the native people and the choice fell upon Henry Kelsey who had come to the Company as a boy of fourteen years. He had learned much about Indian customs and languages and was ready to go. On his first trek from the new post on the Churchill he failed to find the Indians but a short time later, in 1690, he accepted the bigger task of traveling far south and west. At his return two years later he could report success. Company prospects appeared more promising, notwithstanding the presence of the French traders on the Bay.

After a lull of a few years, war trouble began again in 1693. England, under William III, declared war on France in 1689 and there was added reason for hostility on the Bay. It had the character of a long war — and did not end until the Treaty of Utrecht in 1713. Three armed Company ships, having been at York for the winter, moved south to James Bay and in an engagement following, recovered Fort Albany. But nothing was settled by the capture and the English knew the French would be back. Feeling grew ever more intense. The French repeated that the English had no right in being there and the English were just as emphatic that the Hudson, Button, Foxe, and James claims to the territory on behalf of England gave them the best of reasons for being there.

Sure enough, French men-of-war under the command of d'Iberville appeared in 1694 and sailed straight for York where guns were landed. After a nineteen-day blockade, the fort occupants surrendered. Henry Kelsey was among those taken prisoner. But instead of burning the place, the captors spared it and gave it a new name, Fort Bourbon. And so it remained for two years when English ships won a naval race to gain positions at the Nelson River estuary and then recaptured the fort. The Bourbon post became York Factory again.

The French ships would come again, nothing surer. Even the traders anticipated d'Iberville's return and furs shipped in the next year were in armed vessels with H.M.S. *Hampshire* as a naval escort.

York Factory appeared as the most coveted prize on the Bay and the year 1697 was to see the biggest struggles to possess it. The British held York and Albany and the French had Moose and Rupert but nobody was satisfied. A test of strength would come soon, and sure enough, August brought the biggest naval battle in Hudson Bay history. The French were determined to retake York and at the same time drive the British from the Bay, once and for all.

The French plan for a "knock-out" blow had the full support of the Monarch. Pierre Lemoyne d'Iberville, who had taken part in various other attacks along the Bay coast, was to command the campaign and as it turned out, he overcame serious handicaps and won complete victory. He was the hero of the day.

Four French ships — the *Palmier, Profond, Vespe* and d'Iberville's flagship, *Pelican* were assigned to the task but when advancing through the Strait, they encountered ice and became separated. The *Pelican* experienced the least difficulty and as soon as ice conditions would allow, continued on its way, it being d'Iberville's opinion that the other three ships were ahead. The fact was that they were behind and before they could get on their way, two British naval vessels came up and fired on the *Profond,* forcing it to take refuge in the pack ice. Held in the ice, the French ship could use only its two rear guns and the British units continued firing until their officers were sure it was ready to sink. Only then did they sail away toward the Bay.

D'Iberville, not knowing anything about the onslaught upon the *Profond,* arrived at the mouth of the Nelson and failing to find his other units there, simply anchored to wait for them before launching an attack on York Fort.

Very shortly, three British ships — the warship *Hampshire* and frigates *Royal Hudson's Bay* and *Dering* — came in sight. D'Iberville, supposing they were his boats, issued a signal of welcome. But then, finding they were enemy vessels, he realized the weakness of his position. With a single ship, he was seriously outnumbered. He knew, also, that he had to fight or surrender. He elected to fight, notwithstanding the three-to-one odds against him. At once his ship was the target for heavy gunfire which continued for four hours. The British navymen tried to sink or board and capture the *Pelican* but d'Iberville maneuvered cleverly and not only succeeded in staying afloat but returned a full share of well-placed cannon balls.

Then came a sudden turn in events; one of the English ships, the man-of-war *Hampshire,* quit firing, capsized and sank quickly, taking 290 members of crew to their deaths by drowning.[1] The sinking, according to the French, resulted from a broadside shot from the *Pelican.* The British account was somewhat different; unwilling to concede superiority of French guns, the British attributed the loss to a high wind which caught the *Hampshire's* topsail as a sharp turn was being made. There was a strong gale, to be sure, so high that d'Iberville found it impossible to attempt rescue operations. Anyway, the *Hampshire* went to the bottom of the Bay, at a point not far from the mouth of the Nelson.

Another of the British ships, *Royal Hudson's Bay,*

[1]Hudson's Bay Company. *A Brief History of the Hudson's Bay Company,* p. 10, Undated

surrendered and the third sought refuge inside the Nelson River. It was d'Iberville's victory, but while he was accepting the surrender of the *Royal Hudson's Bay,* the sub-Arctic storm erupted with greater violence and drove both the *Pelican* and the English ship aground. Twenty-three members of the French crew drowned when they abandoned ship and attempted to swim to shore.

But the French commander was not through. His other three ships arrived on the scene and the combined crews moved guns to land positions and besieged York. The Company men tried to resist and hold the fort but d'Iberville's strength gave him an advantage. Having lost all hope of naval support, the Englishmen surrendered when given the assurance that the ship hiding inside the entrance to the river would be allowed to return to its home port overseas.

Again the Adventurers of England were reduced to a single fort on the Bay and they wondered how long they would be able to hold it. It was a serious setback and would have meant ruin for men with less determination. But the signing of the Treaty of Utrecht in 1713 brought thirty years of harrying and warfare to an end and restored the lost posts to the English Company. Regained, also, was the undisputed control of the fur trade in the North.

James Knight was the Company officer authorized to accept the return of trading properties following the Treaty. His role for a time was like that of a Rehabilitation Officer. He turned his attention to the construction of a new fort beside the Churchill River. The site was not ideal in all respects, but as Knight pointed out, it could, conceivably, attract the Chipewyan Indians from the west. Previously, these tribesmen remained away from the Company posts on the south side rather than risk encounters with their Cree enemies.

The proposed fort was built and named Prince of Wales. It fulfilled its purpose well enough but men who followed Knight came more and more to the conclusion that the Company's chain of forts needed a central stronghold with imperishable qualities. After all, there was no guarantee that foreign warships would not come again. Perhaps Prince of Wales was in the best location to command and guard the approaches to the

Company's Fur Empire. Leaders resolved to rebuild it, make it the Fort Impregnable. Work on the great stone structure began there at Eskimo Point, across the harbor from the Hudson Bay Railway terminal of later years, on August 6, 1731.

For a structure of large proportions and substance, the work would of necessity be slow. On April 15, 1734, six workers were added to the crew, making a total of thirty-six, enough to "work two wagons with men and one with cattle," in hauling stones and clay. The reader can only conclude that with three wagons in service for hauling materials, the Company had oxen for one and relied upon human draft power for pulling the other two.

With plans for a fort measuring a hundred yards in each direction and constructed from heavy stones, the building task had to be monumental. At that point in history there was no easy way of handling big rocks. All moving power came from either ox or human muscle, but in the hope of escaping some of the toil in breaking stones by means of the hammer, workers experimented with gunpowder and had success.

Experienced stonemasons were brought from England and unskilled workers were obtained wherever possible. Legend had it that men breaking stones were convicted criminals brought from jails in Ireland. In any case, the work proceeded slowly and the great stone fort, with durability resembling that of Egyptian pyramids, was not completed until 1771, exactly forty years after it was started.

Completed, it was something to behold, the strongest fort in the Western Hemisphere. Even in its dimensions it was impressive, 300 feet long, 300 feet wide, 16 feet high, with massive bastions at the four corners. Still more significant was the thickness of walls; three of the walls were built 30 feet thick at their bases, and the fourth or front wall, built to carry 42 heavy cannons and resist all gunfire from ships of that period, was 42 feet thick at ground level. What a contribution to Canadian history!

Standing "four-square" and defying the biggest guns of the eighteenth century, Fort Prince of Wales brought pride to the military engineers who drew the plans and all who had parts in the prolonged and laborious construction. It was also a source of profound embarrassment when, on August 9, 1782, it was captured by French Admiral La Pérouse who sailed into the Bay with three ships and took the great fort without a struggle, without even a shot being fired from guns on the massive walls.

Thirty-seven-year-old Samuel Hearne, who had cut his name on the nearby rocks of Sloop's Cove and dated it July 6, 1767, was in charge of the fort. He had served the Company well, even though that signature in the rock was to keep company with the chiseled sketch of John Kelly, "Isle of Wight," hanging from a scaffold, paying the supreme penalty for stealing a goose. Eleven years earlier, Hearne had trekked far across the northern wastes to discover the source of valuable metal on the Coppermine River. And eight years before the surrender, Hearne had traveled far in a more southerly direction and built Cumberland House on Sturgeon Lake, the first permanent settlement in what was to become the province of Saskatchewan. But surrendering the fort was not a glorious performance in the life of such a vigorous man.

Perhaps it was the fort's obvious strength that spawned its weakness. The d'Iberville raids were forgotten and the idea had grown that nobody in his right mind would try to capture a fort built like Prince of Wales. The big guns were there, but nobody expected to use them.

Just as the sun was setting on August 8, a servant enjoying the scenery from the fort parapet, saw three ships making their appearance on the horizon. Nobody was worried, not even when the ships were identified as French men-of-war. But they drew nearer and were seen to be taking soundings. As darkness settled over the Bay and men of the fort retired for the night very much as usual, there was still no indication of a reason for this visit from foreign ships.

With the light of a new day, however, all doubt was removed. There at the water's edge, drawn up in battle formation, were 400 French soldiers from the ships anchored nearby. Samuel Hearne could scarcely believe what he saw. Doubtless, he thought of the paltry staff of thirty-nine men with him inside the walls, unprepared for battle. He was shocked and may have been the victim of panic. Knowing he had to act quickly, he yielded to impulse; instead of waiting even to parley with the

A group of tourists visiting Fort Prince of Wales. — Saskatchewan Photo Services.

French Admiral, he seized a white cloth and waved it, inviting the assailants to enter at the open gate. To be sure, the surprised Frenchmen entered and took possession.

As discovered later, many of the French soldiers had been ill during the voyage and were seriously weakened. Moreover, they were not well provisioned. But they had courage and audacity and they saw the strongest fort of the continent open its doors to them. It was then for the French admiral to decide what to do with this prize of war. He could not take it with him. He wanted to destroy it and tried. The archway over the gate was blown up; a storehouse in one of the bastions was damaged and a few stones in the walls were displaced. But the task of destruction was found to be too much and the soldiers satisfied themselves with looting. Then, instead of lingering longer, they sailed to take York, a fort they found easier to burn.

Happily old Fort Prince of Wales stands today very much as it did 200 years ago, and Canadians visiting the seaport town of Churchill and venturing across the broad harbor have found it as one of the richest gems in the treasurehouse of North American history.

After the Hudson Bay Railway was completed to Churchill in 1929, the Government of Canada decided most appropriately to restore the ancient structure. It was not a major task. A few stones had to be returned to their niches and cannons which had fallen from the walls required to be reset. But all the essential parts were there and after some reconditioning, the old fort looked about as fresh and formidable as at any time and capable of being one of the finest tourist attractions in the nation. It should be high on the list of Canadian wonders.

TWO HUNDRED FUR TRADE YEARS

For 200 fur trade years Hudson Bay provided the principal trade route between the western part of the continent and Europe. Millions of prime furs went out that way; tons of trade goods came in. It was the English Company's private waterway and helped that organization to survive. The route had its shortcomings, to be sure, but there was nothing better. The northern season for shipping was short, as nearly everybody admitted, and the Strait could be blocked with ice at times. Ship losses occurred, as on other ocean waters, but they were rare. There were delays but almost always the shipments went through and instead of dwelling on the Bay's weaknesses, people of the fur trade period accepted northern shipping as it was and gave thanks for the natural gift of an inland sea.

Only those who were denied the use of the Bay—men of the rival North West Company—spoke bitterly about it, and then only because of their own misfortune in having to transport furs over the long and difficult course to Montreal. They eyed Hudson Bay covetously and schemed for years to gain shipping privileges—by fair means or foul.

The Hudson's Bay Company's monopoly as it applied to the fur country was difficult to protect. The Indian trade was profitable and there was no way of preventing inroads by free traders from the East. They challenged the validity of the Charter and without testing it in the courts, chose to disregard it. At first, those who came were French adventurers and dealers like the La Vérendryes and La Corne, and the competition forced the Hudson's Bay Company to build posts in the interior, beginning with Cumberland House in 1774.

After the end of French sovereignty on the St. Lawrence, there came from the Montreal area more and more free traders with Scottish names like McTavish, McGillivray, Fraser, and Mackenzie. In 1787, those Montreal-based merchants — "Pedlars" to men of the older company — pooled their interests and resources to form the North West Company and prosecute trade with the natives with more vigor than ever. They were shrewd businessmen, tough fellows, practical people who would travel with their brigades and spend spells living as wintering partners in the back country. Man for man, they could outtrade and outwit the servants of the English Company. But the latter had that one huge advantage conferred by Royal decree; they had the Great Bay of the North offering the best and shortest of all avenues to the markets of the Old World.

For the North West Company, the long canoe route from fur country to the St. Lawrence was not only slow and tedious; it was costly. It was a five-months' journey from Athabasca to Montreal. Given equal opportunities and advantages, its men had no fear of competition but with rivals enjoying the exclusive use of the shorter shipping lanes, their handicap irritated sorely.

They searched diligently for the Northwest Passage or a practical outlet to the Pacific—anything to reduce the costly necessity of shipping via Grand Portage and Lake Superior. Alexander Mackenzie's river expedition to the Arctic in 1789 and his journey from Peace River to cross the Rockies and reach the Pacific Ocean in 1793 did not provide the solution to his company's dilemma and he turned his thoughts again toward Hudson Bay, from which he and his people were barred.

Mackenzie, one of the brightest individuals in the trade, was bitterly determined to find a way of obtaining the benefit of shipping rights on those northern waters, even if his company had to buy it. The North West Company, in 1804, was prepared to purchase the rival company outright but the proposal was rejected. Being doggedly persistent men, the Nor'Westers would try again. In the next year they offered the English Company 2,000 pounds annually for shipping privileges through the Bay and Strait and were refused again. The next move was to buy enough Hudson's Bay Company stock to allow Mackenzie and his partners a controlling interest. Mackenzie hoped to secure the necessary shares through the good offices of Lord Selkirk and the plan almost succeeded; Selkirk apparently obtained the equity but decided to use it for what he considered a better purpose—settlement—and again the Nor'Westers were disappointed and probably frustrated.

Hudson's Bay Company post at Fort Churchill, 1910. — Hudson's Bay Company Archives.

But Mackenzie, with the determination of a Highland clansman, decided that the only remaining means of gaining his objective was to simply ruin the English Company through competition. The years which followed, therefore, saw a most bitter struggle for trade — almost ruinous to both companies —and, finally, in 1821, a sensible proposal was accepted and the two trading giants amalgamated. At once York Factory became the main depot in the shipment of goods to and from Rupert's Land, and Montreal was largely by-passed. As Hudson Bay traffic became heavier, the fur interests flourished.

Fort Prince of Wales was the stronghold on the Bay but York Factory became, for all practical purposes, the Capital. It was not destined to become a bustling metropolis but it was to have the distinction of being the oldest permanent settlement in Western Canada. It was never big in population but in relation to resident numbers it contributed more to Canadian history than any place in the country. What other community in Canada could tell of being captured three times by French forces and recovered as many times by the British, of being blockaded by foreign naval ships, of being burned to the ground, and being ruled by a local Governor—James Knight—who would instruct his people to "live lovingly one with another . . . without drunkenness and profaneness," and above all, not to "meddle" with native women?

At a time when seizures and reseizures of trading posts on Hudson and James bays were being conducted somewhat like a game—a rough one—York was the principal pawn. And still, oddly enough, the place remained virtually unknown to most Canadians of later years. Because of relative inaccessibility, it was not surprising that most Canadians had never seen the place, but for its place in history they should have known more about it.

York Factory was the starting point for many of the early explorations and the landing point for just as many notable immigrations. Anthony Henday, embarking upon a mission regarded as urgent for the Company, started up the Hayes River on June 26, 1754, hoping to persuade Indians in the far interior to come down to the Bay to trade instead of taking their furs to Frenchmen on the Saskatchewan River. Evidently immune to loneliness and homesickness, he was absent for almost exactly a year. After wintering with Blood Indians in the park country west of present-day Innisfail, Alberta, he was back at York Factory on June 20, 1755, reporting to disbelieving friends that he had seen Indians riding horses and mountains capped with summer snow. In any case, the man from York Factory was the first of his race to travel so far inland and the first to see the Rockies.

Henry Kelsey set out on his notable journey to the prairies from the same place, leaving on June 12, 1690. Likewise, the John Franklin expedition to explore the Arctic coast in 1820 traveled from York, and George Simpson, starting on regular tours of post inspection which could take him all the way to the Pacific, was likely to leave from York Factory.

Among the immigrant groups to land there were several composed of Selkirk settlers—the West's first real farmers. The first party, sometimes called the Advance Guard, landed late in 1811 and wintered at York Factory. The next to come, genuine settlers, arrived at York in 1812 after sixty-one days on the sailing ship and faced another forty-eight days of overland and canoe travel before reaching journey's end at Pembina. For the settlers in these and succeeding groups, York Factory, 730 miles from Fort Garry, remained in their memories as a sort of "coupling link" between their former homes in Scotland or elsewhere and their adopted land.

York's place of importance lasted almost 200 years and for all of that time it was an unpretentious but moderately self-contained community with a blacksmith, carpenter, gunsmith, and tailor to perform essential work and others who were proficient in brewing spruce beer said to be effective in preventing scurvy. From the time of Henry Kelsey, too, gardens were planted regularly.

Only after the acquisition of the West by Canada and the creation of the province of Manitoba did York Factory go into decline. Hudson's Bay Company freight was beginning to come to Fort Garry via St. Paul, Minnesota. The fur industry was suffering. Fort Garry became the main point of entry, superseding York. No longer were the picturesque brigades of freight canoes loaded with furs going to York Factory.

The first tangible threat to the omnipotence of York and the Bay came when a steamboat splashed its way downstream on the Red River to tie at Fort Garry in 1859. It was the *Anson Northrup,* an architectural monstrosity looking more like a top-heavy coal shed than a riverboat, and the ship's master, by being the first to bring a steamboat to Fort Garry, qualified for a cash prize offered by the St. Paul Board of Trade. Its coming was like an extension of Mississippi river traffic and was a warning to the numerous freighters—mainly Métis—who drove oxen and Red River carts over the 500-mile trail between Fort Garry and St. Paul. And as if that were not enough excitement for one year in the Red River Settlement, Fort Garry got its first newspaper, the *Nor'Wester,* published by two young fellows, William Coldwell and William Buckingham. The paper, by taking a stand against Hudson's Bay Company monopoly, hastened other important changes in that period.

With no advance notice of its coming, when the *Anson Northrup* sounded its whistle it frightened the Fort Garry citizens. But other riverboats followed and as Winnipeg people came to rely upon this new freight and passenger service, they agreed that the long canoe and portage trip between their community and York Factory was not something a person would undertake for recreation. Then, an increase in the movement of people searching for farm land, homesites, and gold on the Saskatchewan and Fraser rivers, added to the volume of river traffic. Boats were traveling as far as Fort Edmonton on the North Saskatchewan and a few went to Medicine Hat on the South Saskatchewan. And then, as more people came to the country and more wheat was available to be shipped out, the demand for an all-Canadian railroad linking East and West became louder.

York Factory lost its continental importance and temporarily at least, Canadians forgot about Hudson Bay.

THE RAILS CAME

The new province of Manitoba was only two years old when the Canada Land Act was passed in 1872 providing for free homesteads in the West, and Scottish-born John Sanderson who filed promptly for a quarter section on the Portage Plains was the first of a great multitude of landseekers coming to farm and make homes under the policy. Four years later a shipment consisting of 857 bushels and 10 pounds of wheat in 2-bushel bags went by riverboat from Winnipeg, the first grain to be sent from the buffalo country. In Toronto, where the wheat was delivered, it was recognized for its superior quality and at once there was an added reason for better transportation.

As the land rush mounted, so did the demand for a railroad. British Columbia had come into Confederation in 1871 with a promise of a rail connection and now men in government were seeing a chance to settle the prairie country and obtain a return from the investment they made to acquire it, all the while bringing the East and West of Canada together in a sort of national embrace.

The rails came, reaching Winnipeg from the east in 1879 and Calgary in 1883. They brought rejoicing, naturally. Settlers saw their isolation vanishing. After years of waiting, the railroad was like an answer to prayer. A railroad connection at the back door or within hauling distance was more attractive than an ocean port a few hundred miles away and most prairie people promptly forgot about that ocean access to which they seemed to have a special claim. Like lady lovers with brand new and dashing beaus, the Westerners found it easy to forget earlier attractions.

The railroad "honeymoon" was great but it did not pass without some disillusionment and the youthful lovers began thinking about earlier romances. Western people thought again of Hudson Bay and what it had to offer for shipping, and sought the opinion of those Canadian scientists who had continued, silently, to gather information pertinent to the coming debate. Henry Youle Hind expressed confidence in the Bay as a shipping route and so did Winnipeg's Dr. Robert Bell. The latter was a medical doctor with training in engineering and an absorbing interest in geology and northern shipping. He communicated his enthusiasm to his chief in Ottawa, A. R. C. Selwyn, Director of the Geological Survey, and succeeded in stimulating fresh interest in Winnipeg business circles.

Early in 1879 Bell was sharing the experiences of adventures along the Nelson River and through northern waters as far as Newfoundland[1]. While admitting the need for more studies on ice conditions, he was confident that a railroad could be built on any of several approaches to the Bay. If and when such a rail communication was completed, grain would be exported with maximum economy and immigrants would be coming to Western Canada by that route, landing at Prince Albert in the time it previously took to bring them to London, Ontario.

Bell knew there were obstacles to a long shipping season. "Two ice streams coming from East Greenland and Baffin Bay down the west coast of Davis Strait" could be expected to bring ice, even in June, he noted. There would have to be precautions. But he could see no major problems within the Bay where, as he believed, water never froze more than "several miles" from the shore.

While making these observations, he spoke with a lone voice. There was still infatuation with the idea of a transcontinental railroad. But Bell was patient, believing that public sentiment would change. "For more than 200 years," he told his listeners, "from two to five sailing vessels per year, frequently with men-of-war convoying them, have sailed from Europe and America to Port Nelson or other ports on Hudson's Bay, returning with cargoes of furs during the same season, via the only available route, Hudson's Strait. The Newfoundland, Dundee and Norwegian sealing steamers, being properly protected, push their way into the illimitable fields of ice in March and April in search of seals having necessarily to seek for ice, as it is

[1]*Manitoba Free Press*, Jan. 14, 1879

only there they can capture the seals. . . . It is therefore not unreasonable to suppose that at the present day, when ice navigation is so thoroughly understood, not only by the captains of sealing vessels but by the masters of steam whalers, that the passage through Hudson's Straits, successfully accomplished for two hundred years by bulky and unwieldy sailing vessels and cumbrous men-of-war—even battleships—should with the aid of magneto-electric lights, become an easy problem."

Bell called for further investigation to determine the earliest and latest shipping dates, and the risks to be expected when ships of appropriate construction were in use. He believed the Hudson's Bay Company had much of the information needed and hoped it would be released from private and confidential files.

Bell and other technical observers of the time guessed hopefully that further research would show the northern shipping lane to be usable for five months each year, enough to give it a major role. Bell was not sure at that time if the new prairie railroad could be counted on to operate through Western winters and a five-months shipping season would make the Bay route appear very attractive.

Coming under the influence of Bell's optimism, Surveyor-General A. R. C. Selwyn was convinced that immediate steps should be taken to test the length of the season and general practicability of the route which would place grain at the mouth of the Nelson River as near to Liverpool as it would be at New York. The effect, said he, "would be to connect the finest grain-producing country in the world with the best market in the world," and help to overcome the existing obstacles of costly transportation when goods are shipped by the Great Lakes.[1]

But much of that optimism was wasted. Westerners preferred to believe that the railroad would supply all their shipping needs. What could be better than a rail connection with Vancouver, Montreal, and Halifax, even though the Hudson's Bay Company had used the northern sea lanes successfully for 200

[1]*Montreal Witness,* Montreal, Dec. 12, 1879

years, even though United States whalers between 1861 and 1874 had taken an average of $124,000 worth of fish oil from the Bay, even though fifty voyages had been made by those whalers in the eleven years and apparently without mishap?

The transcontinental railroad, completed in 1885, was a monumental achievement, both in engineering and financing, and a Montreal port promised to meet all terminal needs. But after the first flush of wonder and joy, Western people—farmers in particular—found the new shipping facilities left something to be desired. Freight rates were high; railroad policy was arrogant and the monopoly feature was most offensive.

Annoyance led to anger and near violence and sent farmers and others searching for redress and possible alternatives. By what other means could Westerners ship their goods to world markets? The more that people thought and talked about it the more they wondered why they had withdrawn their earlier interest in Hudson Bay shipping and why they had left it to Dr. Bell to promote the case for the great inland sea extending itself invitingly toward the wheat country. If Hudson Bay had something practical to offer, why should it not be developed to augment the transcontinental railroad? Competition could be beneficial to all facets of transportation—including the Canadian Pacific Railway.

Manitobans were in a state of extreme restlessness. Their complaints were couched in calls for "better terms." With so many demands for public works in a new province, more revenue was needed and the federal government was being bombarded for bigger grants. At the same time, provincial leaders wanted more space; having been allotted an area of less than 14,000 square miles, they were asking for an extension of boundaries, westward into the Northwest Territories and northward toward Hudson Bay. And not the least of their requests was for the right to control their own public lands and issue charters for the construction of railroads within their boundaries. Federal and Canadian Pacific Railway policies were increasingly irritating. The federal government granted small increases in the subsidies in 1879 and an extension of provincial area in 1881 but refused to relax on lands and railroads.

For a few years the word "disallowance" was on every

Manitoba tongue and people were angry. Its origin was in the federal government's refusal to allow the province to authorize and charter new railway lines and it was the subject of the most bitterly debated issue the province had experienced. Time after time the provincial efforts to bring rail services to new communities were refused and Manitobans felt the impulse of rebellion. The provincial government would issue a railroad permit for construction where a line was needed, only to have it disallowed by federal authority.

The agreement between the Government of Canada and the Syndicate for completion of the Canadian Pacific Railway was signed on February 17, 1881, with the Government undertaking to contribute $25,000,000, certain rail assets in the East valued at some $37,000,000, and 25,000,000 acres of Western land. At the same time the railroad company was to enjoy monopoly privileges in railroad construction south of the main line for twenty-four years. The transcontinental railroad was wanted and needed but the feeling prevailed that Canadian citizens and taxpayers were being asked to pay too much. To add to the irritation the railroad would be permitted to take its 25,000,000 acres in alternate sections on both sides of the main line and be exempt from taxes on that land for twenty years.

The federal government was unbending. Three local charters issued by the provincial government in 1882 were disallowed. Western people who wanted the extra rail lines raised angry protests. However just or sound the federal policies may have been, they were totally unacceptable in the West and before the railway question was settled, the new province was on the verge of insurrection. Spurred by public resentment, the provincial government under Premier John Norquay defiantly brought back some of the legislation previously disallowed, passed it again, and then proceeded to build the Red River Valley Railroad from Winnipeg south on the west side of Red River. It was a clear invitation for a test of strength and authority and there was a hint of troops being sent to block the proposed construction. The issue led to the resignation of Premier Norquay but the wrangling continued until a compromise settlement was reached with the Company surrendering the monopoly features in its charter.

The Canadian Pacific Railway Company offered to buy the controversial Red River Valley Railroad but the Government of Manitoba, under Premier Thomas Greenway, refused the offer and later made a deal with the Northern Pacific Railway to finish the line and add some branches. The latter necessitated crossing CPR tracks. Canadian Pacific officials refused permission for crossings and a showdown became imminent. The CPR, in its refusal to let the opposing line cross, had the apparent support of the Canadian Government and found added strength in the new General Railway Act. The major test came in October, 1888. The scene was about ten miles west of Winnipeg, at the point later known as Fort Whyte, named to honor William Whyte, General Superintendent of CPR operations at Winnipeg at the time.

There was no secret about it: the Government of Canada was supporting the CPR and the Government of Manitoba was behind the builders seeking to effect a crossing. The conflicting forces in what became known as "The Battle of Fort Whyte" came face to face on October 20, 1888. Special constables with provincial authority were hurriedly sworn in and enough able-bodied and irritated Manitobans without any special status joined to make the aggregation look more like a newly recruited army than a policing body. The CPR, with no thought of surrendering in its purpose, erected a fence and even dumped an old locomotive right on the path of the approaching grade. The Company, at the same time, was asking the courts for a restraining injunction.

Manitoba had a big crop that year and farmers hoped to see the new branch line completed for grain handling before the end of the season. Many men from nearby farms offered aid and on the night of October 24 the expanded crowd raided the CPR right of way and lifted enough track to allow a switching spur to be constructed for the new line. Next day the CPR bosses had enough help on hand to remove the switch and repair its own track.

The people of Winnipeg were fired with rage. The Mayor called a public meeting. Worried CPR officials hired a bigger body of guards and kept a locomotive moving back and forth continuously on the embattled portion of track. The deadlock continued until the case was taken to the Supreme Court. While both sides waited for the important judgment, they made sure their forces of constables and guards were maintained vigilantly. A reckless move on either side at this point might have triggered a serious battle and leaders on both sides knew it.

The Supreme Court ruling carried a measure of compromise but was more favorable to the position of the Manitobans than to the railroad company. It brought more comfort to the province of Manitoba than to the federal government and signaled an end to the vexatious monopoly. Provincial authorities felt free to build railroads within their own boundaries as they considered appropriate.

In the meantime, a rail connection with Hudson Bay, sufficient to make Manitobans less dependent upon the CPR, appeared more attractive and more important.

A WAVE OF FRESH ENTHUSIASM

Of course, the transcontinental railway was a boon and a blessing but Manitobans were having second thoughts about those monopolistic features in the agreement which were making the new facility appear more like a master than a servant. They recalled words of counsel and warning which had passed almost unnoticed when sounded. Perhaps Henry Youle Hind, the long-time advocate of the northern shipping route, was right in recognizing York Factory as the coming "Archangel of the West." Perhaps Dr. Robert Bell was correct in his contention that an east-west railroad needed competition such as a Hudson Bay connection would provide. Perhaps business leaders like Winnipeg's Hugh Sutherland were exercising sound judgment in proceeding with plans for one or more railroads to be built to ports on the Bay, regardless of the Canadian Pacific accomplishments.

A railroad from Winnipeg or Prince Albert or other inland centers to the shore of Hudson Bay was regarded as a task for private investors, even though there was some Eastern precedent for the federal government in railroad construction. And business men in the private sector were eager enough. They deserved credit for their pioneer efforts, even though the eternal desire for personal gain accounted for much of the motivation.

Significantly, the earliest private schemes for rail construction northward were proposed before the popular rebellion against disallowance in Manitoba. But the political climate of unrest was exactly what proponents of the railroad connection with the Bay might have desired. If more were needed, it, too, was being provided by reports of evil designs by United States interests gazing enviously at Hudson Bay ports for ocean shipping.

Hadn't Washington authorities bought Alaska from Russia in 1867? Hadn't the same public servants, about a year later, opened negotiations with the Hudson's Bay Company for the purchase of Rupert's Land and the Northwest, with the idea of having unbroken territory extending from the Gulf of Mexico to the Arctic? How could the same people fail to see the advantage of owning the approaches to Hudson Bay and using the great Inland Sea to serve the transportation needs of the Northern and Northwestern States? Patriotic Canadian sentiment was aroused and Manitobans found fresh determination to claim the Bay and build to it.

But as promotors discovered, building to Port Nelson or Port Churchill was not a simple matter. The engineers said they could lay the rails but the bigger problems were political and financial. There was no lack of ideas, no lack of plans. Railroad expansion seemed to enter every conversation and Manitobans were determined that the CPR agreement would not be allowed to stop them, not even in the area where the monopoly clauses applied.

The number of applications for transportation charters coming before the Parliament of Canada during the eighties was astonishingly large. Some of the schemes proposed all-land routes to the Bay, some offered amphibious lines to the same shores. On a single day, April 16, 1880, the House of Commons in Ottawa gave third reading to two Bills to grant charters for companies building to the Bay, one being Hugh Sutherland's famous Winnipeg and Hudson's Bay Railway and Steamship Company, and the other, the Nelson Valley Railway and Transportation Company. About both projects, much more was to be heard — very much more.

The new West was showing signs of rapid development and prosperity and the city of Winnipeg was entering upon a mad real estate boom. Sleeping giants were awakening. The federal government's land subsidies to railroad builders were generous and men in business were eager to participate. Announcements of new schemes for railroad construction were almost as numerous as public protests about disallowance.

Among the Bills to which the House of Commons gave second reading on January 28, 1881, were no fewer than six asking for incorporation of railroad companies; of the six, four were for new rail lines in the West and one of them, the South Saskatchewan and Hudson's Bay Railway, as the name suggested, was to charter still another railroad aimed at the Bay. If rails could have been laid on blueprints and good intentions, the West would have had freight trains to the Bay long before the end of the decade.

Altogether, at least nine different railroad schemes with terminals on Hudson or James Bay were mooted and chartered by federal or provincial governments. Some of those lines would start from points in Ontario and Quebec, most of them from points in the West. One would have been strictly northern inasmuch as it would extend from Lake Athabasca to the mouth of the Churchill River.

The early hints of the United States seizure of Canadian territory to furnish American access to Hudson Bay were all but forgotten, but the advantages of Bay shipping could not escape the notice of businessmen in the Northern and Northwestern States and still more railroad plans resulted. The *Daily Times,* Winnipeg, told of "a gigantic new railroad scheme," the San Francisco, Winnipeg and Hudson's Bay Railway, to carry freight and passengers destined for England, at a saving of "more than 1100 miles over the route via Chicago."[1]

Winnipeg people heard more about it. A few weeks later, a deputation of prominent local citizens waited upon the City Council, arguing that here was an opportunity for Winnipeg to place itself squarely on an international trade route between the Pacific Ocean and Britain.[2] Much of the needed railroad on the United States side was already completed and the construction of a railroad from Bismark, North Dakota, through Winnipeg to Hudson Bay would complete the connection and the west-east traffic from Asia and the Pacific coast would come surging through Winnipeg. "In 20 years," said the spokesman for the plan, "the Hudson Bay will be filled with merchantmen" and Winnipeg would be an international trade center. What he and his associates were seeking was a Winnipeg city commitment to bear half of the cost of a further survey which should be undertaken at once. He believed the Manitoba Government would assume the balance of cost and Winnipeg would then be in a fair

[1]*Daily Times,* Winnipeg, Oct. 30, 1883
[2]*Daily Times,* Winnipeg, Dec. 18, 1883

way to take its place on one of the leading trade routes of the world.

The City Council reacted with proper interest and a few days later, Mayor McMicken and two aldermen were relaying the proposition to Premier John Norquay and members of the provincial government. But the decision was scarcely enough to satisfy the promotors. Instead of authorizing a new survey, as requested, members of Norquay's cabinet decided to send for a copy of the report of work conducted a few years earlier by Dr. Robert Bell.

One point was clear: the northern shipping route as a possible solution to Western transportation problems was back in the news and deep in controversy. Western sentiment was generally favorable. Western politicians were outspoken in their support but many of their Ottawa colleagues were opposed or discreetly silent. As for Prime Minister Sir John A. Macdonald, there was doubt about where he stood on the issue although he was suspected of being opposed. He might not declare himself but until his CPR pet was completed and showing signs of prospering, he would scarcely support any project likely to make competition.

Understandably, newspaper editors — including those within the city of Winnipeg — held totally different views. The great editorial debate began when Eastern papers carried opinions advanced by Hind, Bell, and Selwyn. The most bitter editorials, however, were written in Winnipeg where the *Manitoba Free Press* gave unfailing support and the *Daily Times,* displaying doubt on the point of feasibility because of ice, and fearing an exhorbitant cost of some $20,000,000, advised restraint.

Branding those fears as "nonsense," the editor of the *Free Press* said that "if the Bay and Straits are freely navigable for even four months in the year, the traffic on the railway will give a handsome return for the cost of construction, as the business of the country will all the time be developing in a way that is now out of the question."[1] To doubt "the practicability of the whole

[1]*Manitoba Free Press,* Dec. 18, 1883

route," the editor emphasized, a writer or anyone would have to "set aside the evidence of the Hudson's Bay Company's servants, the American whalers and officers of the English navy as wholly unreliable."

Although he must have known that his opinions were unpopular in Winnipeg and throughout Manitoba at the time, the *Times* editor remained firm. "The only ships that can navigate the Hudson's Bay route," said he, "are those built whaler-fashion."[1] He had another missile: "This Hudson's Bay route is a brilliant scheme, but so was the Aquilitanos trip to the moon."

The editorial ridicule grew in intensity with each exchange. Scornfully, the *Free Press* editor, in his issue of the next day, said the *Times* "treatment of the subject is so trivial that all its arguments carry their own refutations, and its only achievement is the exposure of its ignorance with reference to the whole question."[2]

It was precisely at this point that the Manitoba farmers entered resolutely into the arguments about a railroad to the Bay. Agrarian people as far back as the Selkirk settlers — the first dedicated men and women of the soil in the West — recognized the Bay as their great natural asset and those who came later as homesteaders persisted in their hope for rail connections which would give them the shortest possible shipping route to Europe. But it was not until 1883 that organization permitted the farming people to raise a collective voice.

When the Manitoba and North-West Farmers' Union held its first convention in Winnipeg on December 19 and 20, 1883, the members made three main demands: removal of the customs tariff on farm machinery; an end to CPR monopoly, and a seaport on Hudson Bay.

In propounding a Farmers' Declaration of Rights, the delegates resolved: "That this convention is unanimously of the opinion that the Hudson's Bay Railroad should be constructed with the least possible delay."[3]

One of the convention speakers, Alex Murray, M.P.P.,

[1]*Daily Times,* Winnipeg, Dec. 18, 1883
[2]*Manitoba Free Press,* Dec. 19, 1883
[3]*Manitoba Free Press,* Dec. 20, 1883

won robust applause when he declared that the farmers were underestimating their own potential; one railroad to the Bay would not be enough. Farming people, he said with a statesman-like flourish, should be looking ahead and pressing for no less than two such railroads, "one from Winnipeg and the other from Prince Albert." The CPR, he was sure, "would never be able to move the immense amount of grain that would be raised and three railroads would hardly be equal to the task." Moreover, Murray added, any class of vessel could navigate on the northern route for four months of the year and "with vessels adapted to the purpose, they would probably be able to navigate for eight or nine months."[1]

The executive council of the Manitoba and North-West Farmers' Union, following instructions from the convention, kept the matter of a railroad to the North before the government. From a meeting on March 13, 1884, it issued a statement urging the federal government to grant the province's request for an extension of its boundaries northward to the Bay, allow the provincial administration to charter railways, and assist construction by granting land and money subsidies. The farmers wanted to see Hugh Sutherland's struggling railroad company succeed.

[1]*Manitoba Free Press*, Dec. 21, 1883

HUGH SUTHERLAND'S DREAM

With luck to match his energy and enthusiasm, Winnipeg's Hugh Sutherland would have been selling excursion tickets to Hudson Bay before the last spike was driven in a CPR tie in 1885. For more than a decade he was the leading exponent of the northern route and his sincerity of purpose could not be questioned. His reward was mixed but bitter more than sweet. He had the satisfaction of seeing his pet project started and forty miles of railroad construction, but in the final test to find the finances with which to continue, he had to confess failure. He was close to a glorious success but fate ruled against him.

Hugh McKay Sutherland, with pure Scottish pedigree and Gaelic accent, was born in Prince Edward Island, 1845, and came to Manitoba in 1874, just when the North West Mounted Police cavalcade was starting from Fort Dufferin for the long trek to parts unknown somewhere near the Rockies. Frontier challenges suited Sutherland perfectly and Winnipeg people soon came to know this stocky, muscular and personable young fellow looking more like a well-groomed banker than a lumberman.

He could not hide a Maritimer's interest in politics and in coming to Manitoba he had the earlier experience of one political defeat in an Ontario election. In his adopted province, however, he contested for the federal constituency of Selkirk and won to sit with the Liberal Opposition in the House of Commons from 1882 to 1887. Seeking re-election in the same riding in the latter year, he lost by a margin of eight votes. But regardless of politics, Hugh Sutherland was a man of action and his interests were many. A leader in lumbering and contracting, he controlled the Rainy Lake Lumber Company and operated one of the first sawmills in the area. One of the founders of the Manitoba Club and Manitoba Jockey Club, he held directorates or other official positions with various business concerns, the Canadian Northern Railway, Winnipeg Street Railway Company, Winnipeg Stock Exchange, Canadian Northern Coal and Ore Dock Company, and so on.

Hugh Sutherland, ex-Member of Parliament and financier, Chief Executive Office of Canadian Northern Railway, Winnipeg.

But of all the varied business enterprises with which he was associated, his first love was unquestionably the railroad connection with the Bay, which he fully intended to build. The seriousness of his convictions came through clearly in papers and speeches of his preparation, even when hope of carrying out the proposed program was beginning to fade. He understood the needs of Western settlers and in an address before the Geographical Section of the British Association at Birmingham, September 2, 1886, he said: "When the extent and fertility of the prairie possessions of Canada became fully known, the more adventurous spirits of the eastern provinces began flocking into it, and soon that territory attracted the attention of the world as a field for colonization. Situated far in the interior of the continent, and shut off from all known channels of trade and commerce, the first question that presented itself to those who were anxious for its development, was that of a practical outlet to the markets of the world. Recognizing the enormous agricultural value of that region, the Canadian Parliament hastened to provide a means of communication between it and the provinces of Eastern Canada. . . . But it was soon felt that they were too far removed from the seaboard to ensure that speedy and complete development which the excellence of both soil and climate otherwise rendered possible. . . . The North-West offered a new and practically inexhaustible field for colonization, provided the settlers could be placed within reasonable reach of tidewater and thus be enabled to compete with the world in those staple food products which it was known they could grow so abundantly. But how was this to be done? A land carriage of 1,500 or 2,000 miles between them and the Atlantic was more than the products of their industry could bear. Some other outlet must be discovered, and one presented itself in the great bay of the north. For nearly two centuries ships had visited Hudson Bay from England with the regularity of succeeding seasons."[1]

Writing later, Sutherland explained the great savings in miles which Western shippers would find in the Bay Route.

---

[1]Sutherland, Hugh, Paper presented to Geographical Section of British Assoc. at Birmingham, Sept. 2, 1886, *The Canadian Magazine*, p. 347, Aug. 1894

And, "after all is said and done," he emphasized, "miles count, whether by water or by land." Manitobans had heard it before but perhaps it had not occurred to most readers of the *Canadian Magazine,* that "Brandon is 1,557 miles from Montreal and 650 miles from Port Nelson. Montreal is 2,990 miles from Liverpool, and Port Nelson is 2,966. The ocean distances are practically identical. But there is a saving in land carriage of 900 miles which represents the average advantage that would result to the wheat producers of Manitoba. Regina may be taken as the central point for the entire wheat region of the North-west. It is 1,781 miles from Montreal, and 700 miles from Port Nelson, giving a saving of 1,081 miles of land carriage in favor of the Hudson Bay route. Much of the ranching country is south and west of Calgary which is 2,264 miles from Montreal; the saving in land and carriage would, at least, be as great as from Regina. Edmonton is the centre of one of the most fertile and promising regions of the North-West; it is 2,500 miles from Montreal and less than half of that distance from Port Nelson. An established Hudson Bay route would offer to the farmers of Manitoba the saving on 900 miles of railway haul, and to the farmers and ranchers of the Territories beyond, a saving on from 1,100 to 1,300 miles. We would be brought nearer by these distances to tide water and consequently to the markets of the world."[1]

He realized that his confidence was not shared by a large proportion of Eastern Canadians and wrote again, reciting much of the evidence of successful shipping by Hudson's Bay Company and others over the years, and concluded that Western grain could be "delivered at Port Nelson at a cost of about ten cents a bushel less than the present charge to New York or Boston. . . . A thousand miles less of a land haul — that is the strong point of the scheme that cannot be broken down. And with as free and safe an ocean passage as from Montreal, it would be a crime to withhold the advantage from the struggling settlers of the North-West a day longer than is necessary."[2]

[1]Sutherland, Hugh, "The Hudson Bay Route," *Canadian Magazine,* p. 347, Aug., 1894
[2]Sutherland, Hugh, "Nature's Outlet For the North-West," *Canadian Magazine,* p. 519, Oct. 1894

Long before Manitoba public opinion solidified in support of a railroad to the Bay, Sutherland was drawing plans for the scheme which reached the Parliament of Canada early in 1880. If Manitoba enthusiasm for the northern outlet was not yet fully blown, neither was the Eastern resistance to such an undertaking and the federal acts to incorporate Sutherland's Winnipeg and Hudson's Bay Railway and Steamship Company, and the rival plan, the Nelson Valley Railway and Transportation Company, were passed in the House of Commons with practically no debate and received Royal Assent at the same time, May 8, 1880. Canadian Pacific Railway officials were known to be opposed and if Sir John A. Macdonald, as Prime Minister, was opposed — and it is believed that he was — he was either convinced that both projections toward the Bay would never amount to anything, or considered it politically unwise to raise his voice against them at the time.

The idea behind Sutherland's railroad plan was born right at Winnipeg while the other, with its office at Montreal and Senator Thomas Ryan as Chairman of the Board, appeared more like something created for Eastern investors. In any case, the Nelson Valley scheme was designed to make the maximum use of water on the route to the Bay. It would begin "on the north shore of Lake Winnipeg, or on the navigable waters of any river flowing northward from the said lake," and "extend to a point on or near the Churchill River, at or near the shore of Hudson Bay."[1] By the terms of the same Act, the Nelson Valley company could "own or charter and sail steam vessels" on its route, also construct and operate elevators, lines of telegraph along the right of way and a branch line to connect with the CPR somewhere westward. The Company would be capitalized at two million dollars and be free to accept aid from governments or any like-minded benefactors. Certain things it could not do: it was forbidden to commence construction until the location of the line was approved by the Governor General in Council. In this, however, there was no danger of difficulty because construction was destined to be delayed. More impor-

---

[1]"An Act to Incorporate the Nelson Valley Railway and Transportation Co.," *Statutes of Canada*, Ch. 57, p. 43, 1880

tant was the concluding clause demanding that the railway should be commenced within two years and completed within six years from the passing of the Act of Incorporation.

Hugh Sutherland's Bill 46 was much the same except that the railroad would start at the city of Winnipeg rather than a point on the north side of Lake Winnipeg. It, too, could be constructed in such a way as "to utilize the navigable waters along the route . . . and build and own or charter vessels . . . also build, own, purchase or charter steamships or other vessels for the purpose of transporting freight or passengers from the northern terminus of the said railway to Europe or elsewhere."[1] And for the Sutherland company, as with the rival, "construction of the railway shall be commenced within two years and completed within six years after passing of this Act."

Sutherland may have been pleasantly surprised that the enabling legislation passed in the House of Commons without opposition, but it proved the benefit of three years of planning along with some well-directed lobbying. Having convinced his friends of the merits in the scheme, he was able to secure the support of influential men who agreed to serve as provisional directors, men like Dr. John Schultz who achieved fame for his stand against Louis Riel in 1869 and later served successively as Member of Parliament, Member of the Senate, and Lieutenant-Governor of Manitoba. Among other provisional directors were John G. Haggart, former Mayor of Perth, Ontario, and Member of Parliament for South Lanark, and William Bannerman, Member of Parliament for South Renfrew who introduced the bill in the Commons and escaped without being accused of "conflict of interest." Sitting as a Conservative and on the Government side, Bannerman probably won the Prime Minister's approval before making the formal presentation.

But as Sutherland was to discover, passing of the bill was but the first hurdle and one of the easiest in the long process of taking his cherished railroad with carefully declared gauge of "four feet eight and a half inches in width" all the way to the

[1]"An Act to Incorporate the Winnipeg and Hudson's Bay Railway and Steamship Co.," *Statutes of Canada*, Ch. 59, p. 55, 1880.

Bay. The great need now was for capital and the capitalists preferred to make loans to the Canadian Pacific Railway, especially when the transcontinental company could display land grants as collateral and enjoyed the Prime Minister's fatherly concern.

The federal government's refusal to allow new railroads to be built within the CPR sphere of influence was increasingly irritating to Manitoba people but may have been the means of bringing indirect local support for the Bay-bound projects. Disallowance of the South-Eastern Railway in 1882 led a few editors to advise the companies holding charters for railroads to the Bay to get on with the job as quickly as possible. Both companies, facing exactly the same hopes and difficulties, were anxious to capture all possible from this wave of public favor and placed survey crews in the field with what seemed like precipitate haste.

Inasmuch as the Nelson Valley Railway and Transportation Company would begin building almost 300 miles north of Winnipeg, there could be no direct conflict with the CPR and the location map as submitted received government approval without delay. Not so with the Sutherland projection which would begin from a point at or close to the main line of the CPR at Winnipeg. This time, the proposed route map was submitted courteously for Syndicate consideration and was finally judged to be of no serious importance or threat to existing lines. The desired approval was then granted.

A letter from George Stephen of the Syndicate to Prime Minister Sir John A. Macdonald, written on January 5, 1884, casts light upon the CPR attitude toward a railroad to the Bay.[1] The letter, marked "confidential," displayed more scorn than concern about a railroad into the North and, it would appear, Stephen regarded Macdonald as one who shared his views. The letter begins:

---

[1]Stephen, George, Letter to Prime Minister Macdonald, Jan. 5, 1884, *Correspondence of Sir John A. Macdonald, 1840-1891,* Compiled by Sir Joseph Pope, p. 308, Oxford Univ. Press

"My Dear Sir John:
I have just received the enclosed and send it to you, trust-
ing that you won't mind telling me how I should answer it. The
Hudson's Bay Railway, in my judgment, is a humbug — an
impossibility — but as far as the C.P.R. is concerned I have no
objection to a line to the H. Bay, or for that matter, to the North
Pole, if the promoters will put their own money into the enterprise. It would be a fatal blunder for the Province of Manitoba
to become mixed up with the finance of that, or any other
railway. At least, that is how the matter looks to me. Apart from
this I see no objection to a line being built to H. Bay."

George Stephen had more pertinent information for the
Prime Minister and blamed three "promoters of the H. Bay
Railway" for trying to weaken or destroy the CPR application
for a bank loan. He noted their "great opposition to us" and
attributed it to "envy, hatred and malice."

The East had its skeptics, lots of them, but Manitoba
confidence in the northern route was unshaken. As one
provincially-chartered railroad after another suffered disallowance by federal decree, CPR popularity deteriorated and
Sutherland's plan gained favor. Unfortunately, popularity and
public favor were not enough and while the Prime Minister,
conscious of the crucial importance of saving the transcontinental railway, was helping the CPR to find borrowings, he was
doing nothing of similar kind for either the Sutherland or Nelson
Valley schemes.

For both of the Bay-bound railway projects, financial problems became serious and Ottawa, at length, responded moderately, announcing that the two companies would qualify for land
grants amounting to 6,400 acres for every mile of railroad
construction completed. After the grant of 25,000,000 acres, in
addition to cash subsidies, to the CPR, the federal government
could hardly do less. But it was not enough; the promise would
entail northern land close to the new railroads, not likely to
appeal to settlers and not of much help in securing the urgently
needed cash advances.

Company directors had been known to make personal con-
tributions for administration and preliminary work in the field
but these could not be expected to continue and as officials

approached the majôr task of laying rails, they knew the lack of funds would be crippling. Men of both companies could not fail to recognize the folly of two rival organizations competing for funds which neither had been able to obtain. Amalgamation was proposed in whispers and then accepted as a necessity.

The House of Commons was petitioned to pass a special Act needed to authorize the union and it was finally approved on May 25, 1883[1], the same day, incidentally, that Royal Assent was given to no fewer than four Acts incorporating new railroads for the West: the Saskatchewan and North Western Railway Co.; the Qu'Appelle, Long Lake and Saskatchewan Railway and Steamboat Co.; the Pacific and Peace River Railway Co., and the Wood Mountain and Qu'Appelle Railway Co. — all lines which the government of the day must have considered to be incapable of hurting the CPR.

The new and united company which was expected to result would carry the name of Sutherland's project, namely, the Winnipeg and Hudson's Bay Railway and Steamship Co., and be given a revised Board of Directors, six of whom would be Winnipegers and three Montrealers. Sutherland was satisfied with the Act but before it could be ratified by the two older companies, directors disagreed and the proposed union failed to materialize.

Directors agreed to try again and Parliament acquiesced with another amendment which was passed on April 19, 1884.[2] By the amended terms of incorporation the united company would inherit some slightly modified privileges and instructions, mainly to build "from a point in or near the City of Winnipeg . . . or some other point at or near the Town of Selkirk on the Red River, or on the line of the Canadian Pacific railway west of the Town of Selkirk and east of Portage la Prairie . . . to Port Nelson and Churchill, or some other point on the shores of Hudson's bay . . . and own steam or other

[1] "An Act to Unite The Winnipeg and Hudson's Bay Railway and Steamship Co. and the Nelson Valley Railway and Transportation Co. into One Corporation, Under the Name of the Winnipeg and Hudson's Bay Railway and Steamship Co.," *Statutes of Canada*, p. 62, 1883

[2] "An Act to Amend an Act to Incorporate the Winnipeg and Hudson's Bay Railway and Steamship Co.," *Statutes of Canada*, p. 70, 1884

vessels or ships for the purpose of transport on the route or from the terminus of the said railway to Europe or elsewhere. . . ."

Fortunately for the new company, too, the amended Act extended the time limits for construction; the starting time could be up to two years and completion up to six years from the passing of the new Act. And Sutherland and his friends were going to need all the time they could get — and more.

By this time, with the CPR nearing completion and Hugh Sutherland sitting as Liberal Member of Parliament, the Prime Minister was taking a more benign view of a Hudson Bay railway and actually stood in the House to declare his support. There might have been some doubt about his real convictions because he referred later by letter to "that most hopeless of all enterprises — the Hudson's Bay Railway."[1]

Apart from the matter of finances, circumstances as they applied to railroad construction northward seemed to be improving. Premier John Norquay's government, always sympathetic and still trying to aid Sutherland's purpose, tried to remove some of the lingering Eastern doubts by appointing a Select Committee to conduct hearings on shipping by the northern route and, as expected, the report was a clear endorsation. By that time, 1884, Manitoba was eagerly enthusiastic and the federal government, trying to make amends in Manitoba, authorized an expenditure for an expedition to Hudson Strait to explore for new information which might be essential in making the northern route a success.

Railroad builders had to be optimists, and Sutherland was still hopeful.

[1]Macdonald, John A., Letter to Sir John Rose, Bart., *Correspondence of Sir John A. Macdonald, 1840-1891,* Compiled by Sir Joseph Pope, p. 403, Oxford Univ. Press, Toronto

THE FORTY FRUSTRATING MILES

Prairie people had talked long enough about a railroad to Hudson Bay; the time had come for action. By the amended terms of incorporation, 1884, the Winnipeg and Hudson's Bay Railway and Steamship Company was required to begin construction before the expiry of two years. That meant building grade, laying tracks, pounding spikes, and trying to find the millions of borrowed money with which to pay for it all. For Company President Hugh Sutherland it meant the biggest gamble of his life. He would stake his reputation on the outcome and he understood the risks. "If I succeed in building the railway," he said, "no doubt some kindly things may be said of me, but if I fail, no matter how strong and earnest a fight I make, most likely the reverse will be the case."[1]

Sutherland was right. Historians had to score him high on perseverance, not so high on achievement. Circumstances he could not foresee, and over which he had no control, compounded his misfortunes. When grain prices slumped to depression levels and the waves of shock from the Northwest Rebellion were felt across the hemisphere, investment confidence was shattered. Men of finance were in no hurry to loan money in an area suffering from both depression and strife. They would wait a while; and the resulting delays suited the Prime Minister whose first loyalty was to the Canadian Pacific Railway but whose political sagacity forbade public rejection of a railroad Western people were demanding. To take a stand against the scheme would have been popular in the East but in Manitoba and the Territories it would have been politically dangerous.

Employing well-worn delaying tactics, the federal government authorized another survey in northern waters, this time with the former sealing ship *Neptune* assigned to the expedi-

[1]*Manitoba Daily Free Press,* Jan. 26, 1886

tion, and Royal Navy Officer, Lieutenant Andrew Gordon, named to the command. With less than complete trust in federally appointed officials and observers, the government of Manitoba appointed its own representative to accompany, Charles R. Tuttle, and as might have been expected, federal and provincial observers did not see the Bay and Strait in the same light.

Sailing north in 1884, the *Neptune* party established observation stations at various points along the northern coasts and left men and supplies at each. A year later, another government ship — this time the *Alert* — made the northern trip to relieve the station personnel and collect recorded data. But desiring still more time, Ottawa leaders announced that the *Alert* would go north again in 1886 and Lieutenant Gordon would continue in command.[1] And as further evidence of distrust among the interested parties, the *Alert* carried another observer in the person of Captain Albert H. Markham, a distinguished British explorer, traveling on this occasion as Hugh Sutherland's personal representative and adviser.

But even the extension of the survey program did nothing to resolve the conflict of interest between Western and Eastern people. Tuttle, answering to the government of Manitoba, reported most favorably about shipping conditions in the Bay and Strait, just as Western people wanted and expected of him. He could see reasonable hope for shipping in eight months of the year. Lieutenant Gordon, on the other hand, was neither as optimistic nor as positive. Instead of anticipating at least four months of shipping conditions, he chose to see at least eight months without shipping. As for Markham's observations, they were for the private ears of Hugh Sutherland and the exact content of his report was never made public.

But regardless of what Markham told Sutherland, the latter was as determined as ever to build the railroad. Nothing was changed. The government of Manitoba under Premier John Norquay was making a convincing pretense of confidence in the northern route and the Eastern critics were as skeptical as ever.

Hugh Sutherland was the elected Member of Parliament

[1]House of Commons Debates, March 22, 1886

for the Manitoba constituency of Selkirk at the time, a point his detractors did not overlook. There was the suggestion that he might have entered politics expressly to further his railway ambitions but the evidence did not support such a motive. The year of 1886 found him so occupied with railway plans that he had no time for Parliament and there is no record of him speaking in debate or even attending in the House of Commons. For much of that year he was absent from the country, trying to sell the idea of the Hudson Bay Railway as a good investment risk for English capitalists. As he discovered, it was not easy.

But Sutherland, like any good promoter, presented the image of unflagging confidence. Regardless of any personal misgivings, he was outwardly unruffled and optimistic. He now had the promise of a federal land grant — 6,400 acres per mile of completed railroad — also a million-dollar provincial bond issue secured by that land. But he was still unable to convert either to the cash he needed. He required a railroad in order to qualify for the federal lands and he needed title to the lands to qualify for the provincial bonds. He could see the help he needed but could not reach it. His immediate need was for friends with faith who would furnish interim loans without security.

From England he was sending encouraging reports concerning the interest being shown by British capitalists. It was what Manitoba people wanted to hear, of course — that English business leaders were displaying a growing eagerness to invest in this railway scheme. It was reassuring to hear that William Milburne and Company of Newcastle-On-Tyne and London, one of the biggest private shipping concerns in the world, was ready to send ships to Hudson Bay — as many as would be needed to insure success for the venture.

Sutherland's reports were enough to persuade the editor of the *Manitoba Daily Free Press* that: "The opening up of the Hudson's Bay Route is now only a question of time. There is a strong possibility that work on the railway will be commenced and well under way before the close of the present year. So that while the Government, in the interests of its Eastern friends, is experimenting with a view of convincing itself and others of the impracticability of a route the practicability of which has been established by years of experience, the question will be finally solved by the actual opening up of the route. It is generally understood that capital has been awaiting the report of the exploratory expedition. . . . Not only the British but the American Northwest will experience benefits of the new route which will place Winnipeg almost as close to London as Montreal or New York. . . . The Northwest is destined to become the great food producing section of the Empire. The opening of the Hudson's Bay route will enable it, almost immediately, to fulfill its destiny."[1]

Sutherland, replying to questions from the press about this time, hoped to be able to announce very shortly that all arrangements were complete for the building of the road. "I believe," he said, "that in less than two years a train will run from Winnipeg to Hudson's Bay." This he was saying while admitting to some difficulty in securing all the funds he would need. "It is no easy task to raise $15,000,000, for that is the least it will take."[2] He would remain at Winnipeg a few days to confer with a contracting firm, McLennan and Grant, and then return to England to resume negotiations for funds.

Throughout the summer, rumors about the Sutherland railway were numerous and the President, in London, was kept busy refuting the ones which did not suit his purpose. He may have been responsible for the creation of some of those which placed his company in a favorable light. The news at the end of April told of Sutherland signing an agreement with the contracting firm of Ross and McLennan to build the first hundred miles of grade from Winnipeg, "this year." Another report had Sutherland's company being purchased by the Hudson's Bay Company for the purpose of preventing construction of the railroad and thereby protecting the older company's fur trading interests around the Bay.[3]

Certainly some of the published reports were misleading. According to the news in June of the same year,[4] the first rails

[1]*Manitoba Daily Free Press*, Jan. 19, 1886
[2]*Manitoba Daily Free Press*, Jan. 26, 1886
[3]*Manitoba Daily Free Press*, April 22, 1886
[4]*Manitoba Daily Free Press*, June 17, 1886

were shipped from England via the Hudson's Bay Company sailing ship *Prince of Wales* en route to York Factory. Railroad construction, it was explained, would begin from a point near the estuary of the Nelson River. But when Sutherland answered questions for the benefit of press and public on October 23 of the same year, he reported that "Milburne and Co. vessels are now at Montreal with rails for the railway."

At mid-September, Sutherland cabled from London that final arrangements had been completed for immediate commencement of construction and rails were on the way. This time the announcement seemed convincing and the editor of the *Free Press* waxed eloquent:

"The news is already regarded as signifying the dawn of a glorious day. . . . With an ocean outlet that will bring the prairie Steppes and grain fields of this vast country as near to the British markets as the farmers of Eastern Canada and the seaports of the United States, the grand obstacle of distance will be swept away by a single stroke and the full granaries of this part will be placed on the thresholds of the British market."[1]

The uncertainties of finance notwithstanding, the great day arrived and interested citizens gathered at the right of way, about nine miles northwest of Winnipeg, to witness the "Turning of the First Sod." It was Saturday afternoon, October 9, 1886, and farmers thereabout were busy at fall plowing, hoping to get field work finished before freeze-up. The original plan was to start the railroad construction at the head of Logan Street, "near the race track," in Winnipeg but right of way troubles with one land owner forced the last-minute change of location. It seemed that Company officials were scarcely ready for this dramatic moment when earth-moving would actually begin. Hugh Sutherland, it was noted, was so busy with last-minute negotiations for right of way that he was not present. There was surprise, also, that Premier John Norquay was among those who were "unavoidably absent." But many prominent citizens were on hand, among them Donald Mann of the contracting firm of Mann and Holt, several Winnipeg aldermen,

[1]*Manitoba Daily Free Press,* Sept. 16, 1886

members of the Provincial Legislature, sub-contractors, and many local people who believed it to be an important moment in Canadian history.

As the press saw the event: "About 4 o'clock the Messrs. Egan hitched twelve horses to one of their patent graders and accompanied by those present, proceeded to the staked line of the road. The horses were faced toward Hudson's Bay and without fuss or ceremony the word was given and horses moved on, and the first sod turned for the Hudson's Bay Railway made its appearance. Shortly after the party dispersed, expressing pleasure at witnessing the turning of the first sod of so important an undertaking.

"The Egan Bros., who have the first ten miles, have located on the west end of their contract owing to a difficulty with an owner of property near the starting point, and they will work towards the city. They have about 60 mules and horses and four grading machines. Mr. G. H. Strevel's outfit consisting of about 80 horses and mules, will be on the ground today. Other sub-contractors will be on the ground at once. Over twenty miles are expected to be graded ready for ties this week. Mr. Mann says in three weeks forty miles will be ready for ties."[1]

Manitoba citizens were reassured. At last, the railroad for which they had pleaded was taking shape. The first segment was being built in the direction of Oak Point beside Lake Manitoba, whence it was supposed to veer toward Hudson Bay. But as construction advanced, so did Sutherland's need for money. In supposing that the mere act of building would improve his credit, he was partly right. Two weeks after the sod turning, he was able to report that a provincial order in council had been passed under authority of the Railway Aid Act, granting his company the promised bonds to the extent of $6,400 per mile of completed road for forty miles. The province's security was still the federal land grant and, seeing what he believed to be the promise of better times, Sutherland said that with favorable weather, the contractors would complete sixty miles of grade before being halted by winter.

[1]*Manitoba Daily Free Press*, October 11, 1886

Perhaps the provincial payment of $256,000 would "prime the public pump" and lead to other grants; he hoped the city of Winnipeg would make a donation to a great cause. In view of benefits to the city, a subsidy of $250,000 would be an appropriate sum, the President suggested. Strangely enough, nobody disagreed publicly. Even local editorial writers conceded that it was a reasonable sum to expect the city to contribute.

But Sutherland's glimpse of success was brief; the house he was building was threatened again and again with collapse. After constructing a fraction more than forty miles of railroad, the contractors suspended operations for the winter and the government of Manitoba, without waiting for the federal government to transfer titles on lands Sutherland believed he had been promised, made bond payment for the agreed amount of $6,400 per mile on the completed forty miles. Sutherland, understandably, needed the money in order to make payment to the contractors and the total amount received from the province was turned over to Mann and Holt, all of which seemed quite reasonable because, as everybody expected, the transfer of the federal land — the very basis of Sutherland's financing — was now only a matter of routine.

But as Ottawa officials saw the situation, it was not all that simple and their conduct looked very much like planned obstruction. Was it the result of CPR antagonism and influence or was it the product of the Prime Minister's lack of confidence in the scheme? In any case technical obstacles, one after another, blocked the transfer of land.

The first of these obstacles appeared as an objection to the quality of railroad construction. The work on the first forty miles, the federal government's inspectors said, was substandard and unable to qualify for the land grant. There was instant consternation and it was difficult to know who was the most worried, Premier John Norquay who sensed the possible loss of security for the provincial bonds already turned to the Company's account, or Hugh Sutherland who knew that a determined refusal by the federal government would mean certain bankruptcy for him and his company. While the contractors were called to make such repairs and additions as might bring the railroad to meet minimum standards, Premier Norquay petitioned Ottawa to authorize another inspection of the work and display reasonable consideration.

The Ottawa administration complied and found the renovated construction to be acceptable but before the all-important land could be transferred to the Sutherland company, other technical flaws were discovered. Government officials found that the Company men in their haste had failed to obtain proper right of way clearances from municipal authorities and again the Sutherland men were obliged to take valuable time to obtain the agreements Ottawa was demanding.

Nor was that all of what looked very much like intended obstruction. The Manitoba people understood that the land grants would be made in installments based on twenty-mile segments of the railroad. Such a plan, allowing Sutherland to finance with deeded land as he progressed, was perfectly acceptable but it came as shock when the Ottawa administration insisted that, according to the Eastern interpretation of regulations, the land transfers at the rate of 6,400 acres per mile or 128,000 acres per twenty miles, could only begin after railroad construction totaled fifty miles or more. As it was, the new railroad had less than forty-one miles of construction ending at Shoal Lake, and again the Manitoba Premier, anxious to save his bond investment, went begging to Ottawa for more benevolent consideration.

The spring of 1887 brought no solution to the impasse. No land had been transferred. The provincial government had no security for the bonds turned over to the Company and the money given to the contractors was insufficient to pay for the work they had finished. The Company's single locomotive was idle except for occasional trips over the short line to haul some hay or cordwood or other local freight. The rails were not getting enough use to prevent them from rusting.

Again Sutherland began looking overseas for financial backing but not with much success or encouragement. Again the House of Commons was reminded of the Company's useful purpose when in May, 1887, a Bill was introduced to "Consolidate and Amend the Acts Relating to the Winnipeg and Hudson's Bay Railway and Steamship Company, and Change the Name Thereof.'' The new legislation declared with more of optimism than realism that ''the said Company is making financial arrangements for the completion of the said railway from Winnipeg to Hudson's Bay'' and declared an extension of time for the work to be finished; the main line to the Bay would now have to be completed ''within four years from the 21st of June, one thousand, eight hundred and eighty-seven.''[1]

The Legislature of Manitoba, in the late spring of 1887, while hoping to help Sutherland's chance of extending the railway and attempting at the same time to safeguard the provincial administration's tenuous security in land which the Railway Company had not yet acquired, passed a bill to guarantee interest on certain Company obligations. Sutherland was not giving up the fight and the government of Manitoba was in such a position that it dared not give up. But 1887 was a year of utter discouragement for all concerned. After experiencing one railroad disappointment after another, Sutherland was humiliated by lawsuits launched by his creditors, and then suffered defeat by a very narrow margin of votes when he contested again for the right to represent the constituency of Selkirk in the House of Commons.

There was a change of government in Manitoba in 1888 and Thomas Greenway, Liberal, became Premier. He had been a strong supporter of the Hudson Bay Route and would gladly assist Sutherland with any adequately secured aid. Moreover, the Manitoba Legislators were ready to make a small payment in the hope of obtaining the return of money owing and May, 1888, saw the passing of ''An Act For The Payment of Certain Moneys For The Purpose Of Securing The Payment Of Certain Debentures Delivered To The Winnipeg and Hudson's Bay Railway and Steamship Company.''[2]

[1] ''An Act to Consolidate and Amend the Acts Relating to the Winnipeg and Hudson's Bay Railway and Steamship Company, and Change the Name Thereof,'' *Statutes of Canada,* Ch. 81, p. 100, 1887

[2] ''An Act to Provide For The Payment Of Certain Moneys. For The Purpose Of Securing The Payment Of Certain Debentures Delivered To The Winnipeg and Hudson's Bay Railway and Steamship Company,'' *Statutes of Manitoba,* 1888

The preamble stated clumsily that: "Whereas about forty miles of their railway line have been contracted by said Company, but the same has not been completed to the satisfaction of the Government of Canada. And whereas the Government of the Dominion of Canada refuse to transfer to said Company the land grant for such forty miles of railway until the same is completed to their satisfaction . . . it is important that such land be obtained by said Company . . . it shall be lawful for . . . the Provincial Treasurer to advance the money required to complete said forty miles of railway to satisfaction of the Government of the Dominion of Canada . . . provided the amount to be so advanced shall not exceed $35,000."

For Sutherland, the best remaining chance of extending the railway lay in the hope of qualifying for a federal grant given on some earlier occasions to what classified as Colonization Railways. He believed that the southern portion of the line — the part to run at least as far as the Saskatchewan River — should qualify and he convinced the famous railroad builder, Andrew Onderdonk, who constructed some of the most difficult sections of CPR in the mountains, to come to Manitoba to direct the northern operation. But the federal response to the proposal to classify the next 200 miles of Sutherland's line as a Colonization Railroad was dispirited and Onderdonk withdrew.

Then came one of the cruelest blows of all. The government of Manitoba, facing new financial problems and increasingly worried about Sutherland's failure to gain actual possession of the land he claimed in lieu of forty miles of construction, passed an Act which repudiated its obligation to guarantee the interest on bonds of the Winnipeg and Hudson's Bay Railway Company for twenty-five years, as provided by Act of the Legislature in 1886. There it was, assented to on March 5, 1889, "An Act To Repeal" the essential section of the legislation passed to bring aid to Sutherland's plan.[1]

The repercussions were widespread. The alleged repudiation of statutory guarantees came up for discussion in the British House of Commons in London, and Nicholas Flood

---

[1]"An Act To Repeal Chapter Forty Of Fifty Victoria, Being An Act To Provide For Granting Of Aid To The Winnipeg and Hudson's Bay Railway and Steamship Co.," *Statutes of Manitoba*, 1889

Davin, the Honorable Member from Regina, raised the matter in the Canadian House of Commons on April 29, 1889. He urged the Government to take any steps necessary to protect the reputation of the provinces and safeguard their credit.

"In 1886," Davin explained, "the Legislature of Manitoba passed an Act guaranteeing for 25 years the interest at 4 percent, upon an issue of $4,500,000 of bonds of the railway to connect Winnipeg with Port Nelson on Hudson's Bay. The bonds were issued, the first 40 miles of road were built, when lo! on the 2nd of March last, the Government of Manitoba, without a word of warning, repudiated the obligation to pay interest. If Manitoba is to be allowed to obtain money under a Provincial guarantee one day, and having got what she wants, to repudiate the next, then there is not a Provincial guaranteed municipal debt in all Canada which can be looked upon other than as a fly-trap."[1]

Macdonald's policy was unchanged except that in 1891 — when it was too late to be of much help to Sutherland — he offered an annual subsidy of $80,000 for the essential local services if and when Sutherland's line was built to the Saskatchewan River. Hon. Edgar Dewdney, Minister of the Interior, in introducing the resolution for the assistance, took pains to explain that it was not to be considered as an aid in extending the railway to the Bay and "the Company shall at no future time make any demand on the Government for financial assistance for the construction of the railway northward." The Government seemed to be saying to Hugh Sutherland: "Take this and forget about your pet railway to Hudson Bay. And don't ever come back for more money."

By the acceptance of the subsidy, the old Winnipeg and Hudson's Bay Railway would cease to be anything more than another local line, another "Colonization Road" as the Minister insisted on calling it.[2]

Sutherland learned from bitter experience that there was nobody in the federal cabinet with either feeling or affection for a railroad to connect the Western crop country with an ocean

[1]House of Commons Debates, April 29, 1889
[2]House of Commons Debates, June 25, 1891

port on Hudson Bay. He had been rebuked many times but still he was not surrendering. Twelve years after formulating his plan for the northern railroad and ten years after obtaining a federal charter for his scheme, he was still searching for financial backing, still catching bracing whiffs of the smell of success. And although his road to the Bay never did extend beyond the first forty and a fraction miles, the charter was acquired by Donald Mann and Associates to be built ultimately into what Canadians came to know as the Canadian Northern.

Sutherland certainly did not escape criticism, even in the West. Too often he led Manitoba people to believe that he was ready to make a serious start in building toward the Bay and the editor of the *Edmonton Bulletin* referred to him as a fakir. But Sutherland was no fakir. For his convictions about the need for the northern railroad and his dedication to the task of building it, he deserved the highest praise. If later supporters of the Hudson Bay Route should ever decide to elect a patron saint, they should seriously consider Hugh McKay Sutherland.

ALL THE WAY BY WATER

In the wake of Hugh Sutherland's failure to deliver a railway to the Great Bay of the North came a wave of enthusiasm for the only apparent alternative, an all-water connection between Winnipeg and York Factory or Winnipeg and the Great Lakes. Thanks to those designs fashioned by the untiring hand of Nature, the job of providing the all-water route was already almost finished. If transportation by water was really so much more economical than shipping by rail, why not get on with the dredging and building of necessary canals and locks and bring the big ships all the way to Winnipeg or even Edmonton?

Settlers were not in any way less interested in a railroad to the North but they were disappointed and noticeably angry about delays. They did not blame Hugh Sutherland but charged the federal government with indifference. Impatience showed up vividly in the federal election campaign of 1891 and Western candidates in both parties discovered that anything short of personal declaration of support for a Hudson Bay Railway could be their political undoing. Campaigners seized upon the words of Donald Grant, the contractor: "That sheet of water is not up there for nothing,"[1] and a few of them added: "If the Bay is not up there for nothing, neither are the rivers and lakes between Winnipeg and Port Nelson placed there for no purpose." The effect was to revive an idea which was almost as old as the fur trade. Traders for decades had talked about improving the water courses to facilitate uninterrupted boat travel from Fort Edmonton or Fort Garry to the Bay, and Henry Hind abetted the purpose with his vision of a river highway serving a big prairie area which might never be able to afford railways.

[1]*Manitoba Daily Free Press*, Jan. 22, 1886

Manitoba people had for many years talked about dredging and constructing the other installations needed to let ocean-going vessels come all the way to tie up on the Red River between Winnipeg and St. Boniface. And Edmonton's pioneer newspaperman, Frank Oliver, a consistent advocate of river transportation, advised incoming settlers to recognize the advantages in living near a navigable river and choose the good soil beside the North Saskatchewan instead of a dry-land location close to the new transcontinental railway. "The river furnishes a means by which supplies can be brought in and grain shipped out at far lower rates than a monopoly railroad will give," he wrote.[1] "During the coming summer, parties can be landed by steamer at any point on its [Saskatchewan River] course, with all their effects, quite as cheaply and safely as they can travel out on the CPR, and once they have a surplus of grain for sale they can ship it themselves by means that no monopoly can control. . . . There is twice as much good land along the Saskatchewan as along the CPR between Brandon and the mountains and . . . provided already with means of communication. . . . Next summer the government will commence clearing the channel of the river with the intention, no doubt, of making it one of the great highways of the country, for steamers will run on it all summer. . . . There can be no doubt that the settler whether rich or poor, who settles near any of the principal points on the river will be much better off and much more independent than the one who mortgages himself to the CPR by taking up a half section on the bleak prairies of Regina."

Editor Oliver could be suspected of prejudice but Western people had many reminders of the useful service rendered by riverboats from the time of the arrival of the *Anson Northrup* at Fort Garry in 1859 and they had not forgotten Henry Hind's quite logical proposal. Hind's idea was to construct a dam at the Elbow of the South Saskatchewan and divert part or all of the water into the Qu'Appelle to be delivered to the Assiniboine and Red, thereby furnishing a river highway from Fort Garry to

[1]*Edmonton Bulletin,* Jan. 20, 1883

the Foothills. It would need, according to his estimates, a dam 85 feet high and 600 to 800 yards long and the location would have been close to the site chosen in recent times for the big Gardiner Dam intended mainly for power and irrigation. Hind became enthusiastic about the possibility of furnishing "splendid and probably uninterrupted navigation for steamers of a large size for a distance exceeding six hundred miles."

Hind's observations coincided almost exactly with the arrival at Fort Garry of the paddlewheel monstrosity known as *Anson Northrup,* marking the beginning of the Western steamboat era. Still resembling a warehouse on a raft, the boat came again in 1860 and an attempt was made to place its service on a regular schedule. An announcement appearing in the pioneer paper, *The Nor'-Wester,*[1] informed local people of what they could expect: "The undersigned managing owner of the steamboat Anson Northrup is now prepared to make contracts to transport freight between Fort Garry and St. Paul, and guarantee its prompt delivery at the following rates:

> Fort Garry to St. Paul, $5 per 100 lbs.
>
> St. Paul to Fort Garry, $6 per 100 lbs.
>
> Passengers either way with cabin accommodation on boat, $35.
>
> Four-horse Concord coaches run between St. Paul and Georgetown, connecting with boat.
>
> Time for through passengers, 8 to 9 days.
>
> The Anson Northrup will leave on Monday, 4th inst. at 8 a.m. on this her first regular trip and return in time to leave on the second trip June 1st, 1860."

It was the first direct challenge to the hundreds of Red River carts carrying freight between Fort Garry and St. Paul, and was like an invitation to explore other river courses reaching farther into the Northwest. The result was striking. The steamboat fleet proliferated and extended to Lake Winnipeg and the Saskatchewan River, then into the Assiniboine and as far as Fort Ellice and Fort Pelly. By 1879, at least seventeen of the big, shallow-draft freight and passenger boats were in serv-

---

[1] *The Nor'-Wester,* (Fort Garry), Aug. 28, 1860

ice on the prairie rivers. Of the distinctive and colorful men who were the Captains, many of them gained their earlier experience on the Mississippi.

Most of the steamboats of the time operated on the long river-and-lake route leading from Fort Garry to Fort Edmonton with a single transfer at Grand Rapids as the only major obstacle. A return journey would entail at least 3,000 miles of travel, with stops for freight and passengers at Cumberland House, Fort à la Corne, Prince Albert, Fort Carlton, Battleford and Fort Pitt. And unscheduled stops for cordwood fuel or repairs or river obstructions made it almost impossible to travel on time.

The riverboats were not famous for speed and travelers in a hurry were known to quit the luxury of a big vessel on a twisting watercourse and take to the trails on foot. Nor were the boats considered especially economical by the standards of the time. Freight from Winnipeg to Edmonton was carried at $4 per hundred pounds and passengers paid $40 for a single fare with the luxury of a cabin or $20 for an exposed place on the weather deck.

Notwithstanding their shortcomings, the riverboats drew expressions of familiarity and even affection from the settlers. The best known names were *Manitoba, Minnesota, International, Dakota, Selkirk, Cheyenne, Alpha, Keewatin, Swallow, Lily, Prince Rupert, Lady Ellen, St. Boniface, William Robinson, Colville, Adelaide, Venture, Northcote,* and *Mayo.* They were reaching the peak of their importance and popularity about the time Hugh Sutherland was preparing to build his forty famous miles of railroad and business leaders in Winnipeg were showing interest in a proposal to give the Red River a water connection with Lake Superior. There had been talk about such an undertaking for a decade and finally, on August 15, 1882, delegates from boards of trade and other public bodies in Western Canada and the Northwestern States met at Duluth to consider it.

First, there was a question of location: Should the proposed channel be dug to bring Lake of the Woods into the route or should the choice be for a more southerly course to include Red Lake River, a Minnesota tributary of the Red River, with a follow-through to Duluth? The Red Lake River route was the convention's preference. It was all on United States territory but that was acceptable to the Canadians in attendance because the Americans would have to pay for the 37 miles of actual canals, the 56 dams and 111 locks considered necessary and expected to cost $3,800,000. Obviously, a million dollars at that wheelbarrow stage in North American history would move a lot of earth.

Whether the proposed development were on Canadian or United States soil, the "value and importance to the Prairie Province," according to a Winnipeg editor, could not be questioned.[1] People of the area would be able to utilize more fully the intervening natural waterways and bring new importance to 4,000 miles of lake and river navigation in Western Canada and Western United States.

The editor of the *Manitoba Daily Free Press* tried to be optimistic without loss of objectivity. He liked the idea of a watercourse offering a new approach to Lake Superior and new competition for the CPR. He was confident that "the Canadian North-West and Winnipeg in particular, would be greatly benefited," but after considering the tortuous nature of the Red and other rivers involved, he admitted "reason to doubt."[2]

However the practical obstacles may have appeared, the ambitious plan deserved study. Manitobans were hopeful that their American friends would disregard economics and build the waterway but the Washington administration, refusing to make million-dollar expenditures with later-day abandon, did nothing to implement the plan. Canadians did not forget, however, and alternatives were proposed. Winnipeg was the main spawning ground for new transportation schemes, most of which won publicity and nothing more.

The next proposal to fire public imagination in and beyond Winnipeg was the Hudson's Bay Canal and Navigation Company. Bill No. 52 to incorporate the Company received first reading in the House of Commons on February 5, 1896, and second reading two days later. The politicians then reacted quickly and the House rocked with debate.

[1]*Daily Times*, Winnipeg, Aug. 2, 1882
[2]*Manitoba Daily Free Press*, Aug. 3, 1882

Here was a proposal to simply revive and improve the Lake Winnipeg and Hayes River watercourse to the Bay which traders and settlers had used for 200 years. It looked like another opportunity to make the best use of natural advantages and gain the much-desired economy in transportation. As long as farmers could show that half of the return from sales of their grains was going to pay for freight, nobody could question the importance of the continuing quest. The farmers agreed heartily with a statement made in the House of Commons at the time; "It is unimportant whether a canal or a railway is built, so long as the people obtain some outlet for their products by way of Hudson's Bay."[1]

As the Bill for Incorporation was presented to Parliament, the Company would be permitted by means of canals and dams to improve the waterways between Lake Winnipeg and Hudson Bay, also "all the waterways tributary to Lake Winnipeg." And, having improved the waterways, the Company would be permitted to charge fees and tolls sufficient to realize 10 per cent per annum on the cost of the project.

To the principle of the Bill, the Winnipeg City Council and Board of Trade gave full and hearty support. Nobody objected to the charges to realize 10 per cent on investment but both of the Winnipeg bodies objected to giving the Company full control of all tributaries of Lake Winnipeg, which, of course, would include Red River flowing through the city. That section of the waterway, it was argued, should be developed by the Government of Canada and made available to all parties who could use it.

Company engineers estimated the distance from Winnipeg to York Factory near the mouth of the Hayes River to be 681½ miles. For 616½ miles of that distance, the waterway was considered satisfactory for steamers of light draft and would require no improvement. But for a total of 51 miles, expensive changes involving the digging of canals, building of dams, blasting of shoals, and removal of boulders would be necessary.[2]

[1]House of Commons Debates, p. 4799, March 30, 1896
[2]House of Commons Debates, p. 4803, March 30, 1896

Although the Bill was presented with the blessing of the government of the day, it came in for bitter criticism, mainly from the scrappy Member for Winnipeg, Joseph Martin. Having been in Premier Thomas Greenway's cabinet in Manitoba, he was familiar with the long struggle to gain an outlet to the Bay and while standing as one who hoped fervently to see either rails or canals reaching into the North — either would be acceptable if delivered without more delay — his attack was on the feature of the Bill which would pass the control of the Red River to a private corporation. His speech on March 30, 1896, lasted three and one-half hours and was not intended to win friends. He even raised suspicion that the Company seeking incorporation had more interest in gaining control of Lower Red River and exploiting it than in building canals to the Bay.

Discussion shifted to the overworked but popular subject, the navigability of Bay and Straits and the probable length of shipping season. There was much repetition but, even so, it was appropriate enough because there would be but the weakest case for a railway or chain of canals if grains and other goods could not be exported except during two or three months each year. There would be little or no local freight in much of the North and Hudson Bay fish and whale oil would never pay for the canals.

Again certain Honorable Members from Montreal and the Maritime Provinces derided the idea of shipping "through the Arctic ice," and added an opinion that the proposed waterway would cost closer to 50 million dollars than the estimated 5 million; and again Western members insisted that a shipping season of from four to five months was assured.

After consuming much of Parliament's time, the Bill was not returned for third reading. But later in the year when Canada had a new Government under Hon. Wilfrid Laurier, A Bill To Incorporate The Hudson's Bay Canal and Navigation Company was reintroduced and given first and second readings on September 10 and 11 respectively.

By this time, the Bill which had excited so much attention a few months earlier had lost its novelty and was soon forgotten. Actually, new railway companies seeking charters were appearing with amazing frequency, some of them proposing terminals at Hudson Bay. Among those petitioning before the end of 1896 was the Hudson's Bay and Pacific Railway Company which, with Royal Assent on October 5, 1896, would have the right to build a railroad from a point near Port Churchill to a point at or near Fond du Lac on Lake Athabasca, and from the same point of Churchill to the northwest end of Lake Winnipeg and on through the Territory of Saskatchewan to Prince Albert and Calgary. The first name appearing on the official list of incorporators was that of Admiral Albert Hastings Markham of London who, ten years earlier, accompanied the federal government's technical party to Hudson Bay and Strait as Hugh Sutherland's personal representative and observer. And another of the provisional directors was Wesley Fletcher Orr who is remembered as a Mayor of Calgary.

Still new railway and canal proposals were brought forward and Parliament granted a charter to the Hudson's Bay and Yukon Railway and Navigation Company. Here was one to embrace the best of two principles, water and rail. Assented to on June 29, 1897, the Company was authorized to construct and operate a railway from a far northerly point on Chesterfield Inlet to Great Slave Lake, also from a point on the Mackenzie River to the Porcupine or Yukon River. It was one of the boldest challenges to the Canadian North but as with various other railway schemes of the period, nothing came of it and it was forgotten.

In the light of all the plans and failures to provide an improved transportation route to Hudson Bay in that period, Hugh Sutherland's stubborn attempt to build the railway of his dreams appeared more and more commendable. He alone had the distinction of actually laying rails — even if, as Joe Martin alleged in his speech to the House of Commons on March 30, 1896, those rails were never paid for.[1]

Hugh Sutherland was not impressed by these late proposals to give Winnipeg an all-water link with the Bay but nobody expected the dedicated pioneer railroad promoter to completely reform his thinking. His fancy ran to locomotives and freight

[1]House of Commons Debates, p. 4798, March 30, 1896

cars, not steamships. Nor had this man whose name would have to be enshrined in Hudson Bay Route history, ceased to be a railroad expansionist. It was nothing more than wishful thinking when officials in Government said Sutherland's acceptance of a federal grant for a "Colonization Road" would prevent his return for financial assistance for other projects.

Indeed, the indomitable son of Prince Edward Island, whose Winnipeg and Hudson's Bay Railway Company was the subject of debate for many years, was not giving up. He might not be a candidate for the new prize of one and a half million dollars offered by Premier Thomas Greenway's Manitoba government for the first company to complete a railroad to the Bay within a period of five years, but he was still a subtle force in railway promotion and construction. Anyone with his perseverance and spirit deserved to win, and after a long series of struggles and disappointments, he did achieve moderate success. When he appeared hopelessly in debt and facing what might have been disastrous court action, he blithely accepted his principal creditors as partners and carried on. Men like Mackenzie and Mann and Holt were powerful allies, although a railway to Hudson Bay was not one of their primary aims. In a series of transactions, the old Winnipeg and Hudson's Bay Railway Company became part of the Winnipeg Great Northern and then the Canadian Northern. Partners and circumstances were enough to shunt Sutherland's railroad building energies westward more than northward but it would have brought satisfaction to the Sutherland heart that the Gladstone and Dauphin line, built by the Winnipeg Great Northern, became a link in the Canadian Northern and then, coincidentally, in the line to Port Churchill completed by the Government of Canada in 1929.

Although the all-water export outlets for Western produce — like the one put forward by the Hudson's Bay Canal and Navigation Company — were never realized, neither were they forgotten. Eight years after the House of Commons heard about that scheme and almost twenty years after Hugh Sutherland's heyday, Parliament had a petition from The Great Lakes and North-West Transportation Company asking for incorporation and authority to construct canals and improve watercourses for navigation between Lake Superior and Red River at Winnipeg, and from the latter point to Lake Winnipeg and the Northwest in order to provide transportation from the headwaters of the Saskatchewan all the way to Lake Superior.

Nor did interest in using the natural waterways as a means of finding more economical transportation end there. Even after another fifty-seven years, proposals were advanced for the improvement of the Nelson River system to let freight boats move from Hudson Bay to the heart of the prairie wheat country.

In a background paper prepared for the Resources For Tomorrow Conference held in Montreal in 1961, E. Kuiper, Professor of Hydraulic Engineering at University of Manitoba, sketched the potential uses for Nelson River Basin water and recognized the lakes and streams in the system as great national assets. After discussing flood control, water power, irrigation, and industrial and municipal water supplies, the author turned to navigation and concluded that it would be a simple matter from the technical viewpoint to build shiplocks in conjunction with future dams on the Saskatchewan and Nelson rivers to provide a navigable waterway from "Saskatchewan wheat fields to Hudson Bay or from the Alberta coal mines to Winnipeg."[1]

[1]Kuiper, E., "The Water Resources of the Nelson River Basin," Background paper, Resources For Tomorrow Conference, Oct. 23-28, 1961, Vol. I, p. 337, 1961

FINALLY, A PROMISE

More and more, the Hudson Bay Railway issue was being drawn into the turbulent mainstream of federal politics. Easterners might not have seen it as a national issue in the election of 1891 — Sir John A. Macdonald's last — but in the West and especially in Winnipeg, the voters had every reason to think it ranked with "Unrestricted Reciprocity" as the issue of the day.

Winnipeg citizens who flocked to the last open meeting of the campaign on March 3, came away many hours later speculating about the outcome of this "Hudson Bay Railway Election." A thousand people were turned away from that notable political meeting at Trinity Hall, unable to obtain even standing room. With J. B. Mather as the unfortunate fellow chosen for the role of Chairman, the meeting began at 8 o'clock on the wintry evening, with candidates and prominent supporters from both sides on the platform. But Western people of that pioneer period took their politics seriously and on this occasion, feeling was particularly high. Speakers encountered barrages of heckling and organized interruption and some of those called upon to address the gathering simply gave up after futile attempts to make themselves heard. Degenerating into a contest between obstructionist elements in the two parties, the meeting did not end until almost ten hours after it started.

At 4 a.m., with every chair in the hall still occupied, it was Hugh Sutherland's turn to speak — or try to speak. He was present to explain the difficulties he had experienced in trying to build a railroad to the Bay and lay a share of the blame for his failure upon the Liberal candidate, Isaac Campbell, who had been a member of Thomas Greenway's government in Manitoba. Encountering the same form of partisan resistance as the previous speakers, he shouted above the din that he was "a stayer" and would remain until he could deliver his message, regardless of when that might be. He did stay until the hecklers grew tired and then, according to the Press of the time,[1] "stuck

[1]*Manitoba Daily Free Press*, p. 6, March 5, 1891

to his guns and poured hot shot into Campbell and his friends.'' Sutherland's support was for Conservative candidate, Hugh John Macdonald, ''a sterling and staunch friend of the Hudson Bay Railway. (Great applause).''

''Mr. Campbell then attempted to speak but could not be heard. The meeting closed at 5.45 a.m. with cheers for the Queen and the two candidates.''

Making the best possible use of the party slogan: ''The old flag, the old man and the old policy,'' the Conservatives won the election of 1891 and later in the same year learned of the death of their great Party Chief, Sir John A. Macdonald. His passing was Canada's loss as much as it was the party's.

At the next general election, 1896, the campaign debates were much the same, too much the same, as Frank Oliver saw the contest: ''At every general election,'' said the editor of the *Edmonton Bulletin,* ''Sutherland and his scheme bob up before the public. The road is going to be built forthwith, the Dominion Government is going to furnish the money; and the people of Manitoba are scooped in at the polls—like the suckers they are — and when the election is over nothing more is heard of the building of the railway until the next election comes around.''[1]

Again Western voters demonstrated their conviction that the Conservative Party was the one most likely to provide a railroad to the Bay. In other parts of the country, however, it was different; Canadians were inclined to blame the party in power and its National Policy tariffs for lingering economic ills, and the Liberals came to power. The new Prime Minister, Wilfrid Laurier, had yet to reveal his personal convictions about the route to Hudson Bay and may have wished to emulate his predecessor who skillfully discouraged various private schemes for opening a road to the Bay without ever making a public display of opposition. Laurier's views on the question were scarcely known but he did come to office with determined ideas about immigration, and in the next few years people of many races flocked to the Prairies to claim the coveted prizes of free homestead land.

[1]*Edmonton Bulletin,* May 20, 1895

The result of land settlement was an immediate increase in grain production. Suddenly, the volume exceeded the capacity of the Canadian Pacific Railway to haul it to the Lakehead. "The hopper," according to Sir William Van Horne, had grown "too big for the spout." The dilemma brought demand for additional transportation outlets and a new epidemic of railroad construction. Within the first two years of the new century, the Grand Trunk Railway was under construction, with the promise to make it Canada's second transcontinental line. And then the Canadian Northern — the Mackenzie and Mann railway which had been growing by bits and pieces — began to shape up as the third rail connection between Atlantic and Pacific.

Amid the wild flurry of railway building, fully a score of new Hudson Bay Railway dreams were announced and many of them were officially recognized with charters. Some were grandiose and ridiculous to the point of being laughable. Reports were current in 1894 about an American scheme to build or develop a rail-and-water communication from Mexico by way of Winnipeg to Hudson Bay. The sponsor, Representative McLeary of Minnesota, could foresee no major obstacles in bringing the Mississippi, Minnesota and Red rivers into the system, with the latter two connected by means of a canal between Traverse and Big Stone lakes.[1]

If that international scheme seemed overly ambitious, there was a later plan to far surpass it, a proposal for a railroad to run from Argentina to Hudson Bay.[2] With its northern terminal at Port Nelson, the line would be one of 10,000 miles and pass through Peru, Ecuador, Colombia, Panama, Mexico, Texas, Kansas, Nebraska, South and North Dakota, and Manitoba. The cost of the undertaking was estimated at one-quarter of a billion dollars. Needless to say, the idea did not advance very far.

It was easy to build railways on drawing boards and hope to have them qualify for government favor. Canada's policy of bonusing new railways with land grants looked good to the promoters. It was not uncommon for a company to expose a

[1]*Edmonton Bulletin,* June 18, 1894

[2]*Edmonton Bulletin,* January 6, 1904

hint of greedy purpose in the terms of the charter presented hopefully for government approval. The company, for example, might seek authority ". . . to expropriate or otherwise acquire lands for the purposes of the Company; to acquire, take and receive lands, bonuses, privileges or other aid from the Government of Canada, or of the provinces thereof, or from any municipality, corporation or person towards the construction of the said railway and works. . . ." It may have been correct that many promoters were motivated by the thought of land grants rather than that of rendering the service of a railroad to the Bay.

Between 1887, when Westerners began carrying their fight into federal political channels, and 1908, when they heard the first firm promise of a government-built railway to the Bay, the Dominion Parliament passed legislation to incorporate or amend existing legislation affecting the following companies with schemes for railways to end somewhere on the shores of Hudson or James bays (bracketed dates are those on which Royal Assent was given):

1—An Act to Revive and Amend the Charter of the Quebec and James Bay Railway Company and to Extend the Time for Commencing and Completing the Railway of Said Company (June 23, 1887)

2—An Act to Consolidate and Amend the Acts Relating to Winnipeg and Hudson's Bay Railway and Steamship Company (June 23, 1887)

3—An Act Respecting the Lake Nipissing and James Bay Railway Company (May 4, 1888)

4—An Act to Incorporate the Sault Ste. Marie and Hudson's Bay Railway Company (March 26, 1890)

5—An Act Respecting the Winnipeg and Hudson's Bay Railway Company and to Change the Name Thereof to Winnipeg Great Northern Railway Company (July 23, 1894)

6—An Act to Incorporate the Duluth, Nipigon and James Bay Railway Company (July 23, 1894)

7—An Act to Incorporate the James Bay Railway Company (July 22, 1895)

8—An Act to Incorporate the Hudson's Bay and Yukon Railway and Navigation Company (June 29, 1897)

9—An Act to Incorporate the Montreal and James Bay Railway Company (June 13, 1898)

10—An Act to Incorporate the Toronto and Hudson Bay Railway Company (June 13, 1898)

11—An Act Respecting the Hudson's Bay and Pacific Railway Company (June 13, 1898)

12—An Act to Incorporate the Lake Superior and Hudson's Bay Railway Company (July 7, 1900)

13—An Act to Incorporate the Interprovincial and James Bay Railway Company (May 23, 1901)

14—An Act to Incorporate the Manitoba and Kewatin Railway Company (May 15, 1902)

15—An Act Respecting the Hudson's Bay and North-West Railway Company (May 15, 1902)

16—An Act to Incorporate the Regina and Hudson's Bay Railway Company (June 25, 1903)

17—An Act to Incorporate the Hudson's Bay and Occidental Railway Company (June 25, 1903)

18—An Act to Incorporate the Brandon, Saskatchewan and Hudson's Bay Railway Company (August 13, 1903)

19—An Act Respecting the Ontario, Hudson's Bay and Western Railway Company (July 20, 1905)

20—An Act to Incorporate the Saskatchewan Valley and Hudson's Bay Railway Company (March 22, 1907)

21—An Act to Incorporate the Abitibi and Hudson Bay Railway Company (April 27, 1907)

As titles would indicate, some of these railway programs would have started and ended in the eastern half of Canada and have done nothing for Western wheat growers and shippers. The fact of so many of them being planned to begin at eastern points and terminate at James Bay may appear puzzling but natural resources would have to be high among the reasons. Security was another factor, it being recognized that railways and seaports well removed from the United States boundary would hold benefits in the event of border trouble. But for Eastern promoters and investors, forest, mineral and other natural resources would be the most obvious attractions.

Speaking in Winnipeg on January 24, 1907, J. A. Osborne of the Fort Francis *Times* said he had just returned from the Bay and was convinced that the area would furnish much wealth to the Dominion. "The fisheries have never been exploited," he said. "The Bay is teeming with cod, salmon, whitefish and speckled trout, while there is no doubt that the surrounding country is filled with great mineral possibilities."[1]

Likewise, the Hudson's Bay and Yukon Railway and Navigation Company's intended line from Chesterfield Inlet to a point on Great Slave Lake, and from a point on the Mackenzie River to the Yukon River, would be far from wheat country. Had the planning been a year later it would have been easy to see it as a dream born in the Klondike gold rush. All the other western lines with southern terminals at Winnipeg, Brandon, Regina, Edmonton, and Calgary, were inspired by wheat and cattle. It was difficult, however, to see any of them possessing the natural route advantages offered by the Nelson Valley through which Hugh Sutherland had hoped to build. If Sutherland, after years of trying, was unable to gain the backing for construction, there could not be much hope for the others.

Western people, after hearing about so many private proposals to build to the Bay, lost faith in all of them and renewed in louder terms their call for a railroad to be built by the Government of Canada and operated by a Government Corporation. Just as surely, Ottawa leaders hoped to continue to escape the necessity, even though there was precedent for government in railway building. Had not the Government of Canada fulfilled a promise by building the Intercolonial to connect Halifax with the St. Lawrence River, and had the Government not constructed miles of eastern railway which became part of the Grand Trunk Railway? As Western people saw it, the Government's obligation to build the Hudson Bay Road was clear and positive.

When public pressures mount against a government choosing inaction, the traditional ploy is to order a survey of investigation, regardless of the times the subject has been investigated previously. Prime Minister Macdonald bought time by authorizing a study expedition to Strait and Bay in 1884 and

---

[1]Hopkins, J. Castell, *The Canadian Annual Review*, The Annual Review Publishing Co., Ltd., p. 149, 1907

extending it into 1886. Laurier did about the same in 1897, sending the ship *Diana* into the northern waters under Captain William Wakeham who reported a shipping season of just a little over three months. The Prime Minister repeated in 1903; this time it was the *Neptune* under Captain A. P. Lowe and the report was more favorable than that left by Captain Wakeham in 1897 or Captain Andrew Gordon in 1886. Lowe returned with fresh evidence about the currents in Hudson Strait — two pronounced currents flowing in opposite directions. One of these, he reported, flowed westward along the north shore of the Strait, carrying ice drift from the region of Greenland, so that inward-bound ships could move with the current and the ice. The other current, moving eastward along the south shore and carrying ice toward the Atlantic, would aid outward-bound ships by carrying them with the ice drift. It was the best of news for friends of the Bay route — almost as if designed by Hugh Sutherland — and ship captains traveling either to or away from Hudson Bay could find a current moving in their favor.

In the meantime, Mackenzie and Mann were building, uncertainly, what was to prove a "springboard" for the ultimate leap to the Bay. Their new line to the Northwest was built on the old Lake Manitoba Railway and Canal Company charter acquired in 1896 and was seen as a possible but unlikely first step in the direction of the Bay. Their first objective was to reach the Saskatchewan River at a point from which the build- ers could branch northward — if there was sufficient incen- tive. After building from Gladstone to a point a few miles west of the Manitoba boundary and collecting fertile land at the rate of 6,400 acres per mile of construction within the bounds of Manitoba and 12,800 acres per mile outside of the province as constituted at the time — making what some observers believed were unnecessary curves to increase mileage — the builders showed more interest in the rich Carrot River valley than in Port Nelson and continued the line on to Prince Albert.

It was the first major link in the Canadian Northern Rail- way system but to fulfill a commitment to build to the Saskat- chewan River and keep alive their right to build all the way to the Bay, the men of the Canadian Northern began in 1906 to build a branch line to The Pas. A more direct right of way to the

Bay might have been chosen, one beginning at Mafeking or some other point north of Dauphin and not so far west as Hudson Bay Junction, known originally as Etomami.

Ottawa leaders clung to the hope that if the railway to the Bay had to be built, it would be accomplished by private enterprise all the way, and with this in mind willingly granted the Canadian Northern Railway an extension of time in which it could complete the proposed road to the northern sea.

But the Canadian Northern willingness to build beyond the Saskatchewan River was at a price in land grants and subsidies which the government had no intention of paying. With a big crop in the West in 1906 and less than adequate railway facilities for moving the grain, the clamor for a railway to a northern seaport grew louder than ever and more people were becoming convinced that the federal government would have to build it. Western members of the House of Commons were calling for direct government action, while just as many Eastern members were opposed to the idea.

The House of Commons debate of the year on the subject came on February 22, 1907, with W. E. Knowles, Member for West Assiniboia, speaking to his own motion that: "It is urgently necessary that the Government should take all possible steps for the speedy construction of a railway to the shores of Hudson Bay."[1]

The big wheat crop of 1906 — 89,000,000 bushels and much of it still under the February snow — accentuated the shipping problems. Almost as serious as the freight car shortage limiting grain shipments was the plight of Saskatchewan people who were unable to obtain coal for exactly the same reason. Was CPR policy at fault? Was that Company withdrawing freight cars from the West in order to obtain bigger returns from Eastern traffic? The very idea inspired prairie wrath. But whatever the reason, the solution was to build the road to the Bay. "If you save rail distance, you save money," said Knowles, "and if you save money, you make money." He was sounding the call for an immediate decision. There was grain on the ground in Sas-

[1]House of Commons Debates, p. 3547, Feb. 22, 1907

Belugas (white whales) at Churchill. — Jim Gray.

katchewan which should be in Liverpool and the government should see that such a situation did not occur again.

Western members agreed with Knowles, and Thomas Greenway, representing Lisgar, added that every person in the West now believed the northern railway "to be the solution to the transportation problem."

Knowles and Greenway received unexpected support from a prominent Easterner, Hon. George E. Foster, sitting for North Toronto. As Minister of Marine and Fisheries in the Macdonald administration after December, 1885, he was familiar with the Captain Andrew Gordon expedition to the North at that time. Now, he could speak with the voice of experience and was, at the same time, bringing a refreshing appeal for unity of purpose. ". . . it is all very well to emphasize this question as being peculiarly a western one . . . it is just as much a question for the East as for the West," he said in support of the Knowles motion. "Although an eastern man, I would take just as much interest in the Hudson Bay route as if I were a western man."

Partly in defense of policies when he was a member of the government, he reasoned that the building of the railway to the Bay could not have been justified until there was pressure from overload on the existing rail lines. Now, however, the time had come to build. He believed "a four months' season is perfectly feasible for that northern route" and Canadians should get on with the job of building. "If the old Hudson Bay Company, a hundred years ago, got their punts in there through the ice and storms, and made their ports with great regularity, and had an average season of between three and four months, what can be done with modern forces of invention, with vessels built of any degree of strength you wish, and with any amount of motive power you want to put into them?" the Honorable Gentleman — later Sir George Foster — asked. It was exactly the sort of question asked many times in later years.

Members on both sides of the House looked to Prime Minister Sir Wilfrid Laurier to declare the government's intention. He was not ready to make a promise but he said enough to bring encouragement to those who were arguing for early action. Yes, the West needed the rail outlet to the northern sea and if it would be good for the West, it would be good for the East.

"I agree altogether with what has been said by my friend from North Toronto that the time has come for the construction of this railway . . . and I hope that before the end of the session we will have something to declare upon this subject," he added.[1]

The Canadian Northern branch line from Hudson Bay Junction to The Pas was completed in 1908, bringing a ray of hope for further development in the same general northeasterly direction. At about the same time, Hon. Clifford Sifton, who as Minister of the Interior in Laurier's first government introduced the new and ambitious immigration program, was bringing to the House of Commons a practical proposal for raising the money needed in building the railroad. Drawing attention to the huge acreage of Western land reserved in connection with railway policy, he noted that 30,000,000 acres remained after all claims for grants had been satisfied. Of this, he would set aside 10 per cent or 3,000,000 acres and use the proceeds from sales to pay for the Hudson Bay Railway. In a very few years the land would be worth from $10 to $12 an acre "and you will have provided a fund of some $30,000,000 out of which the Government will recoup itself. . . ." With the adoption of such a plan, he was sure, "there would be absolutely no burden imposed on the exchequer of the country."[2]

He was not one to advocate construction and operation of railways by governments, he took pains to explain to Parliament. He would prefer to see public utilities left to privately owned corporations but "there are cases in which a company cannot be got to undertake an enterprise. A case of that kind was the Temiskaming and Northern Railway. . . . In like manner the Dominion Government would be justified in building the 500 miles of railway to Hudson Bay as a government work provided it first took the precaution to protect itself by making a reservation of land which would be ample to pay the exchequer every dollar of the money expended. Such a reservation would pay the cost of the railway, the wharfs, the elevators and everything connected with it, besides the lighting and buoying of the Bay, the surveying of the channel and all kindred

[1] House of Commons Debates, p. 3577, Feb. 22, 1907
[2] House of Commons Debates, p. 5346, March 20, 1908

expenses . . . and thus the whole thing would not cost the people a copper.''

There was general acceptance for the Sifton proposal and land was marked for a special fund. It had to be realized, of course, that the cash returns would grow slowly and many years might pass before the full sum would be available. Westerners were unwilling to wait and Prime Minister Laurier, knowing that the Hudson Bay Route would be an election issue in the anticipated campaign of 1908 — especially in the West — made the long-awaited announcement: the Government of Canada would definitely build the railway to the Bay. The September timing of the announcement was no doubt dictated by the late-October election but the place — Niagara Falls, beside the Welland Canal, of all places — was a surprise to the politicians. It was exactly where the Prime Minister could have expected the least enthusiasm for another outlet to serve western grain growers but he was apparently anxious to underline two points; first, that he was ready to defend the decision on any platform, and second, that he believed the Hudson Bay Railway would serve the interest of all Canadians.[1]

"If there was one place in Canada where the Hudson Bay Railway was not likely to be a vote-catcher, that place was the district along the Welland Canal," the *Edmonton Bulletin* editorialized.[2] "Yet it was in this district that Sir Wilfrid Laurier made his announcement. . . . Stronger proof of the resolution with which the Government has undertaken the matter could not be given."

The Prime Minister's announcement was welcomed by his Western followers and the same issue of the *Edmonton Bulletin* carried a statement by Candidate Frank Oliver which seemed to recognize the Hudson Bay Railway as the principal issue in the campaign. "Just as the Liberal Government undertook the construction of the Grand Trunk Pacific, it will undertake and carry to completion the Hudson Bay Railway. The railway will cut the distance to Edmonton's ultimate market by 1,000 miles; it will put cents in the pocket of the farmer for every bushel of

[1]See Appendix 1
[2]*Edmonton Bulletin,* Sept. 26, 1908

grain carried to Liverpool, and fractions of cents for every pound of beef shipped. Do you want the Hudson Bay Railway or do you not? That is the question to be answered on October 26th."

The Conservative leaders replied that they had, for all practical purposes, made just such a promise long ago. The claim was debatable but it left the Western Canadian voters with their first assurance that regardless of which side won the election of 1908, they had a clear promise of the railway to Hudson Bay. And as intimated by the campaigning Prime Minister, the engineers were already on the ground of the proposed operation.

JOHN ARMSTRONG'S REPORT

Reports! There had been dozens of them, many quite contradictory, tending to cancel each other's credibility. The authors came from the ranks of fishermen, sailors, soldiers, geologists, chemists, biologists, and medical doctors — just about every profession except that of civil engineer. The Minister of Railways had no wish to invite another protracted study which might further confuse the issue. What he needed was good practical guidance from men who could see the problems in total and relate them in such a way as to spare the Government from needless mistakes and embarrassments.

The man of the Minister's choice was John Armstrong, B.A., B.Sc., C.E., with extensive engineering experience dating back to the construction of the Intercolonial Railway, a man who understood men and felt more at home in a camp cookhouse than in a fancy dining room. In short order, he became the Hudson Bay Route's "Man of the Hour."

The government of the day was quietly preparing to call a general election, and with thought to Western voters, organizers hoped the Prime Minister's intended announcement of a promise to build the railway to the Bay without more delay would be properly and politically timed. It would be particularly convincing if, in committing his government to a program of immediate action, he could say that men were already at work in the North.

The planning was good. John Armstrong was appointed chief engineer at midsummer and told to get on with the job of staking out a route or routes between The Pas and the Bay coast. He was to report to the Deputy Minister, M. J. Butler. As an engineer, Armstrong knew exactly what was meant by "getting on with the job," but he encountered difficulty in finding the needed surveyors and laborers who were not handicapped by inherited prejudices about working in a northern winter. The first crew was sent out of Winnipeg on August 30, to travel by rail to Prince Albert and from there to The Pas by Hudson's Bay Company steamboat on the Saskatchewan. By September 14, the men were "in the field," north of The Pas, ready to begin work, and four days later, Sir Wilfrid Laurier, speaking at Niagara Falls and announcing the government's decision to build the road without further delay, could add quite factually that workmen were already on the job. That the men had not yet had time to break their first shovel handles did not have to be explained.

More work parties left Winnipeg on September 19, the day after the Prime Minister's Niagara Falls speech. These, to go more deeply into the North, were transported by way of Lake Winnipeg and the Nelson River. There was action at last and the government was returned.

The men in the various work crews were active throughout the winter and Armstrong, who was obviously changing his own ideas concerning "the terrors" of the North, could report that with an average of 110 men on the payroll through the winter and into spring, "not a single serious accident or case of sickness" was recorded.

As soon as crews completed their survey work on the railway routes they were directed to harbor surveys at ports Nelson and Churchill, and Armstrong was with them, like a seasoned Northerner, supervising, observing, and probing. For a man carrying the responsibilities of chief engineer on the entire project, he did well to find time for the varied observations transmitted to his Deputy Minister. His reports provided the best general summary of the Hudson Bay Route situation submitted to that time. For an Easterner, he found a refreshing enthusiasm for the Northwest and might well have been writing promotion for the Department of Immigration or The Pas Board of Trade. He knew the numerous lakes and streams along the way were teeming with fish and as soon as the railway was in operation, those virgin waters would supply fresh trout and other kinds for sale in prairie cities, on a 24-hour shipping service. This would be one more "source of great profit to the Hudson Bay Railway."[1]

[1]Armstrong, John, *Report on the Hudson's Bay Railway Survey,* Sessional Paper 20d, 1910

Steam engine on a newly constructed section of the Hudson Bay Railway.
— Saskatchewan Archives.

He was not in a position to estimate the extent of mineral resources, "iron ores, gold, silver, galena, mica and other mineral resources discovered by the Geological Survey at various locations," but he saw great quantities of marble and "unlimited quantities" of limestone not far from The Pas, almost enough to meet the needs of the Western Provinces.

On the subject of agriculture along the northern route, Armstrong had some fresh ideas. In certain parts of the North, the lands would require drainage but "the fact that they are situated within a few hours' run of an ocean port" would give them a value not previously considered and bring rapid settlement. Certainly there would be no climatic obstacle to successful agriculture because, in his opinion, "the climate is quite as favorable for farming operations as that of Prince Albert."

In making his broad assessment, the engineer paused to express his convictions about the waterways of the West. They should be developed for navigation. Even the success of the Hudson Bay Railway should not prevent Westerners from enjoying the practical and economic benefits of water transportation. It may have been unsolicited advice for the Department of Railways but Armstrong was an engineer more than a diplomat and he was telling government officials to make an inventory of navigable rivers at once. Shipping on the Saskatchewan River, which in earlier years had steamboats plying between Fort Garry and Fort Edmonton, should be revived. In the summer of 1908, he noted, the steamer *Alberta* made the journey from Edmonton to Winnipeg and another "good sized steamer" made a return trip on the South Saskatchewan between Saskatoon and Medicine Hat. The rivers were there; they should be used to complement the Hudson Bay Railway.

In the selection of a terminal port, it was not for Armstrong to decide between Churchill and Nelson, but as the engineer charged with carrying out the survey at both places, he would obtain much pertinent information and form a preference. Constantly, he was seeking evidence to show which route and which terminal would present the fewer construction problems. He anticipated no major difficulties on the southern portion of the line to Churchill but troubles would grow with the advance northward. The southern end of the grade would be built

The "Pelican" at Churchill, 1910. — Hudson's Bay Company Archives.

through a tree belt with clay loam soils. The local forest would furnish railway ties and nearby gravel deposits would supply material for ballast. There should be no serious obstacles. The next section would involve an area of exposed rocks but the foundation for a railway would be excellent. Then, between Mile 240 and Mile 360, workers would encounter the roughest country with hills and valleys with which to contend. Finally, the most northerly stretch of right of way — seventy miles of tundra or barrens — was something to frighten the most courageous engineer. Without local forests to furnish ties, without gravel for ballasting, and without promise of grade stability where permafrost was present, Armstrong believed this belt was something to be avoided if possible. Gravel for that northern section of grade would have to be hauled fifty miles or more and who knew how long the muskeg and ice would support it?

Armstrong's preference for the Nelson approach was difficult to hide. The Nelson River would have to be bridged at two places but there would be familiar footing all the way and no worries about permafrost. On top of all else, there would, by his computation, be a saving of $2,682,332 in favor of the Nelson terminal.

The Nelson approach held nearly all the advantages in ease of construction and economy. It was Armstrong's choice, beyond question, but he was anxious to carry out his study and survey without prejudice. This he managed to do, but in submitting the evidence on which he based his personal convictions, he undoubtedly influenced the government decision in favor of Nelson.

Even though Armstrong's reasons for placing Nelson ahead of Churchill did not stand the test of time, the man's comparison of the two terminals was the most enlightening made public up to that time. But the settlement it helped to bring was only temporary and in view of the lingering controversies, the report should be of lasting interest to students of Hudson Bay Route history. That portion of Armstrong's report dealing with ports Nelson and Churchill appears in Appendix 2[1].

---

[1]Armstrong, John, *Report of the Hudson's Bay Railway Survey*, 1909, Sessional Papers, 20d, 1910

Canoes running rapids, 1910. — Hudson's Bay Company Archives.

Armstrong probably misjudged on some points, especially on Port Nelson, but his appraisals were honest and he could be pardoned for some errors in an area which was still unknown to most people. He had one big advantage, however; as an engineer, he could leave it to the politicians to answer for the decisions and mistakes in judgment and they kept the controversies concerning the terminal alive for more than a decade.

"TO HELL WITH OTTAWA; WE'LL DO IT OURSELVES"

After being returned to power in the general election of 1908, one of the first questions Prime Minister Sir Wilfrid Laurier heard, was: "When will the railway to the Bay be finished?"

His promise to build the road was made in good faith but nobody had properly assessed the problem of delivering 500 miles of railway across the unsurveyed rocks and muskegs of Northern Canada to an undetermined port terminal. In spite of all the debates and studies and expeditions, most of the pertinent questions concerning construction remained unanswered, and fortunately for the Prime Minister, he had never actually named a completion date. His immediate concern was to silence the objectors and make a start. There was general agreement among his followers that the road would be built from the Saskatchewan River at The Pas but nobody was sure where it should terminate on the northern shore.

At the time of publicly committing the Government of Canada to the building, Sir Wilfrid could say that engineers with transits and levels and knee-high boots were already on the ground to make the necessary surveys. But when a year passed and then two years without any tangible signs of progress, the project was again caught up in political controversy. Eastern editors and critics succeeded in casting grave doubt upon the scheme. Some of the criticism may have been pure invention, like editorial comment aired in the House of Commons on April 10, 1910. As Hansard recorded it, Thomas MacNutt, Member for Saltcoats, directed Parliament's attention to a Montreal *Gazette* report that survey engineers were forced to discontinue operations because of an "impassable obstacle in the shape of an extensive muskeg which cannot be bridged." The editor, seizing upon it as fresh evidence of national folly, added: "The country may have cause for satisfaction if a physical muskeg keeps it out of a financial muskeg into which the construction of a railway threatens to plunge it."[1]

[1]House of Commons Debates, p. 7187, April 15, 1910

When the same story was carried in the Toronto *Globe* a short time later, the muskeg had grown to become "a bottomless bog," but in reply to the member's question, Hon. G. P. Graham, Minister of Railways and Canals, said he had conferred with his chief engineer, John Armstrong, and was assured that no great obstacle had been encountered and the muskeg was not a serious barrier to construction. "The Government," he added, "had no intention of abandoning but, rather, intended to proceed with all possible speed."

The declaration to proceed with "speed" brought some laughs. A year and a half had passed since the Prime Minister reported survey engineers working in the field, yet no tenders had been called and no decision made about the northern terminal. The Pas community at the end of the Canadian Northern branch line would be the starting point but where would it go from there? Would the new line terminate at the mouth of the Churchill River or that of the Nelson? Nobody knew.

For decades there had been difference of opinion about the merits of the two northern ports, with most observers showing a preference for Nelson. Even the first two railway companies to obtain charters for Bay-bound railways chose different terminals; the Nelson Valley Railway and Transportation Company would build to Port Nelson and Hugh Sutherland's Winnipeg and Hudson's Bay Railway and Steamship Company would end at Churchill.

To avoid the danger of a blunder in making the important decision, the government's chief engineer, John Armstrong, was instructed to stake from the south end and work that portion of the right of way which would be common to both destinations and then run two lines, one to Nelson and one to Churchill. He was further instructed to make those observations which would assist members of the government in coming to a final decision.

Armstrong's preference was obviously for the Port of Nelson. He would admit that Churchill had its points, a superior natural harbor, landlocked and ample, and it would require less dredging for the accommodation of big ships. But the Nelson Estuary had much more in its favor, as Armstrong saw it: The port could be reached with a shorter railway from The Pas and with a saving of almost a hundred miles; the economy in capital expenditure would be substantial, to say nothing of corresponding economies in operation. The Nelson Port would be free of ice earlier in the spring and later in the autumn to make for a considerably longer operating season. Then, noting the more placid river current and more moderate tide at Nelson, he was sure that operational problems would be simplified.

Certainly, the area through which the railroad would run deserved consideration and Armstrong saw the line to Nelson escaping the most troublesome stretches of muskeg and passing through more country suitable for settlement. He did not overlook the fact that Port Nelson, set back farther from the sea than Churchill, would be easier to defend in the event of attack. Enemy ships had intruded upon the Bay before and might do it again.

Savings in time and money by taking the railway to Nelson caught the Ottawa attention at once. Obviously, a shorter railway avoiding the worst of the muskegs could be completed for operation in shorter time and this was a factor of some political importance, especially in the West. And as for the financial savings, they were estimated at $4,292,332 and partly explained by figures presented in the House of Commons by Hon. G. P. Graham on February 8, 1910:[1]

Churchill Route

Railway Construction	$11,351,520
Railway shops and accessories	7,757,152
Port work (Docks, elevators, etc.)	6,675,000
	25,783,672

Nelson Route

Railway construction	$ 8,981,800
Railway shops and accessories	7,444,540
Port work	5,065,000
	21,491,340

It seemed like a clear case of advantage for the Nelson terminal, even though the pioneer student of Hudson Bay, Dr.

[1] House of Commons Debates, p. 3206, Feb. 8, 1910

Robert Bell, had for many years favored the Churchill port and other explorers and would-be authorities were divided in their preferences. In and around The Pas, where many of the residents were familiar with the North, most men argued loudly for Nelson. That the frontiersmen fancied tree country more than tundra might have been a factor but there were other reasons based on years of experience in the North. An opinion expressed from The Pas was that "the eventual success of the Hudson Bay Route is bound up with the acceptance of Nelson as a harbor, and the real reason for the preference is that one can get into it for six or seven months at least."[1]

How would the decision about a terminal be decided? As the cynics said they expected, there would be another government-appointed investigation, this one to be conducted by the staff of the Department of Marine and Fisheries. But it would not be necessary to delay the beginning of construction because the work would start at the southern end where, for the first 150 miles, the grade could be built without regard to the northern terminal.

Of necessity, the first structure to be built had to be a bridge across the Saskatchewan River at The Pas. If the government was serious about building the railway, there was no apparent reason why the bridge should not be undertaken at once. Western people said so. On April 27, 1910, spending estimates brought down in the House of Commons contained an item of $500,000 for "immediate construction" of the road to Hudson Bay. This was interpreted to mean a start on the bridge.

But Western people were finding more and more reason to wonder what the word "immediate" meant in Ottawa. Before the summer passed, however, the government gestured by awarding a contract for the construction of a steel bridge across the river. For very good reason, the Ottawa officials were worried about growing rifts between East and West over the Hudson Bay Railway issue, also about a continuing deterioration of government support in the West. Something new and better in public relations was needed. More publicity was at-

[1]*Edmonton Bulletin*, Sept. 12, 1910

His Excellency, Governor General Earl Grey, visiting Eskimo camp at Churchill, 1910. — Hudson's Bay Company Archives.

tempted. Ottawa news writers began embellishing the program for the railroad and announced that the bridge would be ready for use "next winter." Grading would be hastened and steel was expected to reach the Bay by the end of the next year, 1911. The biggest news of all: "Four Transcontinental Railways Building Lines To Le Pas Junction."[1] It was great to think of big railroading corporations being so eager to gain a connection with the Bay. It made an excellent story but the various trans-continentals never reached The Pas.

It may have been the Prime Minister's idea to elevate Eastern Canadian interest in and respect for the Bay by having the Governor General, Earl Grey, pay a visit there in 1910. Whether His Excellency really liked the idea or not, he agreed to go. Following the traditional Hudson's Bay Company canoe route, he visited York Factory and then Churchill, returning by way of Hudson Strait and the St. Lawrence. If he was traveling to generate a better reception for the Hudson Bay Route, at which many Eastern people were still directing jibes, he was doing it dutifully and well by making all the right comments. It was a delightful cruise, he reported, and as for ice in the Bay and Strait, he did not see sufficient of it "to cool a glass of champagne."[2]

The year 1910 ended with a sod-turning, the only act of moving earth in connection with the railway grade. No con-tracts except the one for a bridge had been awarded. "That railway will never be built by speeches," Western farm leaders were saying, with obvious impatience and disgust. "This road has been promised to the people of the West for the past 20 years. When are we going to see actual construction? Our people are tired of having promises and no fulfillment."

Just as the unhappy marketing circumstances of 1923 and '24 brought forth the Western Wheat Pools, so government inaction and vacillation in building the railway to the Bay gave self-reliant agrarians of the West the idea of building their own road and operating it themselves. "To Hell with Ottawa; we'll do it ourselves," some were shouting defiantly. Why not? Their

[1]*Edmonton Bulletin,* July 6, 1910
[2]*Grain Growers' Guide,* Nov. 8, 1911

own leaders assured them that there were no physical, financial or political barriers they could not surmount. Government engineers had shown how a railway could be built to either Nelson or Churchill at a moderate cost per mile, so "let's build it. We can pay for it while we're waiting for the Government to act."

Presented most effectively by an article in the *Grain Growers' Guide*,[1] the official organ of the pioneer Grain Growers' Associations, and one which was ever ready to champion cooperative endeavors, the idea was debated in livery stables and general stores across the wheat country and gained support. Even the estimated cost running to many millions did not frighten the enraged farmers. If 100,000 Western people would subscribe $100 each, the total would go at least halfway in building the railway, the writer of the article appearing in the *Guide* submitted. The balance of the needed capital could be raised by a loan from the government fund of $20,000,000 accumulated from sale of western land set aside expressly to help in building to the Bay. Failing all else, the Peoples' Joint Stock Company might raise the balance of needed money by the sale of bonds. And with the rails laid close to a succession of waterfalls, these could be developed to "furnish all the power necessary to operate the road by electricity."

The writer did not overlook the possibility that if Western people organized to construct and operate the northern railway, the Government of Canada might then be moved to advance its plans and begin building without further delay. In that event, the Co-operative would let the government finish the building and then offer to take over the operation. In view of Eastern antagonisms toward the railway, it would be better if such a railway utility were operated by a Western body such as the one proposed. The railway would benefit all of Canada but its primary purpose was to serve the West where people "have been and are still exploited without mercy by the great transportation companies . . . and they now have come to the conclusion that the best safeguard and assurance of an escape from the transportation monopoly that has long oppressed them, lies in building a road and operating it for themselves."

[1]*Grain Growers' Guide*, Jan. 11, 1911

The plan now under discussion across the West was put together by a delegation of farmers traveling to Ottawa late in 1910. Perhaps it was E. A. Partridge, fighting farmer from Sintaluta, who made the clearest call for direct action in forming a company to build, own, and operate a railway to the Bay. An organization committee consisting of David Railton, Sr., of Sintaluta, T. W. Knowles, of Emerson, and E. A. Partridge, was struck at once and subscriptions for members and shares were invited. Before the delegates completed their return to the West by train, many of them subscribed to the plan by signing applications in the following form:

"We the undersigned, in the event of the federal government failing to undertake the speedy construction of the Hudson's Bay Railway and its operation through the medium of an independent commission, and from the viewpoint of the interests of our western population in the matter of efficient and cheap service provided throughout the year, desire to express our faith in the feasibility and desirability of the western people, with suitable government assistance, building and operating the road for themselves as a popular joint stock company enterprise, by placing a subscription of $10.00 each at the disposal of an organizing committee, and agreeing when at least 500 signatures be obtained, to sign, if requested, the memorandum of association and take at least $100.00 stock in the proposed company."

In launching the campaign to obtain subscriptions, the committee appealed not only to farmers but to Western people in all professions to write applications and send their subscription money to the Home Bank of Canada at Sintaluta for deposit in the Hudson Bay Subscription Fund. In signing an application and paying ten dollars, the subscriber was taking the first step toward becoming a shareholder to the extent of at least one share with value of $100. The committee would be permitted to draw upon the funds to meet organizing expenses and if the public response was sufficiently favorable, the Company would be formed and subscribing members asked to pay the balance of $100 for each share of stock. In the event of failure to accomplish the purpose, however, the unspent money would be returned to subscribers.

Application forms were forwarded to secretaries of Grain Growers' Associations, Boards of Trade, and other bodies expected to display interest. With the forms went a public appeal over the names of members of the organizing committee:

"People of the West, if the creation of a cheap, efficient and independent avenue of transportation to and from the world's markets by a short route appeals to you as being highly desirable, lose no opportunity in doing your part in making it an accomplished fact. The method adopted to launch the enterprise may seem crude in form owing to the necessity for dispatch, but it is hoped that the auspices under which the movement originated and the personnel of the committee, will be sufficient guarantee of good faith and the likelihood that any reasonable support from the general public will be followed by vigorous and capable action on the part of the committee."

People to whom the appeal was directed were assured that as soon as the organization of the company was consummated, the Government of Canada would be petitioned for a charter and some financial assistance in building. It was proposed, then, that if and when the government decided to nationalize the railroads of the country, the company would be ready and willing to hand over its Hudson Bay Railway; but any attempt by private capitalists to buy out the peoples' railway would be met with a fine and firm refusal.

Just one week after the first general call to action in support of the proposed railway enterprise, the *Grain Growers' Guide* carried a rousing challenge directly from that middle-aged and discomposing campaigner, E. A. Partridge, now signing as Chairman of the Provisional Organizing Committee.[1] It was a "To Whom It May Concern" message, meant to be directed at everybody who might benefit from cheap transportation and find an interest.

"Everybody pays freight charges, express charges and railway fares," he wrote, "and everybody in Canada who does so pays at least double what the service would cost if the railways were capitalized at their physical value and operated at cost, including fair interest on money invested."

1*Grain Growers' Guide,* Jan. 18, 1911

Some people called this forty-eight-year-old homesteader-farmer from Sintaluta an agitator and troublemaker. He was an emotional fellow but he was intensely serious and could become greatly upset by evidence of injustice. And he could be devastating in his denunciation of wrongdoers in big business. Obviously, he was no friend of either the Winnipeg Grain Exchange or the CPR. Now, he was making a plea for a monster co-operative and speaking bluntly: "Never again," he wrote, "will be present so favorable an opportunity to smash the tribute-levying powers of the great Transcontinental roads with their allies, the Beef Trust and the Grain Combine, as that which we, the burden bearers of the western plains, can seize if we have the courage, by co-operatively building and operating a railroad to Hudson's Bay supplied with all the necessary adjuncts for the cheap exportation of the products of the ranch and farm, before the capitalistic interests gain possession or a railway-owned Government boggles the enterprise."

In other words, "those who use the railways should run them" and in so doing confuse those "insolent, cattle-killing, claim-evading, stock-watered, tax-exempted, subsidy-fattened, privilege-drunken corporations that have long dominated parliaments and robbed the people in the guise of common carriers, but in the practical role of highwaymen."

Clearly, the man could be vitriolic but he was also thoughtful and responsible, extremely eager to see his fellow farmers rising to this, the biggest challenge to confront them in their adopted land.

The public response was fairly good but far from being overwhelming. It wasn't every farmer, of course, who could spare ten dollars, even for a good cause, and certainly not many of the rural people of the time could anticipate a hundred dollars of surplus money with which to pay for a share of stock when it became necessary. But some were enthusiastic — like the one writing from Pincher Creek, signing as Bunchgrass,[1] who urged building the road all the way from Hudson Bay to the Rocky Mountains where it would connect with the Crow's Nest Rail-

[1]*Grain Growers' Guide*, Jan. 25, 1911

way and become an outlet to the Pacific, thus giving the co-operative company "the finest transcontinental railway in America, resting on the best harbor on the Pacific Coast and upon the only port of consequence on the Atlantic side."

Whether it was owing to the initiative of the Western farm group or merely the approaching general election, the Government of Canada responded with a fresh display of good intentions. Hon. George P. Graham, in speaking to his annual railway budget on March 11, 1911, announced a government decision to definitely construct the Hudson Bay Railway itself and make arrangements for the construction of terminal facilities and elevators, and for a steamship service between the Bay terminal and the British Isles. The government would "proceed with this work." The first stretch of grade, from The Pas northward, would be undertaken at once.

Was this just another pretty speech or did the government really mean business? A serious intent was indicated by the calling of tenders for the first section of the road. About mid-summer — August 10, 1911 — as politicians were getting into another general election campaign, mainly on the issue of Reciprocity, it was announced loudly and clearly that by a cabinet decision, the contract for construction of the first section of the line — 185 miles from The Pas to Thicket Portage — was awarded to J. D. McArthur of Winnipeg, whose tender was just less than $3,000,000. The contractor was said to be ready to begin work at once, hoping to have a big part of the grading finished before the onset of winter. The party in power, appealing for voter support, hoped also that the work of construction would advance enough to be conspicuous before election day, September 21, 1911.

Having started to build, the government — whichever party happened to form it — could not stop now. E. A. Partridge's drive for the "People's Hudson Bay Railway Company" lost its momentum and before very long was nothing more than a memory.

TWO STEPS FORWARD AND ONE BACK

Progress on the Bay Railway was like that of pilgrims of old journeying to Jerusalem — two steps forward and one reverse. Every promise of an advance in the program seemed to be followed by an unexpected delay or setback. Even the awarding of a contract for the first stretch of road was no guarantee of headway or continuity of effort and the change of government in 1911 did nothing to allay Western fears and end the frustrations.

The principal election issue, Free Trade, was of Prime Minister Sir Wilfrid Laurier's choosing. The United States administration was in a mood to make trading terms which would practically remove the annoyance and cost of border customs. Government revenue would be affected and manufacturers in the Eastern provinces would strongly oppose but Western farmers tired of paying excessive prices for seed drills, binders, and engines, saw those import tariff duties as evil monsters deserving to be destroyed.

The economic principals involved in Reciprocity found academic support and Laurier's Liberals believed they had a winning talking point. But Robert Borden's challenging Conservatives succeeded in making the proposed Free Trade appear as an invitation to United States' domination in Canada and the Laurier administration went down to defeat. Only in Saskatchewan and Alberta did the voters give strong support to the trading proposal. Manitoba's predominantly agricultural population may have favored Reciprocity as much as farmers in neighboring Western provinces but wanted the railway to the Bay even more, and believing the Conservatives with Borden as Prime Minister would end the confusion and deliver the desired communication with a minimum of delay, elected eight Conservatives and only two Liberals.

For the backers of the Bay Railway, however, there was further discouragement and disillusionment. The new administration, for reasons the Western observers could not understand, brought construction — such as there was — to an abrupt halt and Hon. Frank Cochrane, the new Minister of Railways and Canals, was called upon to "remove at once the injunction and allow the work to proceed."

In answering his irate questioners in the House of Commons, Minister Cochrane tried to give assurance that the government would indeed carry out the promises made when his fellow-Conservatives were in opposition and on the campaign trail. "There has been no change of policy," he declared; the cessation of work on the railway was only a pause for the purpose of re-examining the construction program and removing the flaws. Representations had been made to him, he explained, objecting to certain mistakes and omissions; the new railway did not start in the right place; the surveys were inaccurate; the grade for the first hundred miles was laid on deep and dangerous swampland, and so on. "In consequence, the contract has been held up until we have had time to investigate the matter." There would be no more delay than was necessary "for the checking of the survey."[1]

The Liberals bristled at the insinuation that preparations for the northern railway were faulty and tried to send the embarrassment right back to the Conservatives; all guilt in connection with the new delay had to rest with the party in power. Hon. Frank Oliver, seizing the political opportunity of the moment, said this stalling action by the new government was a repudiation of promises and would come as a great shock to people in the West. "The very definite promise made repeatedly by the present Premier are not . . . being implemented as they were understood."

The fact was that Western Members of Parliament in both parties were unhappy about the sudden suspension of work. Valuable time was being wasted. Certain parts of the construction jobs in the North — transportation over soft ground in the roadless country, for example — had to be carried out in the winter when the surface was frozen and the Minister was being inundated with calls from Western organizations and individuals wanting assurance of an immediate return to action.

[1]House of Commons Debates, p. 746, Dec. 4, 1911

Hudson Bay, showing pressure ridges in the distance, July 26, 1913. — Saskatchewan Archives.

Western members sitting with the government were hard pressed to reaffirm their demands for prompt resumption of work without entering into conflict with a colleague and creating rumors of a split in the party. It was a task for the seasoned politicians. Diplomatically, J. A. M. Aikins, Member for Brandon, told the government to get on with the job because no issue of the day was of greater concern to prairie people than the promise of this short, inexpensive and speedy route to the leading markets of the world. Western Canada's people had certain geographical handicaps and needed no more. "The farmers of Eastern Canada can more easily pay the duties under the National Policy than can the farmers of Western Canada," this Member whose party had just won an election on the strength of its National Policy, confessed.

The Member for Brandon, later the Lieutenant-Governor of Manitoba, believed this waiting interval — if there had to be one — should be used to resolve the lingering question about the northern terminal. He made no pretense of having the answer but with barbs for the Liberal opposition he found it unbelievable that a previous government would undertake the construction of a long and costly railway without knowing where it would terminate.

It was a clever diversionary tactic and the debate shifted from the matter of work suspension to the relative merits of ports Churchill and Nelson.[1] Of course, the question of the northern destination of the builders should have been settled earlier but the evidence continued to be hopelessly conflicting and any neutral observer would have agreed. The most recent report, resulting from studies by William J. Stewart, hydrographer with the Department of Naval Services, was not very convincing one way or another. He saw much good in Churchill harbor but criticized it because of shallow water in parts of the harbor which would prevent more than three or four vessels from anchoring at one time. This, Member Aikens saw as a serious limitation because the new port could be expected to handle a hundred million bushels or two hundred millions per year; it would, indeed, be the height of folly to select a port with needless built-in limitations.

[1]House of Commons Debates, p. 1219, Jan. 15, 1912

But the Stewart Report was winning attention on certain new observations. That ice difficulties in Strait and Bay were "not insurmountable" had been noted many times but two new observations were distressing; first, that existing charts were sufficiently inaccurate as to create grave dangers for ships, and second, proximity to the Magnetic North Pole made ordinary compasses unreliable. It was enough to make Western members look glum and inspire some Easterners to whisper "Hallelujah."

While the thorny question of terminal port was still under discussion, James McKay, Member for Prince Albert, introduced another disturbing note, confessing that, in his opinion, the entire line was in the wrong place, regardless of the terminal port selected. The road should have been built from Prince Albert to Hudson Bay and it was not too late to correct the mistake. The Minister of Railways and Canals listened but his problems were already so complex that he did not welcome more bright ideas.

After enduring the long speeches about the previous government's good intentions, the previous government's failures, the present government's promises, the present government's broken promises and the serious congestion in marketing grains from the recent Western crop, the patient Minister made a statement — a very fair one — and set the minds of most members to rest.[1]

"When I took charge of the Department and assumed the duty of looking over the contracts which had been let just before the retirement of the late Government, I was somewhat astonished at the meagreness of the information before the Government in reference to the character of the country traversed, in reference to the building of the road itself, in reference to the harbours on the Hudson Bay, in reference to what was to be done with the wheat when it got there. This meagreness of information led me to hold up the contract for a short time in order to ascertain if we could possibly discover what position we were in. I regret to say that I have not yet been able, from the information of the Department, to discover which is the best

<hr>

[1]House of Commons Debates, p. 1263, Jan. 15, 1912

harbour to bring this railway to. The report of the last expedition does not make it in any way more reassuring, but on the contrary, it seems to mix up things worse than ever before. With all due deference to the Member for Edmonton (Mr. Oliver), I would have to say that were it not that the route has been surveyed, the road located and the contract let, I would not, with the information now before me, consider that the location was the best one. But considering the promises that have been made by Hon. Gentlemen on both sides of the House as to the Hudson Bay Railway being built quickly, and as to its urgency, I find it is too late now to alter it. I have, therefore, ordered the construction to proceed, and the road will be gone on with and completed as fast as possible.''

"If the harbour question were settled today," the Minister added, admitting to his own lingering doubts, ''I would be in a position to advertise for tenders for other portions; but another expedition will be necessary to settle that question. I feel that we ought, perhaps, to go a little slow until we get further information. I do not know that we should be getting on any faster . . . because there is no way of getting supplies as cheaply as we could get them in by the Hudson Bay if the question of the harbour were settled. But it is the intention of the Government to push the construction of this road as rapidly as possible.''

The Minister had another idea about extending the use of the Bay and the new railway, one which most members had not considered — a steamship service from Nelson or Churchill, as the case might be, across Hudson and James bays to the Nottawa River, whence the line of communication would be extended by water and rail to the St. Lawrence River. Such a route would give farmers at Prince Albert and similar northwestern points the shortest possible route to the eastern seaboard, saving some 600 miles. It was enough, at least, to capture and divert the attention of Western members in a provocative mood.

Later in the same summer, 1912, Manitoba was granted a long-standing request for enlargement of the province. The northern boundary was pushed back to the 60th parallel of latitude, to be on the same northern level as Saskatchewan, Alberta, and British Columbia, and slanted eastward to afford

500 miles of Hudson Bay coastline. It was coastal mileage to which Ontario leaders had long believed they had a prior claim but to mollify the provincial neighbors, both Ontario and Quebec were allowed to extend northward, with Ontario being promised a five-mile-wide railway corridor to Nelson and Churchill if such should be wanted.

For years Manitoba officials had called for provincial enlargement. Now, if the Hudson Bay Railway was to be built, Manitoba citizens would be more eager than ever to claim all the land through which it would run. The additional territory brought the province to 250,000 square miles, many times the size of the original "postage stamp" area of 13,000 square miles and the later area of 73,000 square miles. Some of the new territory would be fit for cultivation; some would be forest, some muskeg, some with the rocky surface of the Canadian Shield. The extension would bring the entire length of the old canoe route between York Factory and Fort Garry into the province, also all of the Hudson Bay Route from The Pas to the coast, regardless of which of the two terminal ports was finally selected.

With an increased annual subsidy from the Government of Canada, Manitoba was ready to enjoy its new role and no less eager to see the Bay Railway completed and operating. Construction work resumed. There was fresh reason for optimism. In this "next year" country, it was easy to conclude that 1913 would see greater strides in the construction program.

NELSON, FOR BETTER OR FOR WORSE

Nineteen hundred and thirteen would be the year of the "big push" in the North. Hon. Frank Cochrane, as Minister of Railways and Canals in the still-new Borden government, promised himself and colleagues that he would lift the road to Hudson Bay from the morass of political inaction and demonstrate to a doubting public how a Conservative administration could get things done. The 61-year-old Cabinet Minister and Member for Nipissing, looked like the man to do it if anybody could. He was no stranger to politics and public service, having sat in the Ontario Legislature before entering the federal field, and with a Scottish father and Irish mother, he was bred to reality and quiet determination came naturally.

The task of railway construction on the Hudson Bay line would now be attacked from both ends. There was already something tangible to show at the southern end, a partially completed bridge across the Saskatchewan River, seventy miles of clearing on the right of way, and fifty miles of grade without rails, built by John D. McArthur of Winnipeg who now held the contract for the balance of construction.[1] The most important part of the 1913 program would be the initial work at the seaport end of the line where virgin wilderness was still undisturbed except for a few survey stakes driven into sod by mosquito-bitten engineers during the previous summer.

The railway starting from The Pas was, to be sure, going to terminate somewhere on the Bay coast. But where? Throughout the previous summer, as work went forward slowly at the southern extremity, government officials admitted with growing embarrassment that the decision concerning the terminal was being delayed as long as possible. Evidence about the merits of the two terminal sites was conflicting. If a serious mistake was to be the price in buying rapid progress, delay was

[1]House of Commons Debates, p. 623, Dec. 4, 1912

preferable. The trouble was that even delay was no longer seen as a guarantee against error in choosing the terminal port. The Minister knew that he must weigh the evidence and assume responsibility for the decision to be confirmed by cabinet colleagues. During the summer of 1912, he visited both ports Churchill and Nelson, hoping to see the problem more clearly.

But there was no clarity. On only one point was there certainty: whatever his choice might be, he would have the approval of some students of the North and the disapproval of others. If he fixed upon Churchill, he could take support from conclusions drawn long ago by Dr. Robert Bell who devoted many years to north country surveys, by Lieutenant Andrew Gordon who contended that "Nature seems to have left little to be done in order to make it a capacious port, fit for doing business of great magnitude," and by J. B. Tyrrell who credited Churchill with "one of the most magnificent harbours in the world, probably the finest harbour."

If the Minister adopted Nelson as the terminal, he would find himself siding with just as many other explorers of prominence, among them Henry Youle Hind who as early as 1878 saw the Nelson River system and Port Nelson being developed in a practical way to provide "navigation to sea-going vessels all the way from Liverpool to Selkirk," and Civil Servant John Armstrong who in 1909 would recommend Port Nelson for the same reasons the Hudson's Bay Company made nearby York Factory its principal post on the Bay more than a century earlier.

The Minister concerned might have waited for yet another study of conditions at the two ports but the result would not likely be any more convincing than previous reports and would settle nothing. The Minister would still have to make his choice and then defend it. There was no lack of information about the two sites; the problem was in assessing it accurately. Each location had its attractions. Churchill showed up with the best natural harbor, both in size and shelter, but in accessibility, Nelson held a pronounced advantage. What government men were sensing with growing fear was that long stretch of muskeg — seventy miles of it on the Churchill right of way. True, it was frozen — "frozen since Adam was a kid," as Cochrane noted, "and I have yet to meet an engineer who will vouch for the building of a road across that 70 miles." Perhaps the difficulty could be bridged with a well-laid gravel grade; perhaps it could not. Nobody was sure and nobody was likely to be sure until it was tried. The thought of building to the good harbor of Churchill and then discovering that the grade was disintegrating was enough to frighten the most courageous of public servants. Cochrane's decision was made with trepidation. He could not escape the thought that regardless of his judgment, time could prove him wrong and millions of dollars would be wasted. But he had to take a stand and having regard to a longer shipping season at the more southerly port and an easier and surer railway approach, he declared for Nelson, hoping for a minimum of public attention.

If he was trying for a time when nobody was listening, he was fairly successful. Late in 1912, Hon. G. P. Graham, Minister of Railways and Canals in the former government, inquired across the floor of the House of Commons if a decision had been made about the terminal port and Hon. Frank Cochrane replied in the fewest possible words: "Yes, Port Nelson."[1] Two and a half months later, exactly the same question was presented to the Minister, as if nobody had heard him the first time, and the reply, betraying a trace of lingering doubt, was: "Nelson, unless upon completion of the surveys and inspection it might be thought advisable to decide otherwise."[2]

After another three months, the same question came again, this time from Alberta's Hon. Frank Oliver: "Is it definitely decided to establish the terminus at Nelson?" and the Minister, obviously thinking about the seventy miles of barren land with from "three to seven feet of muskeg on top and difficult to get over," answered: "Yes, it is much shorter."[3]

Oliver responded with an admonition about hidden obstacles in the Nelson harbor. The cost of dredging, he said prophetically, might prove to be "stupendous," to which an Eastern member with strong regional bias and no enthusiasm for any

[1]House of Commons Debates, p. 623, Dec. 4, 1912
[2]House of Commons Debates, p. 4058, Feb. 26, 1913
[3]House of Commons Debates, p. 10940, May 26, 1913

part of the northern operation, added his opinion that it didn't really matter because the Hudson Bay Railway would never bring a "dollar's worth of advantage to Canada" anyway.

While Oliver was offering a warning and Cochrane was trying to reassure himself, the ice was breaking on the Nelson River and government engineers were thinking about the summer work season in the North for which $4,500,000 had been voted. The season would be short and work should be started without delay. Of the total amount, $1,500,000 was the appropriation for harbor installations and Cochrane was determined to spend it and have as much as possible to show for it. Whatever lingering misgivings he might have had about Nelson, he was now formally committed and had to press vigorously with the program as drawn by his engineers.

It would be the biggest and most spectacular year yet for the Hudson Bay Railway, Cochrane declared. It had to be big if the railway was to be completed and ready for use in 1915 as he had practically promised.[1] For Port Nelson it was indeed a spectacular year and in some ways a tragic year. As might have been expected, it was a year of confusion on that northern frontier. Man's ability to shatter the peace in a wilderness community was well demonstrated. When ice went out on the river, the site selected on the left bank, about twenty miles up from the mouth, was still as quiet and desolate as any other unoccupied spot in the Canadian North. But that was to change quickly. To deliver the great tonnage of machinery — including a mammoth dredge — and prepare warehouses, railway connections, wireless communications, living accommodation for workmen, stabling for horses, and navigational aids like buoys and lights — called for the kind of organization that would successfully land an invading army on foreign shores.

Most of the Port Nelson traffic of the year originated at Halifax. Early in July, two government tugs, the *Kathleen* and *Neophyte,* left that eastern seaport for Hudson Bay and these were followed almost at once by the steamers, *Bellaventure* and *Bonaventure,* carrying machinery, supplies, and workmen.

[1]House of Commons Debates, p. 10951, May 27, 1913

About the same time, the two steamers, *Alcazar* and *Alette,* carrying about four million board feet of southern pine lumber for use in building docks and wharves at Nelson, sailed from Port Arthur on the Texas coast. The *Alette* halted at Halifax to take on an additional million feet of Nova Scotia planking and steamed away with her $75,000 cargo. Other ships, *Sinbad, Beothic* and *Cearense,* loaded and sailed. The *Bellaventure* and the *Bonaventure,* after making a delivery at Nelson, returned to Halifax for second cargoes.

Cochrane may have entertained secret fears about the Nelson harbor but he was keeping them entirely to himself and giving his full energy and enthusiasm to the plan. His purchase of the huge dredge bearing the name *Port Nelson* was proof. Said to be the largest dredge ever constructed in Canada, it was built in Toronto at a cost to the government of $272,184. Captain H. B. Saunders, of Lloyds Underwriters, accepted the task of personally directing the giant thing to Nelson. To reach its destination, it had to be towed 3,000 miles and after a forty-day journey it was delivered with nothing more serious than some slight damage from ice.

As viewed from faraway Halifax, the Port Nelson campaign seemed to be going well — at least until returning ships brought reports to the contrary. As seen at Nelson, the operation was almost unbelievable confusion. The engineer to be in charge of the project, D. W. McLachlan, arrived in the second week in August and from that moment, the scene was one of hurry and commotion, as if the circus had just come to town.

All the ships reached the river's mouth without mishap but then faced the problems of unloading in the absence of a wharf and absence of deep water to the shoreline where the freight was wanted. Buoys made from steel barrels were placed in the river to offer some guidance and keep the big ships to the deep channel but there was doubt about them being properly placed, and anyway, they did nothing to overcome the obstacle of shallow water — especially at low tide — near the shore. A shallow-draft boat for lightening or transferring cargo from ships to shore was provided but it was totally inadequate and the movement of materials and supplies was hopelessly slow.

When goods were moved to the site of the wharf, they were

dumped with more thought to the saving of time than the preservation of supplies and workmen returning to Halifax told of machines, building materials, foodstuff, and even coal being dumped together in disorderly piles. The disarray was described as "awful" and the waste of perishables by exposure was no less depressing. It was symbolic of the haste and confusion to be sensed everywhere. Men in authority knew the working season would be short and they were anxious to achieve the objective of converting Nelson to a usable port before the ice filled the river again.

Feeling some of the greatest frustrations were captains of incoming vessels. As they had been assured, the water of Hudson Strait and Hudson Bay was uniformly deep and free from shoals but the approaches to the mouth of the Nelson were made treacherous by silt bars extending far out into the Bay. A channel in the river might be as much as thirty-three feet deep at the mouth, but upstream where the wharf was being built, it was shallower and narrower and made more dangerous for ships moving off course by the rock-strewn shoals on both sides. There was no hope of the bigger ships coming close to the point where cargoes were required and even the *Kathleen,* described as "a beautiful little tug" built for pulling lobster pots, had difficulty and was stranded periodically on river bottom. The tide might be "only half as high as in the Bay of Fundy" but when it was out, the shallows near river's edge was no place for even a small cargo boat. Critics did not overlook the fact that the same tug for which the government paid $10,000, had a speed of about nine miles per hour, which left a discouragingly small margin when working against a river current of six or seven miles per hour.

The first ships, carrying laborers and machines, arrived at the river early in August — just about the time work was being completed on the Saskatchewan River bridge at The Pas and track laying was beginning from the same end. As boats arrived, they anchored near the mouth of the river, about eight or ten miles from the site chosen for the dock, and cargo had to be carried to that spot by small boat. That much should have been anticipated but nobody expected the transfer operations would be so hopelessly slow. The *Bonaventure,* first to unload, returned to Halifax to bring a second cargo, but other boats were coming in faster than they could be unloaded and faced long waits, some amounting to weeks. The ships' owners knew they could collect demurrage from the government and curtailed their protests.

The *Alcazar,* loaded with the best pine lumber, arrived on August 14 and the *Alette,* carrying two scows in sections along with a cargo of lumber, came a few days later. Inasmuch as the lumber was not needed at once, it forfeited its chance for immediate attention and other ships were granted unloading priority. When the port engineer wanted to inspect the scows being carried by the *Alette,* the overburden of lumber was simply thrown overboard to expose the objects of the search to view but nothing more was done to remove them. About a month after the *Alcazar's* arrival, it was still anchored some ten miles below the new wharf, keeping company with the *Alette, Beothic,* and *Cearense* which were in the same waiting position. The long delay was becoming especially irksome to the captains and crews and they may have been guilty of lapsing into carelessness. In any case, on September 14, the *Cearense,* with Nova Scotia coal still in her hold, grounded on the rocky floor at river's edge, her hull ripped open hopelessly. Boat and cargo were soon complete losses.

The reasons for the disaster were debated bitterly in the press and later in the House of Commons. Captain Howard of the wrecked ship attributed the loss to lack of navigational aids and blamed the government. Charts were said to be inaccurate and the buoys were installed in wrong places. He contended, too, that his operator tried without success to make wireless contact with the *Acadia,* anchored not far away, and charged negligence on the other ship. The Minister of Railways had a different version. Speaking in the House of Commons, he countered with a charge of carelessness on the part of the Captain. Why was the ship in shallow water if those in command were attending to duty? And the reason for failure to obtain a reply to the call for help was that Captain Howard's wireless equipment was out of working order with the result that the message was never actually transmitted.

Still the *Alcazar* and *Alette* waited for orders to unload.

With the coming of cool days and frosty nights, the captains entertained fears of being frozen in for a long sub-Arctic winter and appealed to the government engineer for permission to leave, with or without their cargoes. As related in the House of Commons a few months later,[1] Captain Robertson of the *Alette* urged the port authority to allow him to lighten the ship by throwing more lumber into the water and leave the river before the ice formed. The Captain realized that the ship's bottom was already damaged by striking against boulders on the riverbed — "a danger to anything with a draft of over 18 feet" — and this state of affairs coupled with the approach of winter brought him to consider "taking the matter into my own hands to save my men and myself." On October 4 — one day after the *Alcazar* arrived back at Halifax, "carrying nearly all the cargo she had intended discharging at Port Nelson" — the port engineer gave Robertson instructions to sail.[2] The *Alette,* with most of the cargo of lumber still on board, steamed away. But the ship did not go far before being caught by early drift ice and grounded with a hole in the bow.[3] The crew took to lifeboats. The ship was not a total wreck but damage was extensive and Captain Howard and his men were taken on board the *Acadia* for return to Halifax. Nor was it the end of danger for the men of the *Alette.* For the second time in a few weeks they came close to shipwreck when the *Acadia* became caught in ice and they had visions of being trapped there until they died of starvation. But as good luck would have it, an Arctic gale caused the ice field to split sufficiently to let the *Acadia* escape and reach Halifax on November 5.

Of course, Captain Robertson was interviewed by the press. He was critical of government arrangements in the Bay, and in due course, the Minister responsible for the Port Nelson development replied, blaming the Captain for running into shallow water. If the ship had been held diligently to the channel, it would have had a minimum of twenty feet and would have been in no trouble with the ice.

Naturally, however, the government opposition and the

---

[1]House of Commons Debates, p. 677, Feb. 11, 1914
[2]*Halifax Herald,* October 4, 1913
[3]*Halifax Herald,* Nov. 11, 1913

Liberal press tried to make Port Nelson operations appear ridiculous and achieved some success. But there were some independent observers who were ready to speak up on behalf of the northern terminal. H. B. Saunders, of Lloyds Underwriters, after taking the big dredge to Port Nelson, said the critics were overlooking the size of the tasks and the difficulties under which men were required to work. And Captain W. F. Young, upon his return from the Bay in November, said: "Despite the politically prejudiced exaggerations, it can be said in truth that the terminal of Port Nelson is proceeding with as much precision as any similar pioneer enterprise, and additionally the terrors of the sea trail thru Hudson Bay are not as serious as those confronting the navigator of the St. Lawrence gulf and river to Montreal."[1]

Nevertheless, some confidences had been shaken. In the course of his long criticism of government policy and administration at Port Nelson, A. K. MacLean, Member for Halifax, made what many people accepted as the understatement of the year: "Because of the experience of last season, the selection of Port Nelson for the terminal is at least open to some question."[2]

Meanwhile, railway construction on the southern portion of the route was progressing with moderate speed and less grief. The year-end score showed completion of the bridge at The Pas, 137 miles of grade in place and 86 miles of rails spiked down.

The Minister of Railways repeated his forecast that the long-awaited connection with Hudson Bay would be completed in 1915. But the terrible circumstances into which the world would be plunged in 1914 changed many things, including the railway timetable.

[1]*Halifax Herald,* Nov. 11, 1913
[2]House of Commons Debates, p. 677, Feb. 11, 1914

WAR AND SILT

A few hundred hardy men with shovels, picks, sledge hammers, and big appetites were bringing shape to the railway and harbor which would give the prairie West its long-awaited outlet to the sea when, on an August day in 1914, Canadians learned that they were at war with Kaiser William's Germany. It was big news but not many Canadians took alarm. Essentially, they reasoned, it was another of Europe's many quarrels; some of the foreign countries had been at war for generations and it was not immediately obvious to Canadians of various racial origins that they should be involved. Moreover, British might would quickly end the Kaiser's military aggressions and there would be no major disruption of Canadian programs — the building of the railway to the Bay, for example.

Railway contractors continued in their effort to make every day in the short northern summer count for as much as possible, and grade construction was inched forward in the direction of Port Nelson at about an expected rate. The two bridges across the Nelson River were the centers of principal interest, one at Manitou Rapids, which was under construction, and the other at Kettle Rapids, soon to be started. There was no immediate suggestion of curtailment and the Minister of Railways was displaying the proper optimism, except for his revision in the estimated completion date, from 1915 to 1916. Certainly, he declared, the railway would be ready to carry wheat in 1917.

But contrary to wishful thinking, the powerful German war machine was not being stopped. Mercilessly, it ground its way through Belgium, aiming at Paris, and Canadians as well as Britons saw the mounting dangers. If France fell, other nations could expect the same savage assault. Prime Minister Robert Borden, on behalf of the Canadian people, assured Britain of full support and gradually Canada geared for an all-out role in the new war.

Ship in the ice near Charles Island, August 12, 1914. — Saskatchewan Archives.

How would the accelerated military preparations affect progress on the Hudson Bay Railway? It was generally agreed that as long as construction was not impeding the war effort, it should be continued. After all, most of the work in the North was being done under the terms of earlier agreements with contractors and could not be stopped abruptly, even though a case were made for such suspension. And so, there was no apparent change of working pace in 1914, but in the next year, the growing demands of war were adding to the problems of northern construction.

The first Canadians were in the trenches in France in the spring of that year and many more volunteer combat men were in training and on the way, the beginning of some 600,000 young Canadians in four divisions who went overseas to participate in the bloodiest struggle the world had known. Industry and agriculture were being revised to further the war effort and huge quantities of munitions, foods, ships, and other supplies were going forward. Casualty lists were growing alarmingly and Canadians were beginning to realize that they were engaged in a long and costly struggle. There was, already, a serious labor shortage for both industry and farms, and it would grow worse. Non-essential enterprises would have to yield to essential industry.

But neither the politicians nor the Western farm organizations were ready to give up the Hudson Bay Railway until it was positively necessary. The Northern Route was still able to furnish good political fighting ground, and the House of Commons continued to hear arguments for and against. A member of parliament could inquire why the bridge at the southern end of the railway was under guard and closed to all but politically approved citizens.[1] Conservatives, it was alleged, could cross the bridge and travel north on the line; Liberals were not allowed to use the bridge. The reply, when presented, did not deny the discrimination but charged that some local Liberals at The Pas had bribed the night watchman on the bridge and then traveled over the road with a government engine, presumably

[1] House of Commons Debates, p. 606, March 3, 1915

highjacked. Hence the precaution of screening those who tried to enter upon the bridge. It sounded more like a Halloween prank than a political maneuver but the administration chose to take a serious view of the high jinks.

The Minister of Railways, speaking at the end of March, 1915, admitted to the growing difficulty in obtaining laborers and materials for the railway but reported trackage to Mile 214, grade to Mile 293, and one bridge spanning the Nelson, completed. His vote of $4,000,000 for the railway and $1,500,000 for further improvements at Port Nelson, testified to his hope of completing the project, war notwithstanding.[1] He would have wished for faster progress but believed the Canadian people were getting good construction value for their money and a railway which would be commendably and surprisingly straight. The distance from The Pas to Port Nelson as "the crow flies" measured 406 miles and following the railway right of way, it would be only an additional eighteen miles, which any engineer familiar with the terrain would consider a fine achievement.

With the money voted for improvements at Port Nelson in that year, the Minister intended to build permanent docks to replace the temporary structures described as looking like a poor "fisherman's landing" more than an important harbor installation. The new facility would run parallel to the deep water channel in the river and about 1,000 feet from it. Steamer berths would be dredged to allow thirty feet of water at low tide.

It sounded very encouraging but while the Minister was making his Profession of Faith in the new railway and harbor, his engineers were sensing the severity of silting there in the Nelson estuary. It was a big river, draining a big territory, and the volume of silt carried had to be correspondingly high. Much of this burden of solids was deposited where the current was decelerated. And as is often the case with sand and silt bars, their movement was unpredictable. The big dredge built in Toronto expressly for use at Port Nelson was at work but not making much progress against the constantly reshaping river floor bars of sand and silt.

[1]House of Commons Debates, p. 1861, March 21, 1915

Steel bridge at Port Nelson, 2640 feet long, connecting artificial island with the mainland. — Hudson's Bay Company Archives.

Hon. Frank Oliver had warned about just such an impedi-
ment several years earlier and now his hunch was being confirmed. And as usual when rumors of such a situation reach the
public, they were greatly exaggerated and colored. One of the
members of Parliament — an Easterner from near the Atlantic,
of course — brought the matter to the attention of the House in
highly magnified terms, saying: "I have heard . . . that it is
practically impossible to make a harbour at Port Nelson; that
the sandbar there is nearly three miles wide, and that it shifts
every summer, and may shift half a mile in 24 hours. . . . It would
take a fleet of 50 or 60 dredges working constantly to keep the
channel open."[1]

The Minister of Railways, recognizing silence as "the elo-
quence of discretion," made no reply. He would give no indication of how much of that fear he shared, but if he conscienti-
ously believed the silt was not likely to be a serious problem, he
would have said so. The same rumor of impending trouble at the
new northern port was voiced again a few weeks later when the
Member for Oxford North, E. W. Nesbitt, said: "I understand
from people who have been there that dredging will be required
out from the wharves into the bay itself and that the parts
dredged will fill up again. I understand that such a lot of silt
comes down from the river that it will be impossible to keep the
channel open without constant dredging and that it will be like
shuffling snow because as soon as one part is dredged it fills up
again."[2]

This time Hon. Frank Cochrane replied without acknowl-
edging or denying the silt problem and without betraying any
secrets bearing directly upon the question. He said, simply, that
"we have a channel of from half a mile to fourteen miles wide
with water at least 19 to 20 feet deep at low tide." The inference
was that with an ordinary spring tide of 16 feet, there was
nothing about which to worry. But Cochrane's engineers were
greatly worried and Cochrane was probably more worried than
he cared to admit. And Hon. Frank Oliver, to be sure, was

---

[1] House of Commons Debates, p. 2911, April 14, 1916
[2] House of Commons Debates, p. 3378, May 3, 1916

present to say again that Churchill might have been a better choice for the rail terminal.

Yes, engineers at Port Nelson saw their harbor silting seriously. The big dredge delivered in 1913 and a smaller one could not keep up with the rate of silt deposit. Chief Engineer Donald McLachlan resolved upon a carefully revised plan for wharves; he would abandon the temporary wharf on the shoreline and build the permanent structures on an artificial island close to the main river-channel and connected to the shore by a railway bridge. By constructing such an island for the wharves, McLachlan hoped to change the direction of the current sufficiently to make it do its own dredging and keep the channel scoured out all the time.

It was an optimist's dream but work went forward to construct the island, the island wharf, and the bridge to connect island and mainland.

Even in 1917 when it was more difficult than ever to obtain help and materials for northern construction, Minister of Railways Cochrane gave no hint of complete stoppage. When he reported to the House of Commons on June 11 of that year,[1] he expressed confidence in the track being laid all the way to Port Nelson and ballasting "brought to fair shape this year."

Knowing he was expected to furnish some factual comment for the enlightenment of eager members of Parliament, he said: "The bridge structure connecting the deep water wharves with the mainland was completed and 1,600 lineal feet of cribwork of the island placed, built up and filled. The hydraulic dredge worked throughout the season in the channel. The clam shell dredges were employed in dredging stone and gravel from the river bottom for crib filling. During the present season it is hoped that a considerable portion of the island, including the site of the elevator, will be enclosed."

The government of the day, notwithstanding the wartime demands for labor and building materials, and the clamor from certain Eastern members who would employ any excuse to discredit the Hudson Bay Route, appeared to be in no hurry to

[1]House of Commons Debates, p. 2205, June 11, 1917

halt the building program. The Member for Richmond, Nova
Scotia, George W. Kyte, was one of those who appealed to the
Honorable Gentlemen sitting on the Treasury Board to spend
no more money on the northern railway until conditions were
more favorable.[1] Finding it difficult to hide his regional prejudice, he added that any shipping route which could not operate for more than "two months" in the year was scarcely
needed at the best of times. But the Easterner might have spared
himself the trouble of making the speech because the inevitable
circumstances of war were imposing ever more of their own
uncompromising restrictions.

For reasons best known to himself, the Minister of Railways was doing his apparent best to keep the work going and on
June 11 he could report trackage as far as Mile 332 — which
meant Kettle Rapids Crossing on the Nelson River — and
railway grade almost all the way to Port Nelson. The final stage
of track laying was being delayed until the Kettle Rapids bridge
was finished and in use. There had been delays, the Minister
admitted, partly because of the wartime handicaps, partly because of a fire which destroyed the contractor's track-laying
outfit.

Nor would it have been difficult to recognize other forces
working against the railway to the North. Apart altogether from
the effects of war, it was an unhealthy time for Canada's over-
extended railways everywhere. Two of the transcontinental
giants, the Grand Trunk and Canadian Northern, were in serious financial trouble and in danger of collapse. From a commission appointed by the government in 1917 to investigate the
entire railway system in Canada came a majority recommendation for nationalization of all the railways except the Canadian
Pacific. And so great was the demand for iron and steel that rails
were being lifted from some of the most unprofitable lines. It
served to furnish the opponents of the Hudson Bay Railway
with further opportunity to defame it.

The war was, indeed, at a crucial point, demanding everything Canadians could do to aid the cause. Even the coal needed

[1]House of Commons Debates, p. 193, Jan. 20, 1916

to run an additional railway was a consideration. Income tax, as a modified form of conscription of wealth, was introduced. Nonessential enterprises were gradually being brought to an end, although there was continuing debate about which enterprises were not essential. Was the Hudson Bay Railway essential? Perhaps the remaining work could and should wait until war's end. Gradually, the work did come to a halt. With completion of the bridge at Kettle Rapids, operations ceased. It marked the end of another chapter in the long and discouraging struggle, an appropriate time to count the total cost. Accordingly, the new Minister of Railways and Canals, Hon. J. D. Reid, reported total expenditures to the end of the 1917-18 fiscal year as $20,161,000, of which $13,814,000 was the amount spent on the railway and $6,347,000 or about one-third of total, on the harbor and terminal installations at Port Nelson. "The latter sum," the Minister told, "includes expenditures incurred in the purchase of steamships which are now in general service throughout the year, as well as the valuable plant at Port Nelson."[1] The real value of that "plant at Port Nelson" remained to be tested.

[1]House of Commons Debates, p. 2167, May 17, 1918

POSTWAR WORRIES AND NO PROGRESS

At war's end, late in 1918, the count of young Canadians who had fallen in battle, never to return to their homeland, stood at 60,000. The awful price in men and money exceeded that of any other war in history but the end of hostilities brought blessed relief and hope for rapid rehabilitation and permanent peace. Although more or less exhausted from four years of the terrible struggle, Canadians were eager to get on with other things.

Western people accepted the wartime necessity of curtailing and then suspending operations on their darling project, the Hudson Bay Route, but with the return of peace they expected nothing less than full resumption of the railway construction program.

Why not? Wasn't the railway grade — the full 425 miles of it — already completed from The Pas to Port Nelson, with rails laid to a point within 100 miles of the seaport goal? Weren't the big bridges spanning the Nelson River finished and inviting use? Wouldn't one full summer of work bring the program to practical completion to let Western farmers lop off a thousand miles of shipping distance on export cargoes and effect a saving of roughly five cents a bushel on the cost of marketing wheat?

Now that the excuses of war had been removed, how could any government justify delay? Western farmers believed their rail outlet to the Bay should be one of the first postwar projects to receive government attention and government funds.

But those who expected the termination of war to bring an immediate return to work on the railway and port were due for shocking disappointment. They were to discover that reviving a project for which governments over the years had held a half-hidden indifference, was no easier than starting it. If, as Westerners suspected, the Ottawa administration was enjoying the Hudson Bay Railway respite of 1919, they could anticipate a rather long recess.

An appropriation of one million dollars for completion of the railway was placed in the federal budget in 1918 but nobody really expected the money to be used in that crucial year of war. In the next year, however, when Western farmers and others were renewing the familiar call for completion, the budgetary provision was $300,000 to be used, according to Hon. J. D. Reid, Minister of Railways, "to cover ties and finish the Hudson Bay Railway." "The rails," he added, "will be taken from the main line where we are putting on new rails."[1]

The Minister's statement did not satisfy the Honorable Member of Parliament from The Pas, J. A. Campbell, sitting as a Unionist-Liberal. Although he had a special geographical interest in the Hudson Bay Railway, his reaction was exactly the same as that of the organized farmers of the West. The time for patience was passing and what Campbell was asking was: "How soon?"

"It seems rather peculiar," he said, "that a railway which has been under construction for such a long time and which is so nearly completed, has not been finished. Only 92 miles of steel is necessary to complete a railway of 424 miles under construction since 1912 and on which $20,000,000 has already been spent. Lands have been set aside, of which $28,000,000 worth have been sold, $13,000,000 having been already collected. . . . It seems strange to me that under these circumstances that railway should not be gone on with this year."

If Campbell's constituents and the people of the West generally could have been listening to his words, they would have shouted: "Hallelujah."

With one vigorous spurt on the part of the government in 1919, the railway to the Bay would have been completed and Port Nelson, for better or for worse, would have been the terminal. But the spurt was not made. Not only was there no construction but ties from the northern stockpile were quietly moved out to be used elsewhere. Perhaps the delay — deliberate or otherwise — was a blessing in disguise because it gave the federal authorities one more chance to weigh the advantages and disadvantages of Nelson and consider alternatives. Sud-

[1]House of Commons Debates, p. 4688, July 7, 1919

denly and with the sound of thunder in 1920 the suitability of Port Nelson to serve as the railway terminal was called again into question.

While the usual brash questions were being asked again about the usefulness and uselessness of the Canadian Senate, that august body took upon itself on April 23, 1920, to appoint a special committee of its members to consider and report on the future of the Hudson Bay Route. After all the surveys which had been made, another was not likely to excite any public interest and this one went almost unnoticed at first. But the Senators had a serious purpose and were probing for fresh evidence, whether the press and public were watching or not. The Committee held fifteen meetings and called twenty-one expert witnesses, many of whom had extensive experience in the Far North, men like the Manitoba-born Arctic explorer, Vihljalmur Stefansson, and the Tyrrell brothers, J. B. and J. W. It was increasingly evident that the Committee's recommendations would carry authority. The report, dated June 4, 1920, was bold and clear and useful; it was also concise, as the following shows:[1]

"Your committee makes the following findings upon the evidence adduced before them:

1—That the Hudson Bay route is feasible and will probably in time be profitable.

2—That the season of navigation under present conditions is at least four months in length and may by reason of improvements in aids to navigation be considerably increased.

3—That in the opinion of this committee sufficient care was not taken in the selection of Nelson as the terminal of the railway, and that the government should not make further expenditures upon this port without first making a new and thorough examination into the relative merits of Churchill and Nelson as a terminus of the railroad.

4—That the waters of the Strait and rivers tributary to the Bay teem with fish and valuable marine animals, and we believe that the Bay is equally well stocked but there has not been sufficient data collected as to the extent of the fisheries of the

[1]House of Commons Debates, p. 2781, June 10, 1922

Bay to enable an authoritative statement to be made as to their value.

5—That the mines already discovered in the Hudson Bay district are of sufficient number and richness to indicate the existence of great potential mine wealth.

6—Your committee feel that they cannot too strongly endorse the value of the suggestion of Mr. Stefansson as to the cultivation of the reindeer and muskox, and would urge upon the government that the Department of the Interior be empowered to take hold of this matter, earnestly taking advantage of what has been done in this regard by the United States Government.

7—Your committee, although it is somewhat outside the scope of this mandate, cannot close this report without making some reference to the national value of the explorations of Vihljalmur Stefansson. He has completely revolutionized our ideas of the region within the Polar Circle. He has demonstrated that it is possible for white men to live and thrive in that northern region though drawing from no other resource than those afforded by the country itself, and he has proven that those lands which were looked upon as barren and utterly worthless will eventually be a valuable asset to Canada. The committee ventures the hope that the Canadian Government will not be unmindful of the great services performed by Mr. Stefansson, whose reward so far has not been commensurate with the national importance of the work he has accomplished.

8—Your committee expresses its thanks to the gentlemen who have voluntarily come forward and given valuable evidence upon the important matters under consideration.

9—Your committee submit herewith, an extract in narrative form of the evidence given before the committee, and beg to recommend that one thousand copies of this report and extract of evidence be printed in pamphlet form for the general distribution.

> All of which is respectfully submitted
> Geo. W. Fowler (Chairman)"

Western editors and all friends of the Hudson Bay Route seized upon the Senate conclusion that the northern outlet was not only feasible but likely to be profitable. This, said the editor of the *Grain Growers' Guide,* "should effectively silence those eastern newspapers and public men who have endeavored to induce the Government to abandon the project and discontinue construction. . . . It has long been realized in the West that eastern opposition to the route was dictated, not by a conviction of its impracticability but rather by a selfish desire to retain for the East the profits which accrue from handling of traffic, both freight and passenger, between Western Canada and Europe."[1]

But that the Senate Committee would, at this late date, discredit Port Nelson as the railway terminus came as a surprise and somewhat as a shock. If such a warning were considered seriously, it would open an old wound and perchance delay further the completion of the railway. It could not be overlooked, however, that the Committee might have had good and sufficient reason for reviving the old controversy, even though more than $6,000,000 had been spent at and around Nelson.

At about the same time, the *Grain Growers' Guide* carried a scathingly critical article by an Alberta farmer, Bert Huffman.[2] As a Westerner with a dedicated and absorbing interest, he had traveled all the way to Port Nelson to see for himself. To reach that distant point he was able to ride by work train on the new line as far as Mile 214, then by gasoline track speeder to Kettle Rapids or Mile 333. The final ninety-two miles of the journey at mosquito season were made by canoe and on foot.

At Nelson, Huffman saw where the government had attempted "to build an artificial island on a mud foundation, the island to be itself constructed of mud dredged out of the river. One attempt failed and another site for the 'island' was established 4,000 feet farther out in the mud, and there the jumbled, bungling, unscientific job has stopped. A steel bridge was to connect the island with the mainland and the entire immense and spectacular terminal site was to sit on a mud foundation." In addition to all else, Nelson was seen as unsheltered. Surely, the traveler concluded, this was a "wanton and criminal waste of money."

[1]*Grain Growers' Guide,* "On To The Bay", Editorial, July 21, 1920
[2]Huffman, Bert, "The Tragedy of Hudson Bay," *Grain Growers' Guide,* July 14, 1920

Churchill, the Alberta man observed, was not perfect, but it was sheltered and had from sixty to seventy feet of water in the harbor. The sentiment in the North, he stated, was "almost unanimously in favor of Port Churchill."

"I did not walk from Kettle Rapids to Port Nelson and back, 190 miles, for the fun of the thing," he wrote. "I am a producing farmer owning a fine farm within 20 miles of Calgary, and I am interested in transportation from the standpoint of a western farmer. I love this vast north country. It is wonderful, fascinating. Fabulous riches lie buried here for future genera- tions. Vast treasure in fish, fur, minerals, pulpwood, cover its silent and untrodden vastness. . . . I am interested as a Canadian citizen in seeing this splendid national project made a permanent beneficial property for the Canadian people, rather than see it bungled by political manipulation into a perpetual curse and bill of expense."

The solution, according to Huffman, even at the late date of his venture into the North, was to divert the existing rail line or build a new one from some point near Split Lakes to Chur- chill. The new terminal could be made ready for loading wheat in two years. "But Nelson? Well, if a cargo of wheat is shipped out of that port within seven or eight years, the judgment of hundreds of honest and competent men is far, far amiss."

Had it not been for the Senate report, the Huffman article might have been dismissed with only slight notice. As it was, the story was read widely and quoted in the House of Commons. Coming together, the two statements foretold serious setback for the route as it was projected and bewilderment for all who believed hopefully that the long-awaited outlet by way of the Bay was within a hundred miles of realization.

The need for the shortcut to Europe was as great as ever but what was to be done about it? The Senate Committee had advised against additional expenditure on the railway to Nelson until further study of the two ports, and certainly, the govern- ment of the moment was in no mood to authorize either a railway diversion or another investigation.

For Bay supporters it was discouraging. What could they do? With typical Campbell determination and some lingering confidence in the Nelson Port, the Member for The Pas seized the initiative in the House of Commons on March 16, 1921, and spoke on his own motion: "That in the opinion of this House, work on the Hudson Bay railway which was commenced in 1910 and continued to the end of 1918, should be resumed as early this year as possible, and the project completed without further delay."[1]

Western members supported J. A. Campbell in the debate but the climate of the House was not favorable to such a proposal and after almost a month, the motion was withdrawn.

The Senate report casting doubt upon the wisdom of taking the terminal to Nelson instead of Churchill seemed to silence Western voices for a time. It was expected that the government of the day would follow that report with an announcement of a more thorough investigation to make a proper comparison of the two port sites and remove the distressing uncertainties. But the government was taking no steps to resolve the impasse and the inaction produced annoyance in Western circles. Then, when there was disclosure of some railway rails on the northern line being lifted and taken away, Western Members of Parliament became angry. Debate took a more belligerent form.

Yes, it was admitted in response to questions from Rt. Hon. Arthur Meighen on February 12, 1923, rails had actually been removed from the grade between Mile 214 and Mile 334, "for use elsewhere in the West."[2] The removal was on the recommendation of the Vice-President and General Manager of Canadian National Railways, approved by the Board of Directors, and finally authorized by order in council on November 24, 1922.

"What bloody nerve!" men in Manitoba and Saskatchewan were saying. "They'd steal the very rails from our precious road when our backs were turned. It's a dirty eastern trick, but they don't need to think they can block our road to the Bay that way."

Days after the disclosure, March 12, Andrew Knox, Member of Parliament for Prince Albert, eager for a full debate on the subject, moved for consideration of the report from the

[1]House of Commons Debates, March 16, 1921
[2]House of Commons Debates, Feb. 12, 1923

Senate Committee, concerning the Hudson Bay Railway, "with a view to safeguarding the investment of public moneys made in the construction of that portion of the work completed to date," and making "the Government recognize the priority of this undertaking with reference to other transportation projects started subsequent to the Hudson Bay Railway." The motion was seconded by T. W. Bird, Member for Nelson.

The far-ranging debate went on and on and Hudson Bay history from the days of Henry Hudson to those of Sir Robert Borden was reviewed again and again, not always with more than a modicum of accuracy. In one day's debate, reference was made to no fewer than sixteen individual and group reports based on northern studies and submitted to the government. The identifying names making for an impressive list included Bell, Gordon, Wakeham, Tyrrell, Chisby, Crean, Kennedy, Lowe, McKenna, Prichard, Drayton-Acworth, Lower, Melville, Anderson, Armstrong, and the recent Senate report.

But quoting reports did not prove anything because the experts did not agree any more than the members of Parliament could agree. Western members were the most vociferous on the subject, invariably arguing for a government commitment to build a completed railway to one port or another. They were not convinced that Port Nelson should be abandoned. The Member for Nelson, T. W. Bird, expressed the opinion to which more Western people were coming, that Churchill held certain natural advantages but a terminal facility was partially built at Nelson and Nelson could be converted to "a workable and successful harbour." At that latter place, Bird added adroitly, Nature "has left very much to the engineer."[1]

Hon. Frank Cochrane, who had been Minister of Railways and Canals when Nelson became the official choice for terminal, would find it difficult to enter into the new debate. He was speaking defensively when he said: "No doubt Churchill is a better harbour in many respects, but the longer distance by rail and the limited size of the port were reasons that actuated both governments in deciding on Nelson. The latter port, as it ap-

[1]House of Commons Debates, June 10, 1922

pears from the reports I have gone through, is apparently quite safe. It can accommodate any amount of shipping; it is open longer and experiences less cold than does Churchill. . . . The channel [at Nelson] never freezes to any extent on account of the swift current and the heavy rise and fall of the tide. Engineer R. B. Fry who was sent in there by the Laurier Government in 1905 stated that with a light ice-breaker, Nelson could easily be kept open all winter."[1]

While Western members — especially those sitting as Progressives — were ever more eager to argue in support of a revived building program, more Easterners seemed anxious to adopt silence as a means of resistance. Individuals, of course, felt compelled to speak out, the like of J. B. M. Baxter from St. John, who could see nothing good in the northern route. "Eastern Canada is absolutely opposed to this railway," he said, "and the common sense of Canada is equally opposed to it. . . . I understand that Sir Henry Thornton himself started the operation of taking up the rails on this bit of road, which, in my judgment, should never have been built as it was nothing but a wildcat enterprise to satisfy a demand from Western Canada."[2]

The Andrew Knox motion to safeguard the public investment in the Hudson Bay Railway and acknowledge its right to a high construction priority among transportation undertakings, passed on division. But even such an expression of the public will was no guarantee of action and later in the season the Minister of Railways admitted that it was not in the government's plans to do much work on the Bay Railway "this year."

He might have added: "or next year or the year after that."

[1]House of Commons Debates, March 12, 1923
[2]House of Commons Debates, p. 4683, June 29, 1923

AN ON-TO-THE-BAY ORGANIZATION

Sir Wilfrid Laurier said that if the Canadian West needed the Hudson Bay Railway, all of Canada needed it. The trouble was to get the rest of Canada to agree. From its very beginning, the scheme had been plagued by opposition. Regional interests and regional prejudices were serious obstacles and the situation was becoming worse rather than better because Alberta, if not actually deserting the Bay Railway cause, was at least losing enthusiasm and withdrawing support. It was explained by the fact of an improved export outlet by way of the West Coast. After the opening of the Panama Canal, Alberta growers found themselves sending wheat via Vancouver or Prince Rupert and the Panama Canal and delivering it at European ports with less cost than shipping to the same markets through Fort William and Montreal, indeed almost as cheaply as if shipping through Hudson Bay.

Disunity was not a new term in Canada. The hometown outlook hampered the Hudson Bay Route from its beginning. Attitude seemed to depend entirely on how the railroad would touch individuals. Canadians who stood to benefit directly were in favor; those who could see no direct gain were indifferent or opposed. Prime Minister Mackenzie King was right when, in April, 1924, he told a delegation of Hudson Bay Railway leaders that the great need was for a national viewpoint, with dissipation of sectionalism across the country. The Monster of Disunity, having its birth in the germs of selfishness and parochialism, was neither new nor waning.

It was not totally surprising that Maritime and Montreal interests found it difficult to support what they interpreted as a competitor in shipping but it was both surprising and disappointing to sense an apparent withdrawal of support by organizations long thought to be sympathetic and loyal. That Maritime newspapers, Montreal papers, an Ottawa daily, and a leading Toronto weekly would offer repeated opposition had come to be expected. When an Eastern writer said the Route to the North was "criminal folly" and another urged "wiping that railway off the map of Canada," nobody became excited. But that the *Farmer's Sun,* organ of the United Farmers of Ontario, would take a stand against the earnest wishes of fellow agrarians in the West was extremely difficult to accept. Although making a pretense of friendly feeling for the needs of Western farmers, that Ontario paper—as if its editor knew more about the state of Western agriculture than the residents of Manitoba and Saskatchewan — declared: "To go on with building of a railway to connect Hudson Bay with prairie farms would at any time be an act of very doubtful wisdom." To proceed with such a project at the "present time would be an act of supreme folly."[1]

"An act of supreme folly?" the editor of *The Progressive,* published in Saskatoon, queried in amazement. It was "the same old argument as that used against the construction of the Canadian Pacific Railway . . . the same as that used against the settlement of the western wheat fields and the creation of the Progressive Party."[2]

If the stand of the organized farmers in Ontario proved distressing, some of the new reactions from Alberta were more disturbing. One of those irritations appeared at precisely the same time that a leading and responsible farm body, the Saskatchewan Grain Growers' Association was in annual convention and agreeing unanimously that the Hudson Bay Route — needed for the general good of the West — should be completed as early as possible and the provincial governments of Manitoba, Saskatchewan and Alberta should ascertain if a united effort "can be made to set the project moving toward completion as a western undertaking."[3]

That was fine, but when the Calgary Board of Trade, claiming a sense of kinship with agriculture, would declare for further investigation of the northern route before any more government money was spent on it — meaning, of course, more delay beyond the fourteen years already past since construction was started — the farmers were incensed. It was exactly what

[1]*Farmers' Sun,* March 29, 1924
[2]*The Progressive,* Saskatoon, April 24, 1924
[3]*The Progressive,* Jan. 31, 1924

unfriendly Eastern papers had been proposing every time there was a call for Hudson Bay Railway construction. Some of those calls for further investigation had been heeded and Western supporters were beginning to feel that the scheme was being "investigated to death."

Many editors criticized the Calgary Board's position severely, saying it was "striking a blow at western interests." Others tried to be charitable and forgiving, saying, as one editor did, that the Calgary attitude "must be taken as an ill-considered act, born of ignorance, and not a deliberate attempt to embarrass the progress of a campaign which can be shown to be in the interests of Calgary and all tributary territory."[1]

Days later, the Edmonton Board of Trade declined to support a petition for early completion of the railway to the Bay. The position adopted, the *Edmonton Bulletin* attempted to explain with admirable honesty, "is not of hostility but of neutrality. Yet not many years ago the Board and the business men of the city generally were keen supporters of the scheme and anxious that it should be pushed to completion with the least possible delay. That change of attitude is not peculiar to the Board of Trade, nor altogether dictated by the necessity of national economy. It reflects a change of viewpoint on the part of Alberta people generally, due to a radical change of circumstances. The reason is that Alberta is not as much in need of the Hudson Bay route as it was before the Panama Canal was dug. The competition of the waterway freed Alberta of the necessity of shipping grain eastward . . . Vancouver and Prince Rupert are now recognized outlets for Alberta grain en route to Europe."[2]

"Perhaps we need an organization to make us politically more effective," Manitoba and Saskatchewan friends of the Route were reasoning. "Perhaps there is an educational job to be done right here in the West as well as in the East." Nobody proposed a condemnation of Alberta producers for shipping westward instead of eastward if they found it to their advantage. "But we don't want them making needless opposition and trou-

[1]*The Progressive,* May 29, 1924
[2]*Edmonton Bulletin,* April 28, 1924

ble for those of us who are trying to improve our own positions by reaching a seaport with some similarly short rail haul."

One of the first individuals to talk publicly about organization as a means of gaining the objective of a completed railway to the Bay was Dave Ross, of Strasbourg, Saskatchewan, who tried to convince the Saskatchewan Grain Growers in convention at Moose Jaw in January. He favored a company of Bay supporters which would accept the task of enlisting the help of governments and all organizations enjoying influence. In winning the Association's endorsement, he was not successful, but almost the same idea — an organization of boosters, promoters, and workers — was under discussion in Winnipeg.

Winnipeg had its own special reasons for a new concern. If it was the attraction of Pacific and Panama shipping that tended to alienate Alberta loyalty to the Bay Route, exactly the same force was responsible for awakening Winnipeg to aggressiveness and even militancy. The Calgary Board of Trade, with nothing to lose except the good will of prairie neighbors to the east, might abandon the Bay Railway, but the Winnipeg Board had good business reasons for fearing the loss of a huge grain movement to which Winnipeg citizens had grown accustomed. They were eager to safeguard their position in handling and trading western grain and were the first to take up the proposal for a promotional organization.

The idea was discussed informally on Main Street and Portage Avenue and then, on February 22, 1924, the *Winnipeg Evening Tribune* announced: "The first organized steps in Manitoba to effect the completion of the Hudson Bay railway were initiated today in the form of the 'On-To-The-Bay Association', composed of the leading citizens of Winnipeg. The organization meeting was held in the Winnipeg Grain Exchange. Premier Bracken was elected Honorary President, ex-Mayor C. F. Gray, President pro-tem, and a temporary executive has been formed from the following citizens: Irwin C. Nelson, George H. Green, Samuel Caldwell, John Stevens and Senator Watson."[1]

[1]*Winnipeg Evening Tribune,* Feb. 22, 1924

The organization meeting was followed in the evening of the same day by a general meeting of Winnipeg citizens. When, as reported, "Whole streets of citizens in the various municipalities of Winnipeg sent in requests to be present at this meeting," the place of assembly had to be changed to the Board of Trade Auditorium. The impression of enthusiasm on the part of "whole streets of citizens," however, was somewhat at variance with the charge of public apathy concerning the Hudson Bay Railway hurled by J. A. Campbell, Commissioner for Northern Manitoba, who was one of the speakers at the meeting.

But there was no trace of apathy among those elected to temporary offices in the new organization. They recognized publicity and education as their chief purposes, but first of all, they had to complete their organization. Accordingly, another meeting was held, this one in the Marlborough Hotel on March 6, for the purpose of properly installing officers and adopting a constitution being prepared by a special committee. Charles F. Gray was confirmed as President and Sam Blair as Secretary and convenor of the very important Educational Committee.

Eager for action, Blair proposed sending a delegation to Ottawa, presumably thinking that nobody needed the benefits of an Educational Committee more than those in the country's government.

The proposed "invasion of Ottawa" seeemed like a good way of launching the Association's career but why not give the "invaders" the backing of an all-Western organization instead of a merely local or strictly Winnipeg movement? Why not seek the broadest possible backing, especially across Manitoba and Saskatchewan where it would be given willingly? Why not broaden the On-To-The-Bay Association to make it the mouthpiece for all those who had faith in the Hudson Bay Route?

A call went out for a grand rally of friends and supporters of the northern railway and the response exceeded all expectations. Officers of boards of trade, of agricultural societies, and of retail merchants, politicians, municipal officers, and private citizens in various vocations came together in the Winnipeg Board of Trade Auditorium on Friday, April 4, 1924, and numbered over a thousand. There they were, representing all walks of Western life and hailing from three provinces, two American states, and forty-two towns and cities.

In the course of the evening program, fourteen speakers took the platform, and in the best spirit of the times, nobody felt moral compulsion to be brief. Among the speakers were Premier John Bracken of Manitoba; F. W. Taylor, leader of the Conservative party in Manitoba; T. C. Norris, former Premier of Manitoba; Hon. S. J. Latta, representing the government of Saskatchewan; Dr. J. T. M. Anderson, leader of the Saskatchewan Conservative party and later Premier of the province; Sam Blair, secretary of the Association; Sheriff L. G. Calder, of Saskatoon and J. F. C. O'Connor, of Grand Forks, a one-time candidate for the office of Governor of North Dakota, who made the longest speech of the evening and qualified for the loudest cheers. Judging his audience well and entering into the mood of the occasion, the American visitor called for a display of determination: "Say to those in the East who just for a moment forget themselves," he shouted to exuberant applause, "that if they would have a united Canada they must finish this railway and finish it now."

The conference continued on the following day and the On-To-The-Bay Association was transformed from a Winnipeg organization to a Western Canada movement drawing its members and support from all parts of Manitoba and Saskatchewan. Again there had to be an election of officers and again Charles F. Gray, the former Winnipeg Mayor, was elected President. This time, however, O. D. Hill, M.L.A., from Melfort, Saskatchewan, and Major-General R. W. Paterson were named vice-presidents for Saskatchewan and Manitoba respectively.

The conference was unusual inasmuch as there was practically no debate; delegates were in complete agreement about the purpose and maintained their enthusiasm to the end. Two resolutions were passed, the first that "this meeting insist" upon the federal government making good its solemn promise to the citizens of Western Canada that provision be made during the current session of Parliament for the immediate completion of the Hudson Bay Railway.

To give weight to this message, it was agreed that it should be carried to Ottawa by a strong delegation of the Association's members, and no time should be lost. The meeting was in no mood for more compromise. Most of the leaders indicated willingness to join the trek which was to "bombard" the country's Capital, and acting promptly, the chosen group left Winnipeg by train within twenty-four hours from the end of the meeting. The party included one provincial premier, one provincial cabinet minister, one other member of a provincial legislature, one provincial party leader, one sheriff, one major-general and three mayors. It was not a group to be ignored, even in a nation's Capital. The determination of its members was to be heard by as many Eastern audiences as they could reach, Government officials, Boards of Trade, Canadian Clubs and so on. And the principal point of their message, they agreed, would be that all Canada needed the Hudson Bay Railway and the Midwest of Canada simply had to have it.

Members of the deputation met the government and then the party caucuses on April 10. The Westerners talked and the Easterners listened. The reception was all that the visitors might have wished but they should have known that to have the silent attention of the politicians is not necessarily an indication of persuasion. Eastern resistance was really unchanged. Western members of Parliament demanding an appropriation to bring the northern railway to the Port found the opposition about as strong as ever, perhaps stronger. There had been some reinforcing of the resistance; the Montreal branch of the Engineering Institute of Canada had concluded the project as a whole to be unsound, and D. W. McLachlan, who was the engineer in charge of some of the earliest work at Port Nelson, was now reported as saying the enterprise would fail.

In the House of Commons, the voice of Sir Henry Drayton seemed to ring with the greatest influence. He believed most Canadians would regard a government expenditure for completion of the railway as money thrown away. But, he added, if Western people really believed in the northern railway and wanted it, the entire undertaking with all the big public investment to date should be turned over to them or their provincial governments with the federal government's compliments and blessing. He would do more to induce the Western people to take it; he would give them a couple of million dollars with which to finish the construction. The way he said it suggested that he would give the "couple of millions" as a reward for taking the hopeless thing out of federal responsibility and out of the House of Commons forever.

It was the same old story. It only remained for the Minister of Railways, Hon. George P. Graham, who could recall turning the first sod for the railway grade exactly fourteen years earlier, to declare that "Parliament as now constituted is not prepared to vote money for completion of the Hudson Bay Railway."

Writing prophetically and sadly, the editor of the *Grain Growers' Guide* concluded: "The Hudson Bay Railway will not be completed while the King Government is in power; it will be a long time before any Government in Canada will undertake the responsibility of completing this northern outlet to the European markets unless there is a decided change in public opinion, not only in Eastern Canada but even in the prairie provinces."[1]

Members of the youthful and energetic On-To-The-Bay Association were understandably discouraged but not as pessimistic as the editor who, by his own estimate of the progress to be expected, was a better writer than a prophet of Canadian politics. Instead of giving up the struggle, the On-To-The-Bay Association continued to function as a "propaganda mill," one of the most productive and effective the West had known. There was no reason to think its efforts were wasted and its members did not have long to wait for some evidence of returns.

[1]*Grain Growers' Guide,* Editorial, July 30, 1924

"HOW LONG, O LORD, HOW LONG?"

The government's postwar indifference toward the Hudson Bay Railway reached its most aggravating stage in 1924 when even the big body of Western Progressive members of Parliament, upon whom Prime Minister Mackenzie King depended for the survival of his minority administration, failed to generate a commitment for the final stage of construction. Appeals were of no avail, as delegates from the highly regarded Canadian Council of Agriculture discovered.

"If the Hudson Bay Route is somewhat of an experiment," the Council's most reasonable brief stated, "it is an experiment that must be made in justice to the people of the West and also in the interest of national unity and to remove from the minds of the people of the West the steadily growing feeling that this project is being held up by Eastern interests who regard the West simply as a field for their exploitation. In the Hudson Bay, reaching into the very heart of the prairies, the people of Western Canada have the ocean at their doors. The people of Canada will not be worthy of their great traditions if for the sake of the few millions of dollars necessary to complete the line, they refuse to put to the test the possibility of opening up a new and shorter avenue to the sea from the great western agricultural region."[1]

By the beginning of 1925, however, when the life of the fourteenth Parliament was running out and members of Parliament "lightly turned to thoughts" of elections, the sixty-three Progressives began displaying more boldness and political muscle. One of their Western members giving voice to a new impatience was John Millar from Indian Head, a true pioneer, one who had worked with W. R. Motherwell and Peter Dayman in organizing the first Territorial Grain Growers' Association in

---

[1]*The Progressive,* Saskatoon, April 3, 1924

1901, and then served as the organization's first secretary. Now, twenty-four years later, he was visibly troubled. Speaking in the Throne Speech debate on February 10, 1925, he could not reconcile the big expenditures for the Welland Canal and practically nothing for the Western project which was close to his heart. "It strikes the West very strange," he said, "that the Central Provinces have approved the Hudson Bay Railway as far as a certain point, until $21,000,000 have been expended, and then they suddenly felt that it was only a joke; that it was not feasible and that it was time it should be stopped.[1]

The Progressives came again with their slightly aging motion directing the government to give the completion of the Hudson Bay Railway a high priority, which a succession of early promises demanded. The motion was presented by Andrew Knox, a Prince Albert farmer who had made a similar motion two years previously and saw it passed, reluctantly and with no tangible result. This time, his motion submitted: "That in the opinion of this House, it is expedient that more effective consideration be given to the resolution adopted by Parliament on March 12, 1923, recognizing the priority of Hudson Bay Railway, with reference to other transportation projects started subsequently."

Of the "transportation projects started subsequently," the most galling to Western members was, of course, the Welland Canal for which over $99,000,000 had been voted since 1918. They had no quarrel with the Canal but they could not understand why a small fraction of such sum could not be made available for the completion of a railway already well over half-finished.

Said Knox: "We who are pressing for the completion of the Hudson Bay Railway believe implicitly in the feasibility and in the future success of the project. . . . We represent hundreds of thousands of people in the West who today are equally confident of the feasibility and the successful operation. . . . These people believe that it would overcome the great handicap under which the West is today suffering by reason of high transportation costs . . . many of them believe the Hudson Bay was placed

[1]House of Commons Debates, Feb. 10, 1925

as it is by an all-wise Creator for the purpose of serving as an outlet for the great agricultural plateau of the middle West. . . . Mr. Speaker, we certainly feel like crying: 'How long, O Lord, how long?' "

And then the Member for Prince Albert had a tip for the government, one which probably affected the motion's reception: "Now Sir, if the Government [Members] wish to retain, or possibly I should use the word obtain, the respect and confidence of the West, my suggestion and advice to them would be to consider what we are up against in regard to customs tariff and also . . . transportation."[1]

The debate continued throughout the day with most cabinet ministers remaining strangely silent, and about an hour after midnight, the Knox motion was carried.

From 1921 to 1925, Prime Minister King presided over a minority government clinging to power only through the support of the Progressives who disliked the Liberals just a little less than they did Arthur Meighen's Conservatives. Had the members of that relatively new agrarian party used their Balance of Power to the best advantage, they might have seen the rails laid all the way to Nelson in 1923 or '24. But as one of their members, Robert King Anderson, admitted, they had not been very successful in influencing legislation.

Now, however, with the approach of an inevitable election, Mackenzie King was showing more interest in the needs of the West. If he gained sufficient support from the voters, he said, his Liberal government would indeed finish the railway to the Bay. Canadians with short memories and those young enough to be hearing such a promise for the first time were impressed. But the result of the October 29, 1925, election left King with fewer rather than more seats — down from 117 to 101 — while Arthur Meighen's Conservatives increased their elected numbers from 50 to 116. The Progressive party's strength dropped from 65 to 25 Members, but the combined numbers of Liberals and Progressives could still outvote the Conservatives and King carried on. Inasmuch as the voters failed to give him the mandate which he seemed to have de-

[1] House of Commons Debates, May 4, 1925

manded as a condition, he could presume release from the campaign promise about finishing the railway. Nevertheless, the 1926 budget carried an appropriation of $3,000,000 with which to pursue the Hudson Bay Railway goal, an item the Conservatives in opposition insisted was merely a bribe to insure the Progressive backing he needed to stay in power.

But in the wake of the 1926 budget came political chaos. The Conservatives, like hounds bearing down for a kill, charged irregularities in the Customs Department and King, anticipating a vote of censure which the restive Progressives might feel they should support, decided to take the initiative, ask Governor General Lord Byng to dissolve the fifteenth Parliament and make way for a general election. But the Governor General, noting that it was less than a year since the previous election, exercised what he believed was his prerogative, rejected King's advice, and instead of dissolving Parliament, invited Hon. Arthur Meighen, leader of the Conservatives, to form a Government.

In announcing his resignation to the House of Commons on June 28, 1926, King said: "The public interest demands a dissolution of this House of Commons. As Prime Minister I so advised His Excellency the Governor General shortly after noon today. His Excellency, having declined to accept my advice to grant dissolution, to which I believe under British practice I am entitled, I immediately tendered my resignation which His Excellency has been graciously pleased to accept."

King then moved adjournment of the House. The affairs of state moved briskly. Arthur Meighen accepted the Governor General's invitation to form a Government and was at once sworn in as Prime Minister. But on July 1, just two days after taking office, Meighen's new and still rather shapeless administration was defeated on what was regarded as a Want-of-Confidence motion and Parliament was dissolved and an election called. If there existed any unannounced government decision to get on with the Hudson Bay Railway job, it too dissolved.

King, in the ensuing campaign, made much of the "constitutional issue" which students of political science continued to debate. He alleged injustice on the part of the Governor

General and won 116 constituency seats in the election on September 14, 1926, while the Conservatives dropped to 91 and the Progressives to 13.

The On-To-The-Bay Association was active throughout the campaign — as indeed it had been for the two full years since its formation. Its officers could report 150 meetings held in Manitoba and Saskatchewan in 1925, to say nothing of a petition carrying 150,000 signatures for Ottawa's edification. Now, the Association was not going to let the Prime Minister forget his promise to do something positive about the northern railway when he obtained a convincing mandate from the voters.

Mackenzie King had a clear working majority but what supporters of the Hudson Bay Railway saw as even more encouraging was the new Minister of Railways and Canals, Hon. Charles Avery Dunning from Saskatchewan. King brought Dunning into the cabinet just a few weeks before his government's resignation and the new Minister had insufficient time to demonstrate capabilities in either Department or House before dissolution. But he was re-elected and now he was back as Minister in the Department mainly responsible for the fortunes — or misfortunes — of the Hudson Bay Railway. He would be watched, to be sure, by both the friends and foes of the Railway.

Dunning knew the needs and moods of the West as few others did. He had been a seventeen-year-old immigrant when he came in 1902, then a prairie farmer's hired man working to obtain experience the hard way, a homesteader, a leader in the Saskatchewan Grain Growers' Association, a provincial Minister of Railways, and finally, Premier of his adopted province. He was eminently fitted for the new role and Prime Minister King's announcement on February 22, 1926, brought cheers from members of the On-To-The-Bay Association. The same announcement probably helped King's party in the election which was to follow shortly.

Dunning's predecessor in the Railways and Canals portfolio, Hon. George P. Graham, was highly regarded but he was an Ontario man and that was almost enough to make Westerners view his Hudson Bay Railway policies with suspicion.

Everybody knew where Dunning stood with respect to the controversial railway and they knew he was forthright.

While Western Liberals were delighted at Mackenzie King's action in placing Dunning in the important Railways and Canals ministry, the Eastern reaction was less enthusiastic. Opposition members in the House found pleasure in calling him the "Crown Prince of Saskatchewan," and before he was in the Commons very long he was accused of being there to give Ontario "a dose of its own medicine." The critics were convinced that he would be "hostile to Ontario."

Dunning might be new to the Commons and his Department but he knew more about the Hudson Bay Railway than most people on either side of the Commons chamber and was soon seen giving new leadership in the matter. More and more questions were directed to him and his answers were frank and clear. What would the government do with the $3,000,000 in the budget? he was asked and he replied that it would be used to rehabilitate the 332 miles of railroad and make it ready for operation. How much would it cost to lay rails on the remaining 92 miles of grade to Port Nelson? and he answered: $3,153,000. And when asked if he knew for sure where the railway would end, he was honest and said: "We hope it will be Nelson."

Propaganda from the anti-Hudson Bay Route forces increased. Pamphlets published to bring ridicule to the northern railway and port appeared in larger numbers around the House of Commons, and an Ottawa editor won attention with his judgment that money spent to finish the project would be more millions thrown to the icebergs and walruses. But Dunning, appearing as a man with a purpose, was unmoved. Proceeding with caution and steadfastness, he gave weight to the theory that a promise of freedom to go ahead with the Hudson Bay Route development as soon as a few lingering doubts were removed, was one of the conditions he had demanded when he had accepted King's invitation to join the cabinet. He would welcome advice and be prepared to act upon such advice as seemed sound, but he would not be swayed by the propaganda and local pressures. When, as late as April 8, 1927, he was questioned concerning a terminal, he answered with refreshing frankness: "We hope it will be Nelson," then added that he was not through seeking advice.

Nelson was Dunning's hope for the same practical reasons of shorter grade and less muskeg that influenced his predecessors, but Nelson, notwithstanding the big investment already there, was not a foregone conclusion with him. Dredging problems and costs would be very great, the Minister warned his Parliamentary colleagues; they could anticipate the need to move 5,500,000 cubic yards of material from the channel in order to provide a passage with width of 300 feet. Moreover, the silt and clay so excavated would have to be transported by scows for a distance of twenty-two miles to the bay or open sea. It could not be dumped safely in the channel or in the shallows. In other words, those people who raised fears about Nelson as a terminal had some practical reasons, but not enough to deter this Westerner's intention to complete a rail line to the sea.

He was eager to get along with the final phases and late in 1926 decided to seek guidance from at least one more source, this time from someone having extensive port and harbor experience and no prejudices about Hudson Bay. "It was recognized," he said, "in view of the controversial nature of the Hudson Bay project that if any Canadian engineer were invited to make a study of it, in all probability there would be charges or statements that he was prejudiced one way or the other; therefore the Government decided to secure the services of an unquestioned authority on port development."[1]

Dunning was not looking for a man to tell him if the railway should or should not be completed — on that point his mind was made up — but he wanted an outstanding authority who would act as a referee in making a final adjudication between the two terminal points. The search was directed overseas, and with the help of the High Commissioner in London, an arrangement was made with Frederick Palmer, an engineer with an international reputation. The Minister announced the appointment on November 24, 1926.

Members of the On-To-The-Bay Association sneered, saying: "Here we go again; another investigation, another delay."

[1] House of Commons Debates, April 8, 1927

At the Association's annual meeting in Winnipeg on February 5, the President, Brig. Gen. R. W. Paterson, declared that there could be no possible excuse for changing the terminus from Nelson unless it were to appease the foes of the scheme. A Winnipeg editor agreed; the decision to build to Nelson had, for all practical purposes, been endorsed by the people of this country and neither Dunning, Palmer, nor any other person had the right to change the plan at this late date.

The Saskatchewan Legislature, after debating the matter, found agreement for a resolution to the effect that "the construction of the Hudson Bay Railway should be carried out without interruption so that the line may be completed to Nelson and work commenced on the port terminus during 1927."

If Dunning had been looking only for public favor in the West, he made a serious mistake. The general sentiment in rural Saskatchewan and Manitoba was indicated by the formal protest sent by telegram from the Saskatchewan Section of the United Farmers of Saskatchewan to the Minister on April 7: any investigation of Port Churchill would be seen as "a breach of faith and an attempt to play politics with and delay the completion of the project."

In the light of experience over many years, it was not surprising that the people of the West were suspicious and apprehensive. But this time, as events of ensuing months were to show, the critics were quite wrong. They had misjudged both Dunning and Palmer.

ENTER FREDERICK PALMER

Nineteen hundred and twenty-seven was Canada's Jubilee Anniversary of Confederation and the country, after recovering from postwar depression, was enjoying moderate prosperity. Canadians had their first experience with national radio and were becoming accustomed to new liquor laws, short skirts, silk stockings, and self-starter cars. To mark the anniversary occasion, the Peace Tower Carillon was dedicated in Ottawa and the July 1 holiday was celebrated with extra gaiety everywhere.

Members of the On-To-The-Bay Association, in annual meeting at Winnipeg on February 4, had another bright idea for an anniversary feature: a Jubilee Year Excursion to Port Nelson with the northward portion of the trip being made by boat from Montreal or Halifax, and the return by the yet-to-be-completed Hudson Bay Railway. Optimism, of course, had to be the Association's stock in trade but the more practical members admitted that they would be satisfied if the anniversary year produced nothing better than the completion of the railway to tidewater, with or without an organized excursion. By convention time, however, everybody should have realized that nothing in the way of progress could be expected until Frederick Palmer completed his investigation and made his report to the government.

"Who is this man Palmer?" people across the West were asking. The name might be well known to engineers around the world and especially in India where he had served the government as chief engineer in connection with railways, ports, and irrigation, but it was new to most Canadians. When invited to undertake this special work for the Government of Canada, Palmer was the head of the engineering firm of Rendel, Palmer and Tritton of London, consulting engineer for the Port administrations at Glasgow and London, and consulting engineer to the British Government in connection with colonial port development. Highly regarded in professional engineering circles, he was president of the British Institute of Civil Engineers, an office which Minister Dunning described as "the blue ribbon position of the engineering world."

Having agreed to advise the Canadian Government about the two Hudson Bay ports, Palmer came promptly to Ottawa to confer with officials and conduct a search of existing records so that he would have the benefit, as far as possible, of information already established as factual. Later, he would return to visit Hudson Bay and make his own independent observations.

He was in Ottawa for a couple of weeks after arrival on December 23 and before departing, he received from Hon. Charles Dunning a long letter containing instructions and a wealth of background information likely to be useful in the conduct of the study. The letter, an extremely valuable contribution to Hudson Bay Railway record, was dated January 5, 1927, and was read for the benefit of members of the House of Commons.[1]

"Dear Mr. Palmer,

In order that we may have record of the understandings reached as a result of our several conferences, I beg to advise as follows:

In 1911, the Canadian government commenced the construction of a railway to Hudson Bay. In 1912, in order that the road might be placed completely under contract, it became necessary for the Government of the day to make immediate choice between the only two possible ports on the west coast, Nelson and Churchill. After a personal visit to both places by the then Minister, and consideration of the information available at the time, the Minister, on the advice of his engineering staff, recommended the establishment of the railway terminus at Nelson, and plans for harbour terminals were prepared by an engineer specially selected and sent to Nelson for that purpose. Upon consideration of the scheme of development then suggested, differences of opinion arose and the engineer resigned his appointment. A member of the department engineering staff was then assigned to the task of preparing suitable plans, as a result of which the present scheme of development at Nelson

[1]House of Commons Debates, April 8, 1927

was approved and actively prosecuted by the department during 1914 and the succeeding years until the fall of 1917 when the work was discontinued owing to war conditions. During the following winter the construction of the railway was also discontinued upon completion of the bridge at the Kettle rapids crossing of the Nelson river, about 92 miles from Port Nelson.

On the railway $15,245,889 had been expended to March 31, 1926, and on the Nelson terminals $6,242,114.

At the present time that portion of the railway previously constructed is being reconditioned and it is planned to continue the construction of the railway in 1927. This imposes upon the Government early consideration of the question of harbour development in order that the Hudson Bay route may be assured fair trial as an ocean outlet for western grain and cattle, and for such other traffic in agricultural, mineral, forest and manufactured products as may develop.

Controversy has always existed as to the relative merits of Nelson and Churchill as the Bay terminus, and notwithstanding the selection of Nelson in 1912-13, controversy has persisted. In 1920, a special committee of the Senate was appointed to examine and report upon the Hudson Bay project generally and upon the character of the ports and their fitness for terminals. Upon the evidence then adduced, the committee reached the following conclusions upon the harbour phase of the project:

'That in the opinion of this committee sufficient care was not taken in the selection of Nelson as the terminus of the railway and that the Government should not make further important expenditures upon this port without first making a new and thorough examination into the relative merits of Churchill and Nelson as a terminus for the railroad.'

In view of the substantial expenditure already incurred at Nelson, and the shorter rail haul to that point, the Government is naturally predisposed towards Nelson, but desires above all things, that the port chosen, and its arrangements, should afford the best possible opportunity for the development of trade through the Bay.

The problem of harbour development in the two places differs very widely and, as regards Churchill, the use of that port would involve the construction, maintenance and operation of about 90 additional miles of railway. As to the suitability of the terrain between the Nelson and Churchill rivers to railway construction we hope to have definite information in the course of the next few months. Should the survey now being made disclose conditions unfavorable to railway construction, this would, of course, dispose of any question as to Churchill, but if a railway is found practicable, we will require your advice concerning Churchill also. If that port should be found to be capable of such early and economic development as would afford better and safer facilities than Nelson, and more readily available, that would be a factor of great importance to the successful development of the Hudson Bay route. For these reasons we think it unwise and not in the interests of Canada to restrict your investigation to the port of Nelson only, unless, meanwhile, Churchill should be eliminated for railway reasons.

In the event of Churchill becoming a possibility we should have, in addition to relative costs of construction and maintenance, a comparative estimate of the length of time necessary to provide terminals at either port sufficient to enable a proper test of the route to be made. We consider this element of time a matter of prime importance.

We want, also, your opinion of the design of the existing works at Nelson, and as to whether any change could be made there which would either reduce the cost or the length of time required for development, or improve conditions in any way at that point.

What we have in mind as an initial test development — and this is suggested more for your guidance than as a conclusive and limiting instruction — would be the provision of accommodation in either harbour for six cargo ships in port at one time, with working berth for three of the six, the estimated draft of the vessels to be not less than 26 feet. The minimum development projected at each port should, of course, be capable of such progressive extension as future requirements might dictate.

If a railway to Churchill be found practicable, we desire that your report should cover a possible development at both Nelson and Churchill, with estimated cost, your recommendation as to choice to be made and reasons therefor.

In outlining, in this general way, the matters upon which

the Government desires your advice, it is not intended to ask you to consider problems unconnected with port development. We appreciate that, owing to climatic conditions, it will not be possible for you to conduct your personal examination of Nelson and Churchill before next summer. We shall, however, do everything in our power to facilitate your work at both points and would be glad to have your conclusions as soon as possible thereafter, as we are anxious to avoid delay in the prosecution of this important undertaking.

Faithfully yours,
Charles A. Dunning."

Dunning was serious. There would be no more needless delays if he had anything to say about it. He admitted what many Western people were presuming, that the government had given him "full power to proceed with the road as I see fit." He recognized the lingering possibility of a change in plans but as soon as Frederick Palmer reported and the matter of the port was settled, construction would begin from both ends.

In the meantime work crews were busy. There was rehabilitation of that portion of the road built before the war. It had deteriorated seriously. Rails which had not been lifted and removed were badly rusted, and ties suffered from rot.

While waiting for Palmer's advice, too, government engineers were making studies and surveys on the Churchill right of way in case it were the one to be used. Even the preliminary work as it was being conducted, required large amounts of materials and equipment, and to make aviation history as well as Hudson Bay history, Mr. Dunning's Department, early in the year, signed a contract with a western airways company to carry freight and passengers from Kettle Rapids to Nelson and Churchill. In transporting heavy equipment, it was a pioneer effort. Other planes, incidentally, were being used for the first time in patrolling the Bay and Strait for the purpose of obtaining further navigational information for a new Commission under the chairmanship of N. B. McLean from the Department of Marine and Fisheries. Six Fokker planes were acquired for this service and were being manned by officers loaned by the Royal Canadian Air Force.

On June 2, after receiving the opinions of his engineers working in the North, Mr. Dunning had an announcement: the railroad could be built to Churchill with no more technical difficulties than in building to Nelson. Admittedly, the cost of the line to Churchill would be higher; the new construction from the crossing on the Limestone River to Churchill — 154 miles — would cost $7,543,000, according to the Minister, while the cost of completing the line to Nelson would be $2,458,000. The longer route might still prove the cheaper because, as reported at the same time, it could take up to six years to adequately dredge the channel on the approach to the Nelson docks.

Engineer Palmer was back in Ottawa in late July, ready for the all-important, on-the-spot survey of the two northern ports. Accompanying him when he left on the trip to Hudson Bay were Hon. Charles Dunning who was making his second journey over the route in two months; Graham A. Bell, Deputy Minister of Railways and Canals; D. W. McLachlan, government engineer with a long Hudson Bay Route association; A. E. Dubue, a government engineer, and E. J. Buckton, English engineer traveling with Palmer. At Winnipeg, the party was augmented by the addition of C. S. Gzowski, chief engineer for construction in the service of the Canadian National Railways, and Brig. Gen. R. W. Paterson, President of the On-To-The-Bay Association.

Winnipeg reporters interviewed Mr. Palmer, trying to determine if he had preconceived ideas about the best choice of port. He admitted only that he had made a thorough study of earlier surveys, charts, sketches, and other recorded data but found limited information concerning conditions at Churchill. No borings had been taken there, he was surprised to discover, but at his request, government engineers were making them and he would have the benefit of the new information when he arrived at the port.

It was not an easy trip and could not be a fast one. The expanded party, traveling as far as possible by rail, stopped briefly at The Pas on July 30 and then continued over the new railroad to the end of the steel at Limestone River, some 350 miles beyond The Pas. Leaving the rails, the travelers took canoes to reach a camp thirty miles farther north and then transferred to motor boats for the descent upon Port Nelson. After a day given to inspection of the bridge, the island, and the dredging operations, they were on their way to Churchill, traveling by tug. What they saw at the latter point would be very strange to the Britishers in the party. Palmer would be uninspired by the absence of trees and the abundance of big northern mosquitoes, but he found special interest in the borings and currents and tides. There the travelers remained for four days before returning to Nelson on August 8.

At the end of a week, the eminent visiting engineer appeared to have made his decision. He might have been expected to keep his impressions in silence until he could submit them in a formal report, but he could see no reason for keeping his traveling companions in suspense, and before leaving Nelson, he told them that he would recommend Churchill. The big natural harbor with almost unlimited shipping accommodation had impressed him greatly. "It is almost incomparably superior to Nelson in safety, cost of construction and economy of time. It is accessible for 30 feet (of water) at all stages of tide, whereas Nelson can only be made available by extensive dredging for 26-foot ships over periods averaging three hours each, twice in every 24 hours of the shipping season."[1]

Palmer promised to have his preliminary written report ready for submission in August and his final and detailed report as soon after that as possible. But having made a verbal report before leaving the shores of the Bay, his written report would be little more than clarification and confirmation. His advice was clear and, significantly, it proved convincing to all who traveled with him that Churchill should be the Canadian Government's choice. Nelson would be a mistake. The original decision to go to Nelson with the railway, Palmer inferred, was made without an understanding of all the facts. Even General Paterson, whose On-To-The-Bay Association members had so recently voted opposition to the further delay in building to Nelson made necessary by the Palmer appointment, voiced agreement.

There seemed to be immediate relief on the part of all the

[1]On-To-The-Bay Association of Canada, Information issued in October, 1927

officials in the party. The old controversy appeared to evaporate. At once the federal and Canadian National Railway engineers could see what they had to do and the Minister of Railways made it quite clear that he was not waiting to receive the written report. "The Government," he said, "will act immediately on Mr. Palmer's recommendations. . . . Construction will begin from both ends," meaning from the Limestone River on the south and Churchill on the north. And while the rails were being laid over the remaining expanse of about 150 miles, the Minister promised, work would go forward in the harbor "to make it possible to have the port ready for navigation when the line is completed."

Palmer's report, dated August 24, was released in Ottawa five days later. It did not create much of a stir because most people anticipated its contents and 150 men were already on their way to Nelson to dismantle such parts of the port installation as could be used at the new terminal and a dipper dredge at Halifax was being made ready for service at Churchill. Instructions had been given to move coal, supplies, equipment, and tugboats from Halifax. The government administration hoped to move as much of the recoverable materials as possible from Nelson to Churchill in the month of September.

"When will the route be ready to handle grain?" the Minister was being asked by Westerners with renewed hope. Among other things, a large terminal elevator would have to be built, he explained, but he could see a reasonable chance of all being in readiness for some portion of the 1930 crop.

Palmer's report dealt extensively with the port at Nelson. Most of the observations were uncomplimentary to the Nelson prospects as a harbor and supported his earlier contention that the place had been chosen without proper regard for all the facts. The Nelson channel would need dredging for seven and a half miles below the proposed wharf; ships in the harbor would be exposed dangerously to the northeasterly gales; the partly completed artificial island far out in the stream would furnish cramped space for grain elevators and wharf installations; sand and gravel needed in construction would have to be transported between twenty and seventy miles; and, of more than passing political importance, the works at Churchill could be completed for use in about half the time likely to be required at Port Nelson.

Palmer's conclusions, straightforward like their author, left no doubt:

"1—That Churchill is undoubtedly the port to be selected, as affording a real harbour in which shipping facilities can be provided in calm water protected from all storms by the surrounding rocky cliffs.

2—The estimated costs of corresponding accommodation at Nelson and Churchill disclose marked advantages in favor of the latter, the figures showing that, including interest during the period of construction, the cost at Churchill will be less than one-third of what is required to complete Nelson. Even after adding the cost of the extra 87 miles of railway to Churchill, the cost of this place will be only about one-half of the Nelson port estimate.

3—The time for completion of the works at Churchill, namely three years, is one-half of the time needed to carry out the Nelson works.

4—That Churchill provides a completely sheltered port for shipping from the moment the entrance is passed, while at Nelson no shelter can be confidently reckoned upon until the wharf is reached, and then only by the provision of breakwaters.

5—That the annual charges, including interest, operation and maintenance, would be about $1,000,000 greater at Nelson that at Churchill.

6—That at both Nelson and Churchill the sites admit of considerable extensions, but at much less cost at Churchill than at Nelson. The wharf, either in its initial or extended stage, would at Nelson be governed by the limiting nature of its approach, to ships of 26-foot draft during a brief period around high water at neap tides, unless much increased expenditure is incurred in dredging. It is limited to a draft of 28 feet even after this dredging is done, unless still further expenditure of a prohibitive character is undertaken. At Churchill the accommodation proposed will, in the 'initial development,' admit of 28-foot draft ships during the 24 hours of each day, while for extensions there is no practical limit to the draft of ships which can be provided for.

7—The evidence regarding ice conditions at both ports is vague and inconclusive and no satisfactory or reliable decision can be given in regard thereto. It has been stated that the river at Churchill freezes over earlier than the Nelson River and, also, that the bay ice blocks the entrance to Nelson for a later period than that over which Churchill entrance is closed; but in the absence of any evidence dealing directly with the navigation aspect of the question, it is impossible to say that either port is open to ocean-going steamships for a longer or shorter period than the other. Following upon these conclusions, it is strongly recommended that Churchill be made the port terminal for the Hudson Bay Railway because it affords by far the best possible opportunity for the development of trade through the Bay.''

That much was settled. Hon. Charles Dunning was impressed by Palmer's reasoning and conclusions and satisfied to approve the major change of terminal. The Prime Minister was notified by telegram and replied that the cabinet would ratify the Minister's actions. Now, it was a matter of getting on with the job of putting Churchill on the railroad.

FINALLY, THE PUSH TO THE BAY

Suddenly, the friends of the northern route were enjoying a new political climate. A member of the On-To-The-Bay Association returning from an inspection of the new line to Churchill said it was difficult to see everything because there was so much of "Dunning's dust" in the air. Having regard to the dustless character of muskeg terrain, the speaker was exaggerating considerably but the remark served to illustrate the feverish activity which pervaded the working area. "Too bad," the prairie man added, "we didn't have Charlie in the Cabinet years ago; we'd be shipping wheat and cattle out that way and we'd be richer today."

If 1927 was the Year of Decision, 1928 and '29 were years of action. As soon as Frederick Palmer's views were known, contracts were awarded for prompt commencement of grading and track laying to the waterfront and the earliest possible completion. By the terms of the agreements, the new railroad was to be in place from Mile 356.5 to Mile 450 by October 15, 1928, and from Mile 450 to Churchill by September 1, 1929.

When Chief Engineer C. S. Gzowski — a sort of Commander-in-Chief of operations — returned from an inspection of the line in late June, 1928, he reported trains running on the rehabilitated part of the railway at 25 to 30 miles an hour with safety, and construction going forward on the new portion — "the Muskeg Belt" — with all possible speed. Three hundred and fifty men were employed at the Churchill end and more than 2,200 on the railway, most of them recent immigrants and handy with shovels and wheelbarrows.

The railway operation revolved around two work trains, the gravel train from which the roadbed material was wheeled forward on plank tracks and dumped, and the track-laying train ahead carrying ties, rails, and the hoisting devices needed to project the rails into position to be spiked down and bolted together with fishplate clamps. On single track, one of these trains seemed to be constantly in the way of the other.

Construction of the Hudson Bay Railway photographed by Fred Russell (deceased) of Winnipeg near Flin Flon, Man., about 1928. — Manitoba Museum of Man & Nature.

But there was every indication that construction would be advanced the full contract distance before the end of the season, leaving less than seventy-five miles to be finished in 1929. There were setbacks and unanticipated obstacles but when the 1928 season was supposed to have ended officially, Charles Dunning could report with satisfaction that the rails were actually in place as far as Mile 462. Prairie people whose patience had been tried over the years were now properly impressed.

Although the news from the North told of commendable headway, the readers never knew the full extent of troubles and hardships encountered almost daily. Moreover, for hundreds of the men who went north to work, it was their first contact with the unknown part of Canada and demanded some major adjustments in living habits. It brought surprise that a northern winter was no more trying than one spent in Winnipeg. Men worked hard lifting gravel and pushing wheelbarrows but many recognized it as a great adventure. They were impressed or should have been impressed by the native people — Indians and Eskimos — living far from civilization and enjoying life; by the northern caribou, Arctic foxes, ptarmigan, stunted trees, plants and animals adapting to harsh surroundings; by the stillness of the barren ground wilderness, the added brightness of the northern lights, and so on.

Camp rules were strict. Men were there to work. No liquor was allowed and no women were permitted beyond Mile 412. The only exceptions to the latter rule were the nurses who were taken in when needed. There was one serious outbreak of typhoid fever requiring emergency hospital services in tents and cabooses, but men of that generation had to be very sick before they admitted it and not many nurses were seen. Workers had no alternative to saving their wages, their only available luxury being Copenhagen snuff or "snoose," which just about everybody learned to use. The habit was not one which did anything to endear the workers to wives and sweethearts back in the South.

The construction problems were different than any encountered elsewhere and engineers had no reservoir of information or experience from which to draw. For the first hundred miles or so from The Pas, the railway was laid out through

wooded country interspersed with unnamed lakes and underlaid with good conventional clay subsoil. It presented no unusual construction problems. Farther north, however, where
the muskeg became widespread, the problems grew bigger.
Engineers who knew exactly how to cope with clay and rocks
and effect river crossings, were clearly worried by the mile after
mile underlaid with permafrost, that blue ice extending to unknown depths, perhaps a hundred feet, perhaps a thousand feet.
It appeared to be a relic of the Ice Age and likely to remain until
the next Ice Age. Very recent experiments, however, seemed
to show how, with certain precautions, railway grades could be
built right on the tundra muskeg with hope of staying there.

Muskeg moss could be the best of insulation. That much
was known. It was just this quality which protected the permafrost from melting in summer. It was soon realized, too, that
where permafrost was close to the surface, the mossy material
was positively essential for keeping the gravel and tracks se-
curely separated from the frozen material just inches or feet
below. The loss of the insulating layer or anything which would
allow contact between the grade gravel and the ice would result
in melting of the latter and the creation of a new surface depression or gulch. Tractors and other heavy equipment were known
to have settled into the muskeg far enough to reach the ice and
then been swallowed into frigid depths.

There were stories of disaster overtaking an entire construction train working at the northern end of the grade. Darkness had just settled over the tundra and rain was falling when
the steam locomotive jumped the shaky track, plowed awk-
wardly into the spongy muck and took its string of eight flatcars
with it. Fortunately, members of the train crew escaped without
injury. But there was nothing they could do except stare at the
tangled train lying on its side, half submerged. With no other
option, the men began a long walk back over the tracks to the
nearest construction camp where they would have shelter for
the night and from where they could send a telegraph message
reporting the accident and requesting the dispatch of a repair
train.

The unhappy men relaxed to await the coming of the help
and equipment needed to place the train back on the tracks.

When the wrecking train arrived the members of the original crew returned with it to the scene of the accident. When they came to the place of derailment, where locomotive and cars had plunged into the muskeg, no part of the wreck was in sight. It was as though some giant had taken it away. How was this to be explained? Members of the repair gang wondered if this was a hoax and questioned the men of the other crew as though they might be guilty of public mischief.

At length the exact circumstances were recognized. It was not a hoax, but was what nobody had anticipated. The derailed locomotive, in plowing into the muskeg to the depth of the permafrost, had become a first-class conductor of heat to the lower level and the engine and cars had sunk lower and lower through the resulting melt until completely swallowed by the mysterious North.

Even the day-to-day operations of building a railway in that tundra country presented construction problems completely strange to men who were familiar with the conventional dragline technique. Those heavy machines, which under ordinary circumstances would scoop up great buckets of soil and gravel and drop the material on the new grade, had to be abandoned. Even if deposits of gravel were discovered near the surface beside the right of way, they would be so frozen that no dragline shovel could penetrate. Where sizable deposits of gravel were found, the frozen masses were either blasted with dynamite or exposed to thaw, permitting removal one layer at a time. In any case, contractors accepted the necessity of hauling the gravel fill for some miles, sometimes many miles.

Nor could telegraph lines be built by the conventional methods involving the drilling of holes and insertion of poles. Telegraph poles set singly in holes in the muskeg and ice could be dislodged by the heaving force of frost. The alternative was to tie three telegraph poles together and set them up as a tripod on the surface. It required more poles in order to string telegraph wires on tripods but it was more economical than having to constantly reset single poles.

There were many other such difficulties peculiar to the North. Food supplies for men working ahead of the construction trains had to be packed in and deposited in caches, which was all very well until the weather became warm and the pack trails became treacherous from sloughs and bogs. Duckboards, such as those used in the first World War, were brought in and laid down to make miles of paths for the pedestrian workers. It was the least that could be done to protect men against the danger of becoming engulfed in those awful muskeg traps, sometimes quite inconspicuous and often deep enough to devour either a man or a dragline. When construction ended, many of the duckboards found use in snow fences along the right of way.

Yes, in completing the 1928 objective in road construction ahead of the time schedule, the contractors had every reason for satisfaction. They, too, were surprised. Then, strangely enough, the decision was made to continue rail laying through the winter. On March 29, 1929, Engineer H. A. Dixon dispatched a telegram: "Steel reached Churchill today." The amazing message was literally correct but grossly misleading inasmuch as the rails reaching the northern terminal were without grade and without ballast. What was provided was merely a winter or skeleton track. By the adoption of this new and daring technique, the grade would come later — and did.

On the surface it looked like a foolhardy experiment, laying track before there was anything better than a base of frozen muskeg. But it was not really so foolish. In the first place, it was an alternative to a long winter stoppage and Minister Charles Dunning and all others involved were in a hurry. Gravel pits were frozen with a boulder-like solidity and building grade for new track was out of the question. For the winter at least, the frozen tundra offered its own base with all the firmness of the rock of Gibraltar. It was moderately level and engineers, in a hurry too, decided to lay the rails and hope they would be able to finish the job in the summer by simply jacking up the ties and rails and dropping gravel and fill for a roadbed.

Still the plan would have seemed foolish and been foolish had it not been for another overwhelming reason which the critics did not generally understand. It was simply a matter of moving thousands of tons of vital equipment and supplies to the Churchill end of the line where they were needed and doing it as quickly as possible. As the contractors realized, the work program to be carried out before the first commercial cargoes of grain could be shipped overseas would be very big. There was an elevator to be built, and even before that, the terminal community would need shunting yards, shops, a roundhouse, rolling stock, docks, office buildings, rails and ties for construction from the northern end, and countless other things. How were these to be delivered without a long and costly delay while waiting for summer shipping through Hudson Strait and into Churchill Harbor? Air transport had not reached the point where it could offer a solution and winter freighting by means of tractors or horses could not be expected to cope with a movement of such magnitude.

Shipments destined for Churchill were accumulating in southern warehouses. The only possible solution if a major delay were to be avoided was to extend the existing line with a hastily built rail connection over the frozen tundra to Churchill, move the freight over it before the spring thaw, and hope the skeleton structure could be given some muscle and permanency later.

If a small·army of workmen, carloads of steel, tons and tons of cement, equipment including a steam shovel — at least 300 carloads already waiting to be taken north — were to be delivered before midsummer, the only hope was to close the 75-mile rail gap and take the shipments through before the end of winter. Engineers set about to have that strange railway installed and ready for operation before the end of March. Even that would leave little enough time. It was a battle against new hardships, blizzards and the severe cold of a sub-Arctic winter. But the rail-laying car at the northerly end of the work train, conspicuous by its two long arms from which rails could be lowered into track position for spiking, went back into service. Storms raging across the treeless northern wastes buried the work train in snow drifts a few times and there were delays, but progress was generally satisfactory and the goal was reached on time.

When spring came and the ties and the track seemed to be floating on muskeg, there was still some doubt that a grade could be injected under the line with safety. But the Bay Railway, more than most undertakings in transportation, demanded faith; with gravel trains dropping ballast on their northerly extremity, thereby extending their own working range, they proved that it could be done. And so it was that on September 13, 1929, Churchill could boast not only a rail connection with the South but a rail connection complete with roadbed.

In the meantime, Canadians were hearing more than ever about their North and, like the construction engineers, displaying a bolder attitude. The fog of misunderstanding and fear was lifting just a little. Even those Eastern people who had opposed the Hudson Bay Railway were showing some appreciation of the North as a part of Canada. The Northern Commission, under the chairmanship of N. B. McLean, returned after almost two years in and around Hudson Strait and its report was tabled in the House of Commons on April 25. Having been furnished with two ships, several planes, and much meteorological equipment, the Commission had the best opportunity ever to gain understanding of the area.

Chairman McLean confirmed that the Strait never completely froze over but could, indeed, be choked with ice. He recommended two powerful icebreakers, one for use in the Strait and one at Churchill. Needed, also, were radio direction-finding stations and he could report having left behind three radio stations to aid in communication and help to guide incoming and outgoing vessels, one at Cape Hope's Advance, one at Nottingham Island, and the third at Port Burwell. And as for the shipping season, he believed it could well average four months per year with safety and longer with good icebreaker service. One of the strong icebreakers ordered almost at once on the Commission's recommendation was appropriately christened the *N. B. McLean* and was destined to long years of service in those northern waters.

It augured well for the future of the northern route that, as it neared completion, spokesmen for various Western cities began an agitation for a more direct rail connection. The loudest voices were from Winnipeg, the city which had grown accustomed to servicing trainloads of grain en route to the Head of the Lakes and export. Naturally, Winnipeg business leaders wanted the city to retain its role in the grain trade. Requested was a direct rail line which would remove the necessity of the long and circuitous course by way of Hudson Bay Junction.

Without the desired short rail route to the Hudson Bay Railway, nobody at Saskatoon or Regina, for example, would consider shipping to Churchill by way of Winnipeg.

All Manitoba Boards of Trade were invited to send representatives to a meeting in Winnipeg on February 12, 1929. Of course the Board of Trade men favored a more direct approach to the Bay for Manitoba communities but could not agree upon which of several to recommend. Some advocated a railway north from Dauphin; some would take a railway north between lakes Winnipeg and Manitoba. In the absence of agreement, the whole issue was referred to the Union of Manitoba Boards of Trade. Nor did the referral produce a solution, but the federal government, through the Department of Railways and Canals, agreed to conduct an assessment of each of the short rail routes which would give Winnipeg and other Manitoba centers a better assurance of benefit from the expected Churchill bonanza.

Charles Dunning, on September 10, 1929, when for all practical purposes the railway to the Bay was within hours of being finished, reported to the people of Canada. The goal of a Hudson Bay Railway had been reached almost a year ahead of schedule but there was still considerable harbor work to be done, and after consultation with Sir Henry Thornton of the Canadian National Railways, he believed it would be unwise to establish passenger and freight service over the new railway to Churchill until the next year when the proposed grain elevator would be under construction. The original plan was for an elevator of a million bushels capacity; now, said the Minister, the intention was to build a two million bushels elevator. C. D. Howe, of Port Arthur, was designing the elevator and it would be ready for use in the fall of 1931.

"We are making unexpectedly good progress on the harbor work," the Minister added, "but we are not so much concerned that the port should be opened quickly as that it shall be properly equipped and opened just as soon as is consistent with safe and efficient operation."[1]

---

[1]*Edmonton Journal*, Sept. 11, 1929

Dredging was an important part of the harbor work to which Mr. Dunning referred. Two big dredges were working day and night, each capable of scooping up eight cubic yards of silt and clay and rocks at every lift. In conjunction with the dredges, two dump scows were in use, each with 500 cubic yards capacity and both hauling the dredged waste to dump it out in the Bay, about a mile and a half beyond the harbor entrance. The intention was to remove about 2,000,000 cubic yards of soil material from the harbor bottom.

The railway was about finished. The harbor was receiving the attention it deserved. Finally, there was the matter of the townsite at Churchill and the Minister gave assurance that it was receiving the attention of the government of Manitoba and provincial engineers were on the ground. "There is the important question of water supply," he mentioned dutifully.

Later in that same month, Hon. Charles Dunning went over the Hudson Bay Railway once again. It was like a problem child of his adoption, for which he had found increasing affection. Now it was coming to maturity and he believed it would bring credit to those who had befriended it. But this was more than another tour of inspection; it was a farewell, because he was about to leave the Department of Railways and Canals to become Canada's Minister of Finance, a fitting recognition of his worth. Prairie people were hopeful that his successor in the Railways and Canals Department, Hon. T. A. Crerar, would do as well for them.

In being pressed to completion, railway progress was in step with the good times prevailing across the country. Canada's economic position was thought to be healthy and investors bought with confidence — until that day of economic disaster, October 29, 1929. On that date over 16,000,000 shares traded on the New York Stock Exchange, making it a day of record. But it differed from most other days of record sales; it reflected a sudden fear and panic rather than confidence. Almost at once the "bottom fell out" of the markets. Wheat prices began to skid from the previous $1.60 per bushel and did not stop until they reached 38 cents at Winnipeg — which meant about half that amount at country points far back in the wheat belt. Canada, like all other Western nations was in trouble.

Prairie Canada, which was in for a succession of severe drought years, was in particular trouble. Either drought or depression would have been bad enough; the presence of both meant tragedy.

The economic "crash" struck just days after the Hudson Bay Railway was declared to be completed. The latter could not have been "unveiled" at a more unfortunate time.

THE FIRST WHEAT OVER THE NEW ROUTE

Beaver and other pelts — hundreds of shiploads — and some whale oil had been exported through Hudson Bay over the many years when Fur had been King, but things had changed. Wheat, having displaced skins and grease, had become the very lifeblood of the West and, to a greater extent than most people realized, the economic lifeblood of the nation. True, the wheat crop could be temperamental; sometimes it failed disastrously; sometimes it was big enough to tax existing transportation facilities to their limit. It was the main reason for building the Canadian Pacific Railway across the West, the main reason for the Hudson Bay Railway, and wheat growers remained eager.

Small quantities of wheat for seed were imported through the Bay in the early years of the Selkirk Settlement but none was ever exported that way. Now, late in 1929, just as the railroad, "complete with grade," was being finished, the great moment arrived and the first shipment was being made. It was not a big consignment — only one ton — but as the forerunner of what all Westerners hoped would be a mighty movement of grain, it was sufficiently symbolic to rate a ceremony.

The terminal elevator was not yet finished and Hon. Charles Dunning hoped the shipment would not mislead the public by making it appear that the new route was ready for business.[1] Obviously, it was not ready, but there was no problem in handling a token shipment like this one, a mere ton of prairie wheat packed in a thousand small canvas bags for distribution in England.

The honor of sending this vanguard shipment of wheat — No. 1 Northern, grown in southern Manitoba — went to the Hudson's Bay Company, former Overlord of Rupert's Land. James Richardson and Sons, Ltd., another pioneer firm, arranged the shipment and had the bagged grain placed on board a

[1]*Edmonton Journal,* Sept. 11, 1929

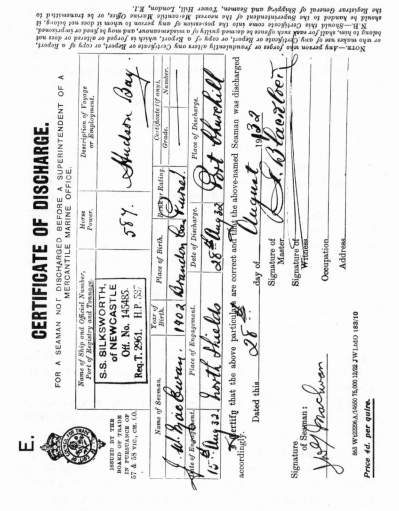

"Seaman J. W. G. MacEwan" sailed to the Port of Churchill aboard the S. S.
Silkworth and obtained his discharge papers on August 28, 1932. He was
ranked as a purser.

Hudson's Bay Company boat, the *Ungava,* to be delivered to the Company's offices in London. From there the two-pound bags of the world's best bread wheat would be distributed by Company officials as souvenirs from Western soil and reminders that the new Route would soon be ready for serious traffic.

It was only the preliminary to the main event still two years away. A ton of wheat in two-pound bags was a nice gesture but the important tests would come when freight boats came to Churchill for full cargoes. And quite obviously, shipping companies would be in no hurry to take the pioneer risks, even for the reward of assured places in history. The government would have to act.

With a total investment of about 50 million dollars and a new 2½-million-bushel elevator which had not been used, members of the federal government knew they could not afford to let the Hudson Bay facilities remain in idleness. R. B. Bennett, who led the Conservatives to power in 1930, had promised to find markets, "blasting his way" to them if necessary, and get the Canadian economy moving again. Both the Prime Minister and his Minister of Agriculture, Hon. Robert Weir from Saskatchewan, knew exactly how most people in the Midwest felt about the Hudson Bay Route. They knew, also, that government aid would be required to start the Churchill shipping traffic in 1931 — prime the pump, as it were.

Having regard to the need of the moment, the government chartered two tramp steamers, *Farnworth* and *Warkworth,* owned by the Dalgliesh Shipping Company of Newcastle-On-Tyne. The Canadian Wheat Pools, unfailing advocates of the northern Route, would furnish the wheat, 540,000 bushels, enough for two shiploads. The wheat, grading 1, 2, and 3 Northern, was hauled to Churchill just a few days before it was to be loaded. The first train, consisting of 24 freight cars, arrived at the Port on September 4. It required 351 cars to complete the delivery.

The first ship to dock was the *Farnworth,* with Captain W. Mouat reporting a trouble-free, thirteen-day voyage from Newcastle-On-Tyne. The government radio stations in the area of the Strait had helped him to keep on course, he reported, and no ice was encountered. A few days later, his ship was loaded with 277,000 bushels of No. 2 Northern wheat and ready to sail.

It was September 18, 1931. Newspapers of that date were reporting another Wall Street market plunge, bringing prices to a record low mark. The gloom of depression was becoming deeper and deeper. No. 2 Northern wheat at Edmonton was quoted at 29 cents per bushel, 2 C.W. barley at 14 cents per bushel, and good butcher steers at $4.25 per hundred pounds. The Premier of Alberta was formally protesting the Canadian Pacific Railway decision to close the Ogden shops and an International conference was being proposed in the hope of finding a remedy for the creeping economic paralysis.

The news of the same date, of course, carried some less distressing information, like the flying achievements of Western bush pilots. C. H. "Punch" Dickens, of Canadian Airways Ltd., was taking off by air from Fort McMurray for the purpose of picking up passengers at Aklavik, of all things, and "Wop" May was flying from Edmonton to Fort Resolution with a load of mail. Both of those daring young pilots were making aviation history and adding to illustrious personal flying careers. And within gunshot of the docks where the *Farnworth* was loading, was a United States party of scientists under Captain Flavel M. Williams, planning to camp there for six weeks to take motion pictures in color of the northern lights, part of a broadly based study program. Altogether, it was an exciting as well as a tragic time but the loading of the *Farnworth* managed to capture a substantial share of newspaper headlines across Canada.

The ship's clearance papers, signed by T. Ross Moulton, Customs Official, were made out on September 17, in favor of Thomas Harding, Montreal, who had chartered the two Newcastle-On-Tyne ships on behalf of the Government of Canada. As part of the last-minute preparations for sailing, the ship's "trimmers" were at work filling hundreds of bags with wheat to prevent cargo shifting. And then, at 10.30 a.m., September 18, when the tide was high and the autumn sun was peeking intermittently through the clouds as if trying to catch a glimpse of the *Farnworth* spectacle, shrill siren blasts from all the ships in the harbor joined in signaling departure. Loud cheers arose from workmen and other spectators lined up at the dock and the *Farnworth* "slipped its moorings" and floated free, bow pointed in the general direction of London.

The unruffled Captain Mouat anticipated no difficulty in navigating the Bay and Strait. It should be a comparatively easy voyage, he said confidently. The cargo of wheat had been sold to Spillers of London, making destination quite firm and members of the crew could expect to be there in two weeks.

As the *Farnworth* moved away from the dock, the sister ship, *Warkworth,* came alongside to take on the remainder of the 545,000 bushels in the test shipments and leave the Churchill elevator empty again. But there was no hurry about loading that balance of 267,769 bushels because the wheat was still unsold and its destination uncertain. It was expected, hopefully, that John I. McFarland, serving as administrator for the Canadian Wheat Pools at their moment of financial distress, would be able to wire definite shipping instructions before the ship was loaded or far on its way.

The Department of Railways and Canals congratulated itself on having successfully carried out the initial task of loading and sending wheat to sea. Hon. R. J. Manion, Minister of Railways and Canals in the Bennett government, was at Churchill to witness loading of the *Farnworth,* and in Winnipeg a few days later he announced that it would be government policy to begin at once to move an additional million bushels of wheat to be stored at the Churchill terminal for loading as soon as ships could arrive in the following season.

Sixteen days after clearing the Churchill dock, the *Farnworth* arrived at London. The Captain reported the trip as having been made in "record time" and totally without navigational troubles. The term "record time" might have been questioned because no other ship of similar size and purpose had ever crossed with a cargo of wheat. Nobody, however, would have denied him the satisfaction of having completed a pioneer mission in very satisfactory time.

Various prominent Britishers were present at the London dock on that Sunday evening to witness the arrival and pay their respects to an initial shipment which, according to the editor of the *Edmonton Journal*: "brought the grain growing areas of the prairies 1,000 miles closer to British markets."[1] Malcolm MacDonald, Under Secretary for the Dominions, and son of Prime Minister Ramsay MacDonald, was in attendance as a representative of the Imperial Government, and Lt. Col. George Vanier — later the Governor General of Canada — was present to represent the Canadian High Commissioner who happened to be in Canada at the time.

There were those individuals on both sides of the Atlantic who appeared surprised that a ship loaded with wheat had succeeded in making its way through the northern waters without mishap. But the Captain said again that he saw no particular reason why his ship should not come through unscathed at that season of the year. In any case, Rt. Hon. L. H. Thomas, Secretary of State for Dominion Affairs, using stiff and proper terms, sent a cable message of congratulations to Prime Minister R. B. Bennett: "On the occasion of the safe arrival in London of the *Farnworth,* bringing the first direct shipment from Western Canada to this country by the Hudson Bay Route, His Majesty's Government of the United Kingdom wish to convey to His Majesty's Government of Canada hearty congratulations on the successful inauguration of this great Canadian enterprise and express hope it may lead to increased trade and prosperity for all concerned."[2]

The most disappointing feature in those initial shipments was the rate of insurance charged by the underwriters. As admitted by the insuring company's spokesman, the rate of about 2 per cent was some six times as high as that charged on the St. Lawrence River run. Perhaps it had to be that way in the first season but there was the hope that the premium would drop substantially after the two trial shipments were made without mishap.

Three days after the *Farnworth,* the *Warkworth* drew away from Churchill with its cargo of wheat, still unsold and destination still unknown. But as everybody realized, international sales were extremely slow and difficult. The fact remained that for the new route, the test, as far as it could be conducted at that

[1]*Edmonton Journal,* Oct. 5, 1931
[2]*Edmonton Bulletin,* Oct. 6, 1931

stage, was a complete success and Western farmers were reassured. And, strange to tell, the general Canadian attitude toward the new northern route was more kindly, perhaps more sympathetic, than at any time in the past. The former opposition had not vanished but Eastern editors could bring themselves on this, the occasion of an initial shipment of wheat, to voice a few words of congratulations, even hope. The critics seemed to be conceding that the new railway might be a success. And if an outlet to the Great Inland Sea were found to be practical, other provinces would wish to share in the advantages. Ontario resolved to extend its existing Temiskaming and Northern Ontario Railway to James Bay. The line had been built about the beginning of the century as a colonization railway into the northern Clay Belt and, now, as the idea of an additional outlet to salt water became attractive, plans were made to build to Moosonee at the mouth of the Moose River emptying into James Bay. Nor did the lure of the Bay end there. The Canadian Pacific Railway construction in a northeasterly direction from Saskatoon was seen as a first step in giving the Saskatchewan "Hub City" a direct connection with an ocean port.

Simultaneously, the government of Manitoba was granting a charter for a railway to run the full north-south length of the province, linking Emerson and Churchill. Even the Province of Quebec was reacting with enough fresh interest to consider building to tidewater at Rupert House, at the mouth of Rupert River. It was distinct change of sentiment but not something likely to last very long. Only the Ontario railway to Moosonee was actually built.

While the Eastern attitude had become more conciliatory, Western editors used the reports of success from two trial shipments to remind Western people of some practical problems yet to be overcome. Said the editor of the *Edmonton Journal:* "The arrival in London of the first ship with a cargo of grain from Churchill is an incident in the history of transportation that deserves widespread attention. . . . As over fifty million dollars has already been spent on the route, it would be most unfortunate for the country if this should turn out to be money sunk to no good purpose. . . . It will take more than a few experimental shipments by the Government to furnish an adequate test of the commercial possibilities of the route. Canadians as a whole must rejoice that the first grain cargo has reached the British metropolis from Hudson Bay without any untoward happenings on the voyage and trust that the traffic will reach steadily increased proportions. It is well to face the fact, however, that there are many obstacles still to be overcome before the new avenue of commerce can be said to be thoroughly established. It is only entering on its initial tests."[1]

Equally timely, useful, and prophetic were the views expressed by the editor of the *Country Guide,* another consistent advocate of the northern route: "The fact that the physical facilities of the route are complete is no guarantee of its success. There are powerful interests who have opposed the building of the Hudson Bay Railway from the time the project was first mooted until today. They take the narrow view that our traffic should be routed East and West and seem unable to realize that in the normal development of Canada there is ample traffic to make the Hudson Bay Route a success without injury to other routes.

"The Hudson Bay Route," the editor continued, "must be given a fair chance. Its success can be retarded and the Route crippled most effectively by unreasonably high marine insurance rates on ships and cargoes passing through the Bay and Straits. The navigation record of the Hudson's Bay Company would warrant rates as favorable as those on the Montreal route although present marine insurance rates are much higher on the Hudson Bay Route. Only the Dominion Government can bring about equitable insurance rates and it may be necessary for the Government to go [into] the insurance business. The prairie people upon whose insistence the Hudson Bay Railway was built must not be lulled into security by the fact that construction is now completed. They will need to be on the alert to ensure that it has a fair opportunity to demonstrate its feasibility and to bring the full anticipated benefits to this country."[2]

[1] *Edmonton Journal,* Oct. 5, 1931
[2] *Country Guide,* Oct. 1931

Canadians accepted 1931, when two government-chartered ships came for wheat, as a test year, an important test year. But it was a test of only one phase of operation and the next year, 1932, when decisions about coming to Churchill for cargo would rest with the intensely practical shipping companies, would be even more important as a test year. Without Canadian Government chartering, would the ships come to Churchill?

DAILY NON-IMMIGRANT REPORT

Churchill Man. Aug. 29, 1932

(A) CANADIAN CITIZENS BY BIRTH	1	*Mr J. K. G. Macewan*
(B) BRITISH SUBJECTS WITH DOMICILE		
(C) CANADIANS NATURALIZED WITH DOMICILE		
(D) ALIENS WITH DOMICILE		
(E) PERSONS RETURNING		

Readmitted

National Revenue Canada
Customs and Excise
AUG 29 1932
CHURCHILL, MAN.

(F) TOURISTS, ETC.

*First Person to be admitted
to Canada, by Customs and
Immigration via Churchill.
S.S. Silkworth*

Inspector   *INSPECTOR*

The author was the first person to be admitted to Canada by Customs and
Immigration via Churchill, August 29, 1932.

THE DIARY OF A 1932 PASSENGER

The official certificate in the author's files declares "J. W. G. MacEwan readmitted to Canada, August 29, 1932." Dated at Churchill, it bears the notation: "First person to be admitted to Canada by Customs and Immigration via Churchill," and is signed by Federal Inspectors T. R. Moulton and Hubert Legg. The following notes are from the "passenger's" diary:

August 11, 1932 — My first trip overseas has not been marked by luxury but it has been a great experience. It is fashionable for my academic friends at the University of Saskatchewan to travel overseas on scholarships; I came on a cattleship and the company of our cattle on the nine-day crossing from Montreal to Manchester was moderately congenial. After seeing 112 head of our experimental animals marketed at Birkenhead and Smithfield, I set out to see as much as possible of the Old World. I enjoyed England, loved Scotland and was captivated by the Channel Islands. My only disappointment is the necessity of having to return home to Saskatoon by way of Montreal — the way I came over — when I had hoped so much to obtain passage back by Hudson Bay and Churchill in order to make a study first hand of the new northern shipping route. But the last message to reach me from the office of the Canadian High Commissioner in London, reported tersely: 'Hudson Bay appears to have dried up. No more ships expected to go there this year.'

It leaves me with no choice; I will sail tomorrow for Montreal on a Manchester ship.

August 12 — I celebrated my 30th birthday by boarding the S.S. Manchester Citizen at Manchester. The ship was due to leave at 12 o'clock noon. At 12.15, as I sat at the lunch table on the ship — 15 minutes after the scheduled time for leaving — I was handed a telegram from W. A. Wilson, Agricultural Agent for Canada, Canada House, London, advising that if I could get to Newcastle-On-Tyne sometime tomorrow, I would be permitted to go with the S.S. Silksworth, sailing for Churchill for a cargo of wheat. Excitedly, I repacked my travelling bag and dashed from the ship as though it were burning, reaching the dock just as the signal was given to lift the gangplank. The officer on the dock looked in surprise and gasped: 'W'at the bloody 'ell's the matter with you?'

Trying to recover my breath, I explained that I had a chance to sail to Churchill instead of Montreal, and he grunted: 'Bloody fool! You'll wish you hadn't. But Blimey, if a man wants to drown in iceberg water, I wouldn't stop 'im. Go right ahead.'

The Manchester Citizen pulled away and I made my retreat to the nearest bus depot, prepared to travel all day and all night in order to cross England and be at Newcastle-On-Tyne in plenty of time for the sailing I dearly wanted to make.

August 13 — The bus on which I left Liverpool yesterday continued on what seemed like an unsteady course and unschedule until shortly after midnight when the driver announced: 'We're at Darlington and this is as far as we go tonight.' I stepped out into the darkness and looked about for some sign of a hotel. Seeing none, I asked the driver if there was one nearby and he replied: 'No, and if there was one it wouldn't be open at this late hour.' There was a moment of silence and he asked: 'Where are you from?' I answered: 'Canada.' 'Well,' he said, while locking the door of his bus, 'you'll have trouble finding a place to sleep unless you've made a reservation somewhere, but if you'll come with me I think I can find something for you.'

Obediently, I followed on foot and then discovered to my surprise that he was taking me to his home and directing me to the spare bedroom kept for visiting relatives. I slept well. This morning there was a pot of hot tea at my door and I used it but not for drinking. Because I do not care for tea and find that hot water for shaving is almost unknown over here, I used the hot tea for shaving, just as I have been doing rather often in England, often enough to give my face a distinct smoked-ham complexion which I do not need or want. I tried to pay my host for the room and his kindness but he would take nothing and I left muttering: 'I was a stranger and ye took me in.' I shall not forget the genuine generosity of U.W.Key, 86 Geneva Road East, Darlington.

August 15 — I spent part of this forenoon and the lunch hour with Robert Dalgliesh, President of the Dalgliesh Shipping Company and former Lord Mayor of Newcastle-On-Tyne and found him excellent company and quite sympathetic to Churchill shipping. The two boats taking wheat from Churchill last year belonged to his company, likewise the Pennyworth which sailed to Churchill about two weeks ago and the Silksworth on which I will now return to Canada. He believes the practical season for shipping through the Straits will be from August 1 to October 15. This year the underwriters specified that an ensured ship must not pass Cape Chidley before August 10th. The Dalgliesh ship, Pennyworth, left Newcastle two weeks ago to reach Chidley on the very first permitted day for entrance to the Straits. Mr. Dalgliesh explained that British Board of Trade regulations prevent him from carrying passengers on the Silksworth, sailing this afternoon for Churchill, but I can sign on as member of the crew.

But that's all right with me. I'm travelling to observe. I will pay for my cabin and my food and will receive no wages but I should be able to learn much about the new route and I was happy to accept the plan as he presented it. After meeting Captain G. Blacklock of the Silksworth, I signed on and moved into a very comfortable cabin which will likely be my home for the next 10 days or two weeks. At 3 o'clock, the good ship left its moorings and steamed away for Churchill.

August 16 — A splendid day but we struck some rough seas on the north of Scotland, Pentland Firth way.

August 17 — Cool and windy. I'm getting acquainted with the ship and sailors. The S.S. Silksworth appears to have had good care even in this time of depression when many ships have been neglected, and the members of crew impress me more than the sailors I met on the Manchester Division.

August 18 — Cool and windy.

August 19 — Cool and not so windy.

August 20 — Fog and rain.

August 21 — Fog and a harsh warning of danger. At mid-morning there was a mild impact and the signal was given to cut

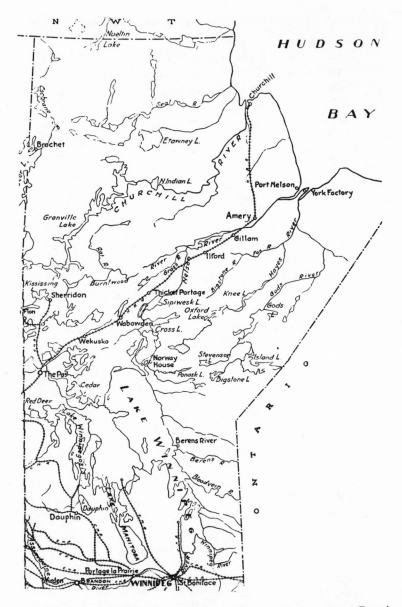

A map of the Churchill Railway prepared for Manitoba Government Travel and Publicity Department in 1949.

the power. The ship had struck a 'growler' or small piece of ice. It did no perceptible damage but was a frightening warning of the folly of proceeding with less than perfect visibility, especially in these waters off the southern point of Greenland. When the fog lifted, momentarily, we could see a dozen mountainous icebergs uncomfortably close to us, which explained the penetrating damp cold.

Captain Blacklock admitted that advice from Ottawa was to stay away from the point of Greenland by 100 miles to avoid most of the bergs moving down from the Arctic, skirting the Greenland coast. The Gulf Stream, it appears, strikes the Arctic and rebounds southward along the east coast of Greenland, bringing the giant bergs with it. As it is, we are right on the path of the bergs. In the light of the warning we've just had, we'll probably not turn a propeller until we can see exactly where we're going. We'll just drift with the current and hope we drift with the bergs rather than into them. Blacklock is a good head and I'm enjoying his company but he has the Englishman's irritating opinion of his own judgement.

August 22 — No progress today. Fog continues and the proximity to bergs gives an Arctic feeling to the air. With much time to spare, I have been doing a lot of writing. When I ran out of writing paper, I resorted to English toilet paper which is thicker than Canadian. When I became tired of writing, I tried my hand at fishing. I borrowed a thousand feet of line from the steward, also a few sausages for bait, then let my baited hook over the edge of the ship and unrolled the line full distance. The sailors told me I might get a halibut there. As it turned out, I caught no halibuts, didn't even get a nibble from a deep sea fish, and lost my sausages. At least, I can boast of having done deep-sea fishing.

August 23 — Fog lifted sufficiently to let us get a view of the southern tip of Greenland and be on our way at 9 a.m. It's still cold enough to be Greenland's icy mountains.

August 24 — Better day but still very chilly.

August 25 — We passed Cape Chidley and entered Hudson Straits at 9 a.m. For most of this day we could see ice floes and occasionally a berg. There was a two-hour stop this morning on account of fog and the dangers it might be hiding. But Captain

Blacklock said again that he would prefer coming over this route than going to Montreal. Here there are more ice hazards but no shoals, not more than a slight current and no narrow channel about which to worry. And as he points out, the best insurance against icebergs is in the fact of knowing they are there and refusing to travel blind. If a ship is stopped when the fog limits visibility, there is not much risk of accident. Ice floes, of course, are quite another matter.

August 26 — Still a few bergs but we have visibility and are making fair progress. Today I had a lesson about compass aids. Early on this season's trip I learned from a Manchester sailor that the Hudson Bay Route would never be a success because the magnetic compass is unreliable in the northern waters. It sounded serious. The sailor was partly right; due to northern mineral deposits or proximity to the magnetic North Pole, the magnetic or conventional type of compass is definitely unreliable. But apparently my informant did not know about the use of the gyro compass which does not depend upon magnetism at all. In principle, the gyro is a high-speed spindle making something like 15,000 revolutions per minute. At such high speed, the gyro axis assumes the same direction as the axis of the earth. And the Silksworth has both compass types, magnetic and gyro, side by side, on the bridge. With the Captain's cooperation, I have been able to study them and make comparisons. The gyro compass is costly but it is available, very reliable and ships so equipped can qualify for lower rates of insurance.

August 27 — We entered Hudson Bay last night about midnight. No ice, no fog, and water as still as that of pond.

August 28 — A perfectly delightful day on the broad Bay. Hardly a ripple on the water. I believe we have changed courses only twice since entering the Straits.

Near sundown, we came within sight of Churchill, at least within sight of the big elevator which can be seen for many miles across the water. Breaking the horizon like a skyscraper, that elevator can be misleading, too. One of the sailors standing beside me rejected my warning that this was not a big city centre likely to afford all the shore-leave pastimes in which sailors like to indulge, and exclaimed as he gazed at the elevator tower and the flat rocks looking slightly like buildings: 'What you trying to tell me? That place is as big as Newcastle.' Poor fellow, he was due for some disappointment.

August 29 — We anchored outside the harbour last night, entered first thing this morning and docked at 9.30 a.m. It is a grand sensation to set foot once again on my own Canadian soil — indeed, any soil after two long weeks on the ocean.

Our first operation after tying up at the dock was to unload the water ballast. It seems incredible but there it was, the spectacle of pumping out the 3,000 tons of Atlantic water the S.S. Silksworth had carried across the ocean — for ballast. Surely there was something we could have brought to better advantage. As Robert Dalgliesh reminded me, the northern route will be severely handicapped until it is assured of two-way freight movement. It is all very well to be taking wheat from this Manitoba seaport but wheat should not have to carry the cost of operating the ships in both directions. The charges against our wheat will be substantially reduced when incoming ships carry valid cargo instead of the thousands of tons of water pumped in at a British port and pumped out at the Churchill end.

It doesn't take long to see the town; a fine 2½-million-bushel elevator and not much else. It takes longer to inspect the relics of history, mainly across the harbour. This afternoon I began exploration beyond the harbour and was intrigued by Fort Prince of Wales which dates to 1733 and took 40 years to bring to completion. It is one of the rarest treasures in all of North American history and even today it shows only a slight trace of the erosion of time. A few stones have fallen from the walls and most of the big guns have come to rest in the soil but the main structure stands four-square and solid, 300 feet long, 300 feet wide and about 16 feet in height of walls. Three of the walls are approximately 25 feet in thickness and the fourth wall which was to carry the cannons, is just about 40 feet thick.

One can only imagine the toil involved in transporting and shaping those huge boulders and building them into walls. Some of the partition walls have developed fractures but the outer ones have the character of timelessness. On the Churchill side of the harbour are an ancient powder magazine and a lime kiln used no doubt by those early men of the Hudson Bay Company.

I made my way along the shore line on the fort side of the

harbour to inspect Sloop's Cove where rocks bear the etchings of familiar names, including that of Samuel Hearne for whom spells of inactivity must have inspired the desire to imprint his signature on the register of the immortal rocks. One of the nearby sketches depicts a John Kelly from the Isle of Wight, hanging from a scaffold, paying dearly for the sin of stealing a goose.

At various times today we watched the white whales performing playfully in the harbour. There they were in quite big schools, running the risk of being hunted by the native people for dog feed or for sale to the whale-oil rendering plant. Whale hunting is a popular pastime and I am sorry I have not seen these Indian and Eskimo 'cowboys' — or 'whaleboys' — riding bareback on the belugas. The hunters, I was told, pursue the whales with motor boats and when alongside, a man with nothing more than a sharp knife will spring from the speeding boat to land on the whale and ride it and knife it until it gives up or succumbs. It is then a simple matter to tow the body to shore.

This evening I walked out into the tundra to inspect the sparce sub-Arctic flora. Although the vegetation is predominantly mosses and lichens, there are many beautiful northern flowers blooming at present. They do well growing less than 16 inches above the permafrost.

A cairn has been erected here, the plaque of which bears the following: 'Port Churchill. Discovered in 1619 by the ill-fated Danish expedition under Jens Munck. In 1689 the Hudson's Bay Co. built the first Fort Churchill which in the same year was destroyed by fire. In 1717 the Company rebuilt Churchill, for nearly 200 years its most northerly post on the Bay, and starting point for many Arctic explorations. The Hudson Bay Railway was completed to this point on 1st April, 1929.'

August 30 — I will be unable to remain to see the Silksworth fully loaded and sailing but this morning I saw the great streams of prairie wheat pouring into the ship from a four-belt conveyor system. The gallery along the dock is 1400 feet long which will allow three grainboats to berth under the gallery spouts at one time. Four streams of grain can be discharged at the rate of 20,000 bushels per hour for each stream.

Before boarding the 'Muskeg Special' for the 510-mile rail journey to the Pas, I accepted my 'honorable discharge' from the Silksworth, on a British Board of Trade form. Until today I did not know my official rank with the ship's crew but now, from the discharge certificate I discover that my post bearing recognition of the British Merchant Marine was that of Assistant Purser. Perhaps it should be added that I was the Assistant Purser on a ship which had no Purser and nothing to purse. But I shall be ever grateful for the opportunity of travelling over the new route. After saying 'farewell' to Captain Blacklock and other members of the congenial crew, I boarded the southbound train, known in these parts as the 'Muskeg Special.' The train's passengers are a cosmopolitan lot, a couple of Eskimo men, a few Indians, the vice-president of the Canadian National Railways and Bishop Arsene Turquetil, Bishop of the Arctic, who has been serving the Roman Catholic Church there since 1900 and probably knows the Eskimo people better than any other living white man.

The roadbed consisting of gravel and a cushion of moss and base of ice feels surprisingly good and we travel along at 30 miles an hour. The countryside is strange and a little terrifying, mile after mile without a railway crossing, a road or sign of human habitation. The Churchill end, of course, is treeless tundra with water in abundance, then the 'land of little sticks' and ultimately forests and park country. It is vast and lovely and lonely. Nature has found uses for it. How much use man will find for it remains to be seen.

Noting the names of stations and sidings on this new line is like a lesson in Canadian history. I'm glad to see names with a Canadian ring about them instead of those we have so commonly imported. That is not to quarrel with Old World names and heroes; it's just time we recognized our own. The second station south of Churchill, at Mile 493, is Digges, a name which recalls Sir Dudley Digges who helped equip the ship Discovery for Henry Hudson in 1610 and in whose honor, also, Digges Island at the mouth of the Bay was named.

The next station is Bylot, Mile 485, with its name taken from that of Robert Bylot who was Henry Hudson's first mate on the Discovery. Then there is Lamprey, Mile 477, commemorating one of Jens Munck's ships with which he entered the harbour at Churchill in the autumn of 1619. Farther south on the line is Back, Mile 434, carrying the name of Captain George Back, a member of the Sir John Franklin expedition of 1819.

We come to Gillam at Mile 326 and then Nonsuch at Mile 295, taking their names from Captain Zachary Gillam and the ship Nonsuch which sailed from Gravesend to Hudson Bay in 1668 and carried out much of the experimental work upon which the Hudson's Bay Company was founded. The railway point of Munck, Mile 269, is of course, named to honor Jens Munck who, sailing under the Danish flag, wintered and suffered at the mouth of the Churchill River in 1619-20. Stitt, at Mile 243, bears the name of a prominent figure at early Red River, and the Bridgar name encountered at Mile 218, is in recognition of John Bridgar, one of the very early Masters at Albany House.

La Pérouse who sailed into the Bay and captured Fort Prince of Wales in 1782, gave his name to the siding at Mile 171 and William Lyddal, an early Governor of the Hudson's Bay Company did the same for the siding at Mile 148. Then there is Wabowden at Mile 136, named for W. A. Bowden, a Chief Engineer in the Department of Railways and Canals. There are Button and Tyrrell stations at Miles 114 and 101 respectively, reminding travellers of famous northern personalities, and Turnbull at Mile 93 named for Thomas Turnbull, another engineer on the line during the years of construction. Rawebb at Mile 54 is for Ralph Webb, former Mayor of Winnipeg and always a vigorous supporter of the Hudson's Bay Railway. It's time Canadians acknowledged that they have some history.

August 31 — I arrived at the Pas, Mile 0, almost 24 hours after leaving Churchill. There is more history here and the community retains the marks of the frontier. The Pas, like other settled areas, did not escape the painful pinch of depression and I could have bought a polar bear skin, nicely tanned, for $10. The trouble was that I did not have that much money for investment in non-essential wares at this time on my journey. The people here are intensely enthusiastic about the Hudson Bay Railway, and they should be. It could do much for this town with its roots penetrating deeply into the fur trade era.

It was here at the confluence of the Saskatchewan and

Pasqua Rivers that the LaVérendryes — Pierre and Louis Joseph — built a trading post in 1751 and called it Fort Paskoyac. It became an important landmark for explorers and travellers and freighters. Henry Kelsey passed that way on his historic trip in 1691 and Anthony Henday stopped to fraternize and drink a little French wine when making his famous cross-country journey in 1754 and '55. And there on September 10, 1910, the Hon. G. P. Graham, Minister of Railways and Canals, turned the first sod for the Hudson Bay Railway.

From here I take train to Melfort for a short visit with parents and then to Saskatoon and my employer, the University of Saskatchewan.

THE "BRIGHT FAN" AFFAIR

Ten ships crossed the Atlantic to load wheat at Churchill in 1932. Considering that only two subsidized vessels loaded in 1931, the 500 per cent increase seemed most encouraging. But percentages could be misleading and of the ten ships to load in the later year, only nine completed delivery of cargoes; the tenth, the *Bright Fan,* struck an iceberg in Hudson Strait and went to the bottom, taking its load of 253,000 bushels of wheat with it. Happily, no lives were lost.

The tragedy on October 1 made it a sad and disastrous day for the new Hudson Bay Route struggling to gain public confidence. The accident could not have occurred at a more inopportune or critical time because the inquiring eyes of the entire shipping world were on Hudson Bay and Hudson Strait. It was generally agreed that the successes and failures of the season would determine insurance rates and the readiness of shipping companies to send their boats to Churchill in succeeding years.

The sinking of the *Bright Fan* may have produced some mirth among people who were bitterly opposed to the new northern route. It certainly cast a cloud of gloom over the rural communities of Manitoba and Saskatchewan. And with shipping everywhere feeling the awful pinch of worldwide depression and many freight boats lying idle in home ports and insured far above their sale value, there was the inevitable gossip about the possibility of premeditated destruction for the sake of insurance payment.

The *Bright Fan* was the eighth ship to load wheat during the season. Weather was turning cool, giving a hint of winter blasts to come, and sailing time as specified by the insurance underwriters was running out. With a cargo of slightly more than one-quarter of a million bushels, the ship left Churchill on September 25, facing what appeared to be fine sailing conditions on the Bay. Captain Oliver was aware of the possibility of icebergs in the Strait but he was not one to be frightened easily.

After a few merry days and nights at Churchill, he might very well hope to "catch up" on sleep.

The journey across the Bay was uninterrupted and splendid and at the moment the month of September was yielding to October, the *Bright Fan* was entering the Strait and steaming forward through the night — not very fast because the ship was not capable of more than moderate speed. The vessel's position was eighteen miles northeast of tiny Wales Island, close to the south shore, and about 150 miles inside the western point of entry to the Strait. Most crewmen were sleeping peacefully when, at 4.20 a.m. on that first day of October, the loaded ship rammed into an unnoticed iceberg lying precisely across its course. The awful impact would make no noticeable impressing upon the floating mountain of ice with most of its bulk below the water's surface, but it was more than the ship could stand. The fore part of the *Bright Fan* was hopelessly stove in and the vessel began to fill with water.

There was no hope of either repair or rescue. Crewmen seeing the damage could readily anticipate the result. Two hours and forty-eight minutes after the collision, Captain Oliver ordered members of his thirty-man crew to take to the lifeboats. Fifteen minutes later, the big ship heaved pathetically and sank in 115 fathoms of water. Fortunately, the icebreaker *N. B. McLean* was not far away — not far, that is, as distances are regarded in the vast North — and picked up the *Bright Fan's* distress signal. In abandoning ship, the *Bright Fan's* radio was left to operate as long as possible, thus giving the other ship an indication of location. Radio signals ceased at 7.23 a.m., about three hours after the collision, presumably the moment of sinking. But by this time the *N. B. McLean* was coming on with all possible haste and about two hours after the *Bright Fan* disappeared, the icebreaker reached the scene and rescued the crewmen packed in two lifeboats, and took them to Wakeham Bay, a sheltered inlet on the south coast of the Strait.

In the troubled prairie country where anticipation of shipping economies was like a lone ray of sunshine in an atmosphere made dull by depression and drought and drifting soil, the news of the first casualty on the new route brought sadness. "What's this going to do to the future of shipping through the Bay?" was the question men were asking sullenly when they met in livery stables and general stores across the West. They did not have the answer.

If underwriters and opponents of the Route were to insist upon using the record of 1932 as an actuarial basis — one loss out of ten ships coming to Churchill in the season — it would be difficult or impossible for the government to plead convincingly for lower insurance premiums which were considered so essential to the route's success.

Not that there was anything new about icebergs. Skippers on the North Atlantic run saw them often and worried about them occasionally. Ships had collided and sunk but there was sufficient body of actuarial data to insure against a single sinking making much difference to rates. Premiums bore a reasonably just relationship to risks. An occasional accident was anticipated and accepted on those long-established routes. But the Hudson Bay run was a new experience for shippers and insuring firms and they could be expected to pursue policies of extreme caution.

As any seasoned observer would have guessed, the House of Commons was to hear much about the *Bright Fan* tragedy. Western members of Parliament, apprehensive about the Eastern reaction to the sinking and eager to make the best possible case for more favorable insurance rates, would place the blame for the disaster upon human frailty more than shipping conditions. B. M. Stitt, Member for the Manitoba riding of Nelson, Cameron McIntosh from North Battleford, and Hon. W. R. Motherwell, who had been Minister of Agriculture in Mackenzie King's recent government, were the principal inquisitors, apparently convinced that stories about the Captain's days of celebration when at Churchill bore some relationship to an alleged failure to maintain a proper lookout and take reasonable precautions when the ship was moving through water with a reputation for ice.

Stitt, in whose constituency Churchill was located, spoke with characteristic north-country bluntness and aroused some emotions: "There are no marine handicaps in Hudson Bay or Straits," he said, "in spite of the fact that we lost a boat this year, a boat that looked around two days before it found an iceberg. . . . There is no question about that. The boat was deliberately sunk."[1]

Hon. Mr. Motherwell brought the matter of the *Bright Fan* back to the House on February 10, 1933,[2] and precipitated a long debate about what actually happened and the future of the Route. Borrowing a phrase from the Honorable Member for Nelson, Mr. Motherwell said it was generally conceded that the *Bright Fan* "looked around a few days and then banged into that iceberg for some purpose or other. I do not think the idea was to do damage to the route; I think it was to collect insurance upon an old boat which had been insured heavily. These rumors should be settled and I was wondering if the Government had taken any steps . . . to get to the bottom of this."

Yes, the government had taken steps to determine the facts of the case. The Minister of Railways and Canals could report some of the findings of an investigating commission headed by Mr. Justice Mellish. One general conclusion, in the Minister's words, were that "the ship had not been handled very well, that the only lookout was a boy of eighteen years of age. . . . As to looking around for an iceberg, as the Hon. Member for Nelson so picturesquely expresses it, we must realize that the ship is at the bottom of the sea, and it would be rather difficult to find out if it did really look around for an iceberg."

Mr. Motherwell wanted to know if the boat was heavily insured and if the insurance was paid. The Minister was sorry that he did not have the answers. He had heard that the ship "was not in the best of condition. . . . The ship was not particularly valuable, but no ship is valuable at the present time."

William Duff, Member for Antigonish-Gysborough, Nova Scotia, rose to object to insinuations expressed by certain Westerners. The fact of a ship being old and well insured was no reason for any Honorable Gentleman suggesting that as a sinking victim, it was cast away. "The statement should not be made that this ship deliberately ran into an iceberg."

And as for the person on the lookout being of the tender age of eighteen years, Mr. Duff, with a Maritimer's loyalty to men

[1]House of Commons Debates, Nov. 10, 1932
[2]House of Commons Debates, Feb. 10, 1933

of the sea, said an eighteen-year-old would likely have better vision than a man of more advanced years. Even the Minister, at the age of eighteen, would no doubt see icebergs better than "he can today."

Nevertheless, the investigating commission believed that a proper lookout had not been kept because, "apparently" the only person on the ship who had opportunity of seeing the approach of danger was the helmsman, "an apprentice of eighteen years of age." As the Minister quoted from the report: "The court cannot too strongly intimate that a lookout should be maintained under all circumstances by some person or persons whose sole duty for the time being is to keep a lookout. It appears that such was not the practice on this ship. Under the circumstances disclosed in this case the court regrets that it is unable to exonerate the master and first officer of the Bright Fan from default contributing to the loss of the ship in failing to see that such a lookout was maintained."

Again Mr. Duff came to the defense of the captain and first officer. He could tell of attending the hearings and listening carefully to the evidence. From what he had observed, he was impressed by Captain Oliver who, in Duff's opinion, did all possible to obtain information about icebergs and avoiding them from the icebreaker, *N. B. McLean.* "It was just an accident such as happens every day in the marine world."

Duff may have been convinced but he did not convince B. M. Stitt and the latter repeated what was his considered opinion, that the boat was scuttled. "I shall go to the grave with it," he added with determination. "I have had no reason whatever to change my mind about the sinking . . . and as far as the Bright Fan looking for an iceberg is concerned, if Hon. Gentlemen will read the evidence, they will see that previous to striking the iceberg, the Bright Fan sailed only 16 miles in six and one-half hours, although she was a seven-knot boat."

It was all very well to review the evidence with the idea of determining how it happened and affixing responsibility, but the most important question of the day concerned insurance and the probable future of the Hudson Bay Route. How would the recent tragedy affect the insurance premiums and the hope of reducing them? How, indeed, would it affect the entire future of

Hudson Bay shipping? Had the sinking of this ship destroyed all the happy dreams about marketing economies for Western farmers?

Hon. W. R. Motherwell submitted the questions and heard some answers from the Minister of Railways and Canals. First of all, the Minister believed the loss of the ship would wipe out the insurers' reserves from collected premiums. "Naturally," he added, "the Imperial Shipping Committee will not be enthusiastic about lowering rates. At the same time, the Government, through the Marine Department, which handles that branch of the work, has been impressing upon the Canadian High Commissioner in London, and through him the Imperial Shipping Committee, the importance of lowering insurance rates, and I can assure my honorable friend that the Government will do everything it can to have the rates brought down."

It was too much to expect that insurance rates would fall materially in the wake of the great misfortune of 1932. They didn't. But regardless of insurance, Western spokesmen continued to press doggedly for information pertaining to the sinking. Mr. Motherwell, with a sheaf of unanswered questions, came again and, on May 11, 1933,[1] received some answers. First, the certificates of the Master and First Officer of the *Bright Fan* were not canceled by Judge Mellish. Second, the Department of Marine had been informed by the High Commissioner in London that no further action had been taken by the British Board of Trade. And third, in response to the Motherwell question about the price the last owner of the *Bright Fan* had paid for the ship, the reply was guarded: "No official information — press report stated £8,625."

The fact was that nothing had changed very much. Many Easterners remained critical and even hostile toward Hudson Bay shipping; Western people managed to retain their confidence, and insurance rates were no worse and not much better. In the best tradition of the wheat country, "next year" would be better.

---

[1] House of Commons Debates, May 11, 1933

THE YEAR OF THE OX

Wheat growers were not the only Western producers looking hopefully at the short shipping route to Europe. The British market for beef cattle attracted Canadian stockmen from an early date and trade had been spasmodic and spasmodically encouraging. George Lane of the Bar U Ranch in the foothills took a trainload of four-year-old steers to England in 1887 — the summer following the severe winter — and netted slightly more than the $35 per head he had been offered in Calgary before shipping.

The great obstacle to marketing cattle in Britain was, of course, the distance, which meant higher costs for shipping and higher shrinkages. A reduction of a thousand miles, it was argued, was exactly what was needed to make export shipping both profitable and practical. And in addition to other considerations, the Hudson Bay Route would be cooler than others in the summer season and less likely to result in losses.

Cattlemen in convention could become enthusiastic about the Hudson Bay prospects, as a news item from May 1, 1890, showed clearly: "A deputation of cattle range owners from the Northwest waited upon Mr. Dewdney on the 24th to urge the importance of the early construction of the Hudson Bay Railway. It was pointed out that the shrinkage in weight and deterioration in quality of beef in consequence of the long distance by rail to the seaboard as at present was a great drawback to the cattle trade of the Northwest and that a shorter and cooler route via Hudson Bay is what is desired to make cattle raising profitable. Mr. Dewdney fully concurred and expressed himself strongly in favor of the proposed new route to Europe."[1]

[1]*Macleod Gazette,* May 1, 1890

Snow plow on the Hudson Bay Railway. — Hudson's Bay Company Archives.

Hon. Edgar Dewdney, Minister of the Interior in the Sir John A. Macdonald government of the time, was, to be sure, sufficiently familiar with Western needs and Western moods, to concur heartily.

Nobody west of Winnipeg disputed the alleged advantages in shipping beef-on-the-hoof to Britain by the short and cool route but forty-three years elapsed before the first animals were exported that way.

After a year of mixed responses in 1932, there were moderate hopes for the 1933 shipping season. A slightly reduced rate on insurance and an extension of the late season shipping without extra premium from September 30 to October 7 were encouraging. Another Dalgliesh ship, the *Pennyworth,* was the first to arrive for wheat and a few others followed. Then, at midseason, the stores of grain in the elevator terminal became depleted and the Port of Churchill went suddenly dead. As newspapers reported with evident astonishment and farmers read with undisguised anger, the year's operations had ended.

What was wrong that the elevator had been allowed to become empty? Did this situation relate to a recent reduction in shipping rates on the Great Lakes which could partly or completely nullify the advantage in shipping through the Bay? How did it happen that the Lake rates were dropped at this particular time? Was it by any chance an attempt to destroy Western interest in Churchill at what might be a crucial moment? One point was clear: if fears of the new Northern competition was the real reason for the reduction in Lake rates, then the Hudson Bay Route was indeed paying a first and quite handsome dividend, as noted by the editor of the *Lethbridge Herald:* "The Port of Churchill . . . has served the farmers of the West splendidly this year. For we learn that the lake freights on wheat today are as low as 2¾ cents per bushel, as against an average over many years of six to nine cents a bushel. . . . Because it is there ready to use, farmers who are shipping their grain via the Lakes and Montreal are getting three to five cents a bushel more for it. That's a worth while consideration."[1]

---

[1] *Lethbridge Herald,* September 7, 1933

As a further consequence in the same chain of events, Churchill terminal storage rates were dropped and grain began moving again. After an embarrassing midsummer lull, it was announced on September 12 that ships were steaming toward Churchill, among them the S.S. *Brandon,* equipped to carry cattle as well as wheat. Here was a challenge for which nobody in the cattle trade was ready. But cattlemen were eager for a test shipment and there was a flurry of excitement, with the principal task of assembling 200 head being assigned to the Saskatchewan Livestock Co-operative Association and the Western Stock Growers' Association. Hurriedly, holding pens at the seaboard end were made ready for the trainload of cattle being collected at Prince Albert.

According to the news from Prince Albert: "The first shipment of Canadian cattle for the British Isles via Churchill and Hudson Bay, left here this morning [Sept. 29, 1933]. The shipment consisting of 200 head, 15 percent of which are high quality killers, will reach Hudson Bay Junction tonight and will be loaded on the S.S. Brandon at Churchill on Monday."[1]

The loading was carried out as planned and the crossing to Birkenhead was without any unusual incident. The returns from the sales in England gave enough encouragement that Western stockmen requested a bigger test in 1934.

Yes, the S.S. *Brandon* would be coming again for wheat before the end of the 1933 season and plans were made to send more cattle. Neither growers nor governments would miss an opportunity to move cattle. Panic resulting from drought, feed shortage, and ruinous prices continued to bring frustration to the livestock industry and farmers and ranchers were quick to seize any new market opportunity. Good to Choice steers in August were quoted at Calgary and Edmonton at $3.00 to $3.50 per hundred pounds; cows at $1.00 to $1.50, and stockers and feeders at $1.50 to $1.75 per hundred. With insufficient feed available, a herd might be seen as a liability more than as an asset and governments were assisting with large-scale liquidation.

[1]*Lethbridge Herald,* Sept. 29, 1933

An export shipment via Churchill would furnish no more relief from current troubles than a shipment through Montreal but it could, if successful, do something for the cattlemen's depressed morale and enhance the Churchill record. Again, as plans were being made for the 1934 adventure in export, W. E. Cutt, Agent for the Saskatchewan Livestock Co-operative, and Jack Byers, Manager of the Western Stock Growers' Association, assembled the cattle for shipment, concentrating this time on grain-fed cattle of baby-beef ages and weights.

The cattle train left Prince Albert on August 11 and stopped for an hour at Melfort to add the equivalent of a carload of choice Aberdeen Angus yearlings belonging to Alex H. MacEwan of that place. Another halt was called at Hudson Bay Junction to feed and water and the train arrived at Churchill late on Sunday evening, August 12. The running time from Prince Albert was thirty-eight hours, just a fraction of the customary freight time to Montreal. Jack Byers and William Cutt, directing the shipment, insisted that the stop for feed and water at Hudson Bay Junction was unnecessary and by eliminating it, the traveling time from Prince Albert to the boat could be brought well under thirty-six hours.

In departing Churchill, the S.S. *Brandon* cargo consisted of 324,000 bushels of wheat for London delivery and 290 head of cattle consigned for sale by the Co-operative Wholesale Society, Eastwood and Son, and Brown and Co., cattle brokers at Birkenhead. With Captain John Begg as Skipper, the crossing was completed in twelve days and Alex MacEwan, who was accompanying his own cattle from Melfort, reported that although freight and other charges were slightly higher than would have been charged on the Montreal run, the shrinkage was so much less that he was convinced his net return was greater.[1]

With the cargo on the *Brandon,* the 1934 season, ending six days ahead of the specified closing date, was the best in the three-year history of the new route. Fifteen ships carried away 4,000,000 bushels of grain, 580 head of cattle, 2,000,000 feet of lumber, eight tons of honey, and a couple of small shipments of

[1]*Melfort Moon,* Oct. 25, 1934

miscellaneous goods. No accidents occurred to mar the season and Western people were pleased that something appeared to be going for them.

EIGHT YEARS AND SIXTY-FOUR VOYAGES

An initial period of Hudson Bay shipping ended with the outbreak of World War II in 1939. Disruption was rather general. Almost at once, all United Kingdom shipping in the Atlantic was taken over by the British Shipping Board and charter sailings for Churchill were promptly canceled. It was a policy with which nobody could argue and the relatively idle years which followed for northern shipping, 1939 to 1945, gave friends and foes of the Bay Route a chance to analyze their record of performance and consider the future.

As members of the still-active On-To-The-Bay Association saw it, the record of the first eight years of shipping fell far short of expectations but was not totally discouraging. Nobody had any right or reason to suppose that completion of the railway in 1929 would put an end to all pioneer shipping problems. Clearly, it was one thing to construct a railway of the peculiar kind, quite another to insure its full and proper operation.

There was an unsteady expansion for five years after 1931 and then shipping fell away seriously in 1937 when only two boats came for wheat and together took only 603,982 bushels. The next year, the last prewar year, experienced only slight improvement, with three ships taking less than a million bushels total. It was not good enough and the tally for importations was far worse than that for exports.

Robert Dalgliesh, President of Dalgliesh Steamship Company, speaking to the Board of Trade in Saskatoon, in August, 1933, proclaimed the essential importance of two-way trade, coming at least close to balancing exports with imports. Everybody agreed with the principle but nobody at the time could foresee the difficulty of inducing even a moderate volume of imports through Hudson Bay. Importers as well as exporters stood to benefit but not many purchasers could wait for the short Hudson Bay season or would take the trouble to specify delivery via Churchill.

A shipment of cars and tractors unloaded off a boat from the United Kingdom, c. 1957. — Jim Gray.

The trade route could be maintained with wheat alone and all cargoes moving in the same direction, but it could not reach the zenith of success and economy until the ships were carrying goods in both directions. Mr. Dalgliesh was informed by his captains, he told his Saskatoon audience, that the Hudson Bay shipping lanes, taken with care, presented no obstacles to use and Churchill had one of the finest harbors in the Western Hemisphere. But these facts did not reduce the necessity of finding incoming freight to take the place of water ballast being carried across the ocean and help to carry the cost of the outward carriage of wheat.

The import freight, generally carried by a single ship coming to Churchill each season in those early years, consisted mainly of coal, glass, and what was classified as "general cargo." The total in 1931 was 390 tons and it rose to 2,619 tons in 1933 and then dwindled to 1,930 tons in 1938. Even though the quantity brought to Churchill in 1933 might seem moderately impressive, it represented only a small fraction of a normal load. The 4,293,501 bushels of wheat exported from Churchill in 1936 represented sixty-five times the cargo weight of the coal and glass and general cargo imported and laid out at the same port in the year. Every member of the promotional organization was aware of the seriousness of the imbalance but unable to correct it.

Members of the Association were familiar with the other problems, also, mainly the relatively short shipping season and the high cost of insurance. There had been some improvement but much more was needed if Churchill and the shipping lanes were to rise to their full potential.

Even before the completion of the railway to the Bay, the Government of Canada made its petition for reasonable rates on marine insurance. The Imperial Shipping Committee, which assembles factual information about risks and makes recommendations concerning rates, was asked to consider the special case of Hudson Bay shipping and advise the Joint Hull Committee of the Underwriters Association of London, the authoritative body in fixing marine insurance and rates. The 1931 rates were exorbitant, as just about everybody admitted, but the underwriters at that point had no information on which to base

Grain car being emptied inside Churchill terminal elevator. — Saskatchewan Photo Services.

risks and could not be criticized in trying to protect themselves. To their credit, they used the meager data from only two ships and a single season to effect at least a slight reduction in rates to apply in 1932. Insurance was still costing far more than for corresponding ships going to Montreal, and Western Canadians continued to call for adjustment. Some further relief came in 1936.

The report on Hudson Bay Marine Insurance Rates, 1936, as submitted to Prime Minister Stanley Baldwin, mentioned the unwarranted disparity between Churchill and Montreal shipping. In the course of five seasons, it was pointed out, there were ninety commercial crossings of Hudson Bay — forty-five inward and forty-five outward — with one total loss in Hudson Strait, and "one minor casualty." The "total loss," to which reference was made, was, of course, the *Bright Fan*, the ill-fated ship crashing into an iceberg in the Strait in 1932 and going to the bottom with its cargo of wheat. The "one minor casualty," on the other hand, suggested the *Avon River*, a ship which went aground on Mansel Island, near the western approach to the Strait, in the course of a storm in 1936. Without much comment about the "minor casualty," the "total loss," the report added, "was found by a competent court to be due to negligence and was such as might quite likely have happened on the St. Lawrence route."

The important points about the report were the decisions from the Joint Hull Committee:[1]

1 — "That the coming season shall open on 5th August, instead of 10th August as hitherto, subject to a provision that no vessel must pass Cape Chidley before 10th August until the Captain has received advices from the Canadian Government patrol ship that it is safe to do so.

2 — "That the coming season shall close as hitherto on 15th October but that the surcharge for late departure from Churchill will be enforced for the five days 11th October — 15th October, instead of the eight days 8th October — 15th October."

[1]Imperial Shipping Committee, *Seventh Report on Hudson Bay Marine Insurance Rates,* 1936, as submitted to Rt. Hon. Stanley Baldwin, by D. Carter, Secretary of the Imperial Shipping Committee, April 24, 1936

It was further conceded that a ship equipped with a gyro compass would be entitled to a reduced rate of insurance.

The ninth and final prewar report on Hudson Bay Marine Insurance Rates was directed to Prime Minister Neville Chamberlain, under date of July, 1939, just weeks before Europe's "walls came tumbling down." It offered a timely summation: "There have been during the nine seasons since the route was opened 64 voyages to Churchill, and in our opinion the stage of development may now be considered as over. The way is adequately charted and equipped with the usual aids to navigation, and the exceptional circumstances on account of which the warranty is imposed — ice, fog and magnetic disturbance — are known and have been provided against by gyro compass, direction-finding and radio, and the very efficient service of the Canadian patrol vessels. With the sole exception, therefore, of the difficulty which might arise of securing adequate salvage if a vessel should be wrecked late in the season, it is the view of the Committee that the Hudson Bay route need not be considered as more risky than the St. Lawrence. The Underwriter's representatives have agreed to regard the past nine seasons as closing the development period of the route, the casualties which have occurred being regarded as paid for by the premiums received. . . . But in consulting our Chairman, the Joint Hull Committee has taken note of the fact there are already at Churchill for shipment from the 1938 season's crop some eight cargoes of wheat, and they have agreed that if some 20 cargoes in all are brought away from Churchill in 1939, and no serious loss occurs, they will be prepared to give favorable consideration to the question of recommending a further reduction in 1940 from the rates of premium chargeable in 1939."

But war is war and the 1939 shipping season was arrested rudely. Apart from taking on a military role, Churchill lapsed into temporary quiescence.

BEGINNING AGAIN

For six war years the big terminal elevator at Churchill was as quiet and dormant as a haunted house. The enforced holiday was inevitable. Britain and her allies had trouble enough in keeping the older Atlantic sea lanes open for traffic without undertaking to protect shipping against the menacing submarine attacks in northern waters also. But war brought a new role for the Churchill community and in 1942 a large United States military base was built south of the townsite. There, both ground and air force personnel were stationed for the duration and near the end of overseas hostilities, the base was reordered for use in a joint Canada-United States "cold-weather" research and training operation.

After the lapse of several war years, members of the pioneer promotional organization known as the On-To-The-Bay Association, called for a fresh appraisal of purpose. Their original reason for organizing was — as the name implied — to press for completion of the railway to tidewater. That aim had been fully achieved and the Association persisted simply because members believed they could still be useful. The time had now come, however, to disband or to accept a new challenge and a new name.

Although the railway to the Bay was an accomplished fact, its success was not yet assured. The volume of trade had not reached the level of expectations and in Eastern parts of Canada the route was not even fully accepted. Setback was inescapable; much of the prewar momentum generated in support of Hudson Bay traffic had dwindled seriously during the war years. Members of the Association were fully conscious of the reverse and believed that at war's end they would be obliged to begin again from about the point they were at in 1931. But in working to rebuild, the virgin enthusiasm of the earlier years might be missing. Western farmers had not forgotten the earlier attractions of the Bay Route and the lovely theories of economies.

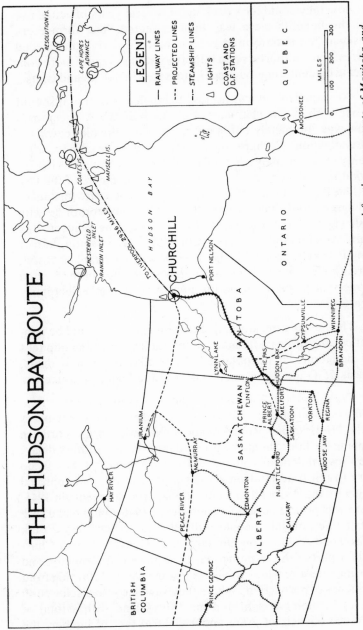

Map of the Hudson Bay Route, showing shipping routes to Europe; prepared for the governments of Manitoba and Saskatchewan in 1953

But now they could look back upon several years of actual use and the benefits were less than 'expected. The former enthusiasm had deteriorated perceptibly. To revive the needed interest, both exporters and importers would require more convincing evidence of advantages measured in dollars and cents.

An organization was needed as much as ever but it should be one with a new character. Inasmuch as the Association's name was completely outdated, there was a double reason for reorganization. Perhaps most clubs and associations, after twenty years, need overhauling. Anyway, a meeting was held at Saskatoon, November 15, 1944, at which members of the On-To-The-Bay Association acknowledged the new circumstances and agreed to disband in favor of a new body corporate with fresh vigor and a new name. Immediately, the Hudson Bay Route Association was born, with Walter G. Streeton, farmer from Plunkett, named to be President, and Frank Eliason, currently Secretary of the Saskatchewan Section of the United Farmers of Canada, to be the new Association's Secretary-Treasurer.

The new organization, like its predecessor, would be non-political and draw its financial lifeblood from membership fees and donations to be obtained, hopefully, from individuals, Boards of Trade, farm organizations, and business concerns.

Came war's end and great stocks of grain and other food products awaited shipment to Europe and elsewhere. Members of the Hudson Bay Route Association believed the northern shipping facilities should be pressed into service without delay. The Government of Canada did not disagree but was in no hurry to reinstate Hudson Bay as a trade route, and approval sought by the Association came too late for shipments in 1945. There was promise of trading activity in 1946 and to make sure that the responsible people did not forget, Secretary Frank Eliason and Association Director A. J. Hanson were at Churchill for part of the shipping season, gathering information and exerting pressure where it might do some good. Returning from the scenes of port activity where they saw one ship discharge 40 tons of incoming freight and nine ships load with a total of 3,000,000 bushels of grain and 1,000,000 feet of lumber, the

Board of Directors of the Hudson Bay Route Association, 1959. L-R: Jim Cameron, Youngston, Alberta (deceased); Cameron McIntosh, North Battleford, Sask. (deceased); Jim Gray, secretary manager, Saskatoon, Sask.; J. S. Woodward, president, Saskatoon, Sask.; Walter Streeton, Plunkett, Sask. (deceased); Willis Richford, Norquay, Sask.; Frank Appleby, Kindersley, Sask. (deceased)—Jim Gray.

Association officers embarked upon an educational program and a massive drive to sell Association memberships.

For the new leaders, the purpose was clear, but the reward of increased shipments was not to come quickly. Officers in the previous organization saw their principal duty in drumming up enthusiasm and generating political pressures. The new men were taking a more studied approach to the problems. Western Canada needed the Churchill seaport, they were convinced, as always, but it was no longer sufficient to simply say so. They had to furnish proof and make sure that Montreal opposition, Ottawa indifference, and Western compliance did not combine to render the whole scheme impotent.

Some new concepts were emerging boldly and clearly. More than ever before the Association leaders were catching a vision of a multi-purpose North being served by a multi-purpose railway. For previously unsuspected reasons, the Hudson Bay line, won with great hardship and difficulty, might prove to be a source of huge benefit and blessing. If the northern rocks proved to be rich in minerals, the Hudson Bay Railway would be needed urgently to haul out the wealth. If Hudson Bay fishing were found to be profitable, the rails would have an added purpose. If the Nelson Valley land was useful for farming, as more people were coming to expect, the railway would be ready for service as a colonization road. And if Canadians and tourists from many lands were to gain an understanding of the vast and fascinating Canadian North, just such a railway communication would be necessary.

The idea of Churchill becoming a tourist attraction was beginning to catch attention. Here, indeed, was opportunity for travelers to see white whales playing in the harbor; here was a chance to observe and study the distinctive northern vegetation; here was an invitation to become better acquainted with the Northern Indian and Eskimo cultures; and here was the best of all chances to view old Fort Prince of Wales, one of the rarest of Canada's historical exhibits.

The federal government, displaying more interest in tourism than in northern shipping, was already taking steps to restore the old fort, situated just across the harbor from the railway terminal. Workmen with picks and shovels were already digging into a long-buried chapter in Fur Trade story, reminding spectators of the prolonged searches for the illusive Northwest Passage to Asia, of northern battles for the Bay and supremacy in trade, and of grim experiences on the part of incoming settlers who were obliged to winter there. The forty massive cannons, which were supposed to have rendered the stone fort impregnable, were being excavated from rubble and returned to their commanding places on the walls from which they had fallen.

Men of the Hudson Bay Route Association were convinced that the railway and terminal could become many-sided assets but, as they realized, the task of convincing Canadians elsewhere would never be easy. If citizens, both Eastern and Western, could be induced to travel into the North and visit Churchill, it would be helpful. Beginning in 1947, organized excursions to Churchill were conducted by the government of Saskatchewan for the declared purpose of making prairie people more familiar with their northern seaport. The Canadian National Railway conducted a similar service and then the Hudson Bay Route Association assumed the responsibility for the annual rail tours. Many Western people, a few Eastern people and some from the United States joined for the holiday and educational outings via "Churchill Special."

The new Association's vigor was everywhere apparent. In addition to the annual excursions to the Bay, there were essay competitions for school children and lecture programs on Hudson Bay topics with speakers being made available for meetings anywhere. Paid-up memberships in the Association reached the remarkable total of almost 8,000 in 1949. Such a large body of Association backing gave leaders a strong voice when presenting petitions in Ottawa or in the course of public hearings anywhere.

The Association petitioners did not always get their way, certainly not without some distressingly long waits. They wanted increased elevator capacity at Churchill — which was obtained in 1954 — extra loading berths at the Churchill docks, competitive internal freight rates to give Churchill shipping an advantage consistent with the shorter rail hauls involved. They were requesting the appointment of soliciting agents to obtain more freight traffic, both export and import. And perpetually, the leaders were asking governments to press for relaxation of regulations governing length of shipping season and the costly rates on marine insurance.

Although they experienced many disappointments as they sought concessions for the Bay Route, they enjoyed reasonable encouragement too. The increase in volume of traffic was not spectacular but it seemed to follow the hope of the English shipping magnate, Robert Dalgliesh, whose enthusiasm and loyalty for the Bay Route were unfailing. The Dalgliesh dictum instructed friends of the Churchill outlet to work for steady increases in shipping rather than dramatic jumps which would carry no assurance of lasting worth.

For thirteen years after 1946 when the movement of wheat from Churchill was resumed,[1] the export volume increased steadily if not spectacularly. In the earlier year, nine ships took 2,929,000 bushels of grain, and in 1959, a total of fifty-eight ocean-going ships loaded a total of 21,787,126 bushels of wheat. Imports, on the other hand, remained meager, with volume — excluding petroleum products — ranging between 40 tons in 1946, and 7,650 tons in 1951. But even the higher import figure could not be seen as more than a trifling amount in a year when twenty-one ships came for grain and loaded out with more than 200,000 tons of wheat. It represented a lingering imbalance — almost an embarrassment — which members of the Hudson Bay Route Association were eagerly anxious to correct.

Much of the Association's strength and effectiveness in those years after 1946 came from the assistance of Board Director R. H. MacNeill, of Sherridon, Manitoba, one of the best authorities on Hudson Bay matters either within or outside the organization. A Prince Edward Islander by birth, MacNeill had embarked upon a journalistic career and sat in the House of Commons Press Gallery in Ottawa between 1906 and 1908. In the latter year he was the Federal Government's appointment to the post of secretary for the Hudson Bay Railway. In 1910 and 1911 he was engaged in the conduct of photographic and

[1]See Appendix 3

topographic surveys of the region adjacent to the Bay and Strait. From time to time for the next twenty years he was engaged in activities related to the construction and operation of the Hudson Bay Railway. On various occasions after 1946, he was the Association's mouthpiece as representations were made to governments and commissions. So it was on June 9, 1949, when the Hudson Bay Route Association was presenting a brief to the Royal Commission on Transportation, of which Hon. W. F. A. Turgeon was Chairman.[1]

Supported at the public hearing in Regina by M. A. Mac-Pherson, legal counsel, W. G. Streeton, President of the Association, and Frank Eliason, Secretary, MacNeill seemed to be speaking to Canadians everywhere. "The whole purpose behind the building of the Hudson Bay Railway and the development of Churchill," he said, "was to bring the prairies closer to tidewater with the logical expectation that the substantial advantages of reduced rail haul would be directly reflected in reduced freight costs. The expectation has not been fully realized . . ."

MacNeill's plea was for a better deal in marine insurance, an enlarged shipping season, new rail lines to serve as feeders to the Hudson Bay road, and a review of domestic freight rates with a view of correcting existing inequities which were keeping the Bay railway from being competitive with other Canadian lines. MacNeill's summary of the internal needs to make the route a success won praise: "In summary, therefore, we submit:

1 — That it is the earnest objective of this Association to develop, by all means possible, traffic both inward and outward over the Hudson Bay Railway and the Hudson Bay Route.

2 — That the present freight rate structure applicable to the Hudson Bay Railway is on a level which fails to reflect adequately the shorter distance of prairie points to tidewater at Churchill and a revision of the rate structure is essential to make the Route more attractive to prairie importers and distributors.

3 — That the Commission give careful consideration to our

[1]MacNeill, R. H., *Submission to the Royal Commission on Transportation, June 9, 1949*. Transcript published by Hudson Bay Route Assoc., Saskatoon, 1949

request for railway extensions in the North (Branch Lines lead-ing to the H. B. Railway).

4 — That due consideration be given to colonization of the fertile Nelson River area.

5 — That a Freight Soliciting Agent be appointed for the specific purpose of promoting traffic for the Hudson Bay Route.

6 — The Association further recommends that a full scale test of capacity of Hudson Bay Route in the export of Prairie grain be inaugurated.''

The Commission chairman wanted to know what sort of "full scale test" Mr. MacNeill had in mind.

"The shipment of 25,000,000 bushels in one season," the Association man replied. The wheat in that year of 1949 amounted to about 5,500,000 bushels, the biggest yearly ship-ment to date, but for a test of 25,000,000 bushels in one year, MacNeill and the friends of the Bay Route were obliged to wait another twenty-three years.

WATCHING THE "MANHATTAN"

By 1969, Canadians were feeling a new sense of Northern Destiny. Northern mines were proving productive and new claims were being staked with feverish haste and optimism. What, according to some observers, might prove to be the richest iron-ore reserve in the world was on Baffin Island, awaiting mining operations. Another iron-ore deposit of fabulous magnitude was identified in the northern Yukon and reserves of copper, lead, zinc, and other mineral substances were known to be big. The cool and rocky areas contiguous to Hudson Bay and Strait were seen as good hunting ground for resource treasures and the possibility of offshore drilling for oil was being considered.

Suddenly the North was capturing the attention and enthusiasm of oil scouts and drillers, and oil men meeting on the main streets of Edmonton and Calgary were known to part with the friendly greeting: "I'll be seeing you in the Arctic." Even the Government of Canada became a partner in a consortium known as Panarctic Oils Limited, drilling on Arctic islands. Some of the most intense searching for oil then shifted from the high Arctic islands to the Mackenzie delta where the indications were favorable.

But the most spectacular resource news of the period came out of Alaska, telling about sensational oil strikes in the vicinity of Prudhoe Bay on Alaska's northern slopes. What was there? Perhaps 10 billion barrels of crude.

Of course it would be handier if all the rich resources were scattered near the International Boundary where most Canadians chose to huddle, but inconvenient as they might be, great stores of minerals, including oil and gas, were deep in the North and if Canadians and Americans wanted them, they would have to find ways of taking them out. Northern transportation was a matter of growing importance. A railway to Hudson Bay, a highway to Alaska, and air lines to widely scattered points would increase in importance but they would not be enough.

The first major test would be in transporting the much-needed oil from Prudhoe Bay. Because of a mounting fuel and energy crisis in the United States, the petroleum industry was in a hurry. The United States ratio between proven reserves of gas and oil on one hand and annual consumption on the other was becoming narrower at an alarming rate.

Per capita consumption of fossil fuels was growing annually while the supply was shrinking and leaders admitted the necessity of importing bigger percentages of the country's needs in oil and gas. If oil in Alaska or elsewhere in the Far North could be moved in economical and practical ways, it would alleviate the alarming threat of fuel shortage. But how was oil from inside the Arctic Circle to be moved to areas of consumption far to the south?

Various proposals were offered. The Alaskan oil interests favored a trans-Alaska pipeline — one of about 800 miles which would deliver oil to an all-season harbor at Valdez on the Pacific side, whence the product could be taken by ocean-going tanker to more southerly Pacific ports. Ecologists objected and Canadians, worried about the risk of marine accidents and pollution damage to their British Columbia coastline, shouted their protests.

Oil spills in the recent years had been costly and terrible. Citizens recalled the *Torrey Canyon* disaster of 1967 when 100,000 tons of crude oil left a 35-mile slick on the Atlantic water and coastline of southern England. Then there was the later spill from the break-up of the tanker, *Arrow,* on the east coast of Canada — and still later the *Santa Barbara* tragedy off the coast of California. The results were similar, heavy loss of bird life and a lingering and sickening mess necessitating costly clean-up.

Most Canadians favored a Mackenzie Valley pipeline as a means of moving the Alaska or Mackenzie delta oil. It would be extremely costly to construct but, they reasoned, it could be accomplished to carry oil from both Alaskan and Northern Canada fields to Edmonton and the International Boundary.

Other schemes were proposed. Some people favored a railway with a daily complement of from twelve to twenty trains running in each direction to facilitate the oil marketing, and, of course, there was the idea of boat transportation through the ice-infested northern channels. It was difficult to be optimistic about Arctic sea lanes but they had to be considered. Shipping from Churchill where ice problems would be slight compared with those inside the Arctic Circle, had appeared difficult enough, and ice encountered in Hudson Strait had taken tolls. The loss of the *Bright Fan* in 1932 had not been forgotten and then, as recently as 1963, there was the loss of another big freighter, the *Kastela,* also loaded with wheat. Details about the latter were lacking. Perhaps the cause was ice. It happened in a year of exceptionally heavy ice. Anyway, this was a Yugoslavian vessel of 7,000 tons displacement, built as a liberty ship during the years of World War II.

The *Kastela* left Churchill on July 31, loaded with 323,333 bushels of wheat, bound for Liverpool. It was the intention of Captain Bruno Mazer to use the escort services of the Canadian icebreaker *N. B. McLean* as soon as ice was encountered but when his ship was in the vicinity of Digges Islands, at the western entrance to the Strait, according to a member of the crew, it was discovered to be taking water in Number One Hold.[1]

It was early morning of Saturday, August 3. There was an immediate stir and the pumps were put to work. But water was coming in faster than it could be pumped out and distress signals were sent to the *N. B. McLean.* As the situation became steadily more serious, the Captain ordered eighteen crewmen to leave the ship in two lifeboats while the remaining sixteen continued at their posts with the slight hope of averting a sinking.

The government ship arrived, picked up the crewmen from the lifeboats and stood by to render any other assistance as an effort was being made to save the freighter or ground it as a means of saving the cargo. By midafternoon, however, the *Kastela's* fate was clear and the Captain ordered abandonment. Hours later, at 7.30 Sunday morning, the great ship tipped like a big toy and went to the bottom in about 1,300 feet of cold water.

[1]*Winnipeg Free Press,* p. 3, Aug. 16, 1963

Members of the crew — all without injuries — returned to Churchill with the *N. B. McLean* and were then taken by air to Winnipeg, Montreal, and back to the homeland. Yugoslavian authorities may have probed for a full explanation of the sinking circumstances but with the ship at the bottom of the Strait and members of the crew in Southeastern Europe, the Canadian opportunities to study causes were slender indeed.

It was a great misfortune — like any similar sinking — but the loss of the *Kastela* created less damage to Hudson Bay Route reputation than was the case when the *Bright Fan* went down. No doubt the *Bright Fan* affair had caused ice conditions in the Strait to appear magnified and many Canadians were led to think of that area as a treacherous ice field, ever ready to swallow a ship making an imprudent move. Nobody could deny the presence of ice and ice hazards at certain seasons but by the year of the *Kastela* misadventure, more Canadians were recognizing Hudson Bay Route maturity. More than previously, they could accept an occasional accident as something which must be expected on any ocean run. The record of thirty years was showing that with proper care and good guidance, the Hudson Bay Route risks were small.

Certainly, shipping conditions in the Strait appeared in a more favorable light after the public heard about the depth and hardness of ice encountered and obstacles overcome in the Arctic channels by that massive oil tanker *Manhattan* in 1969. After the inevitable comparisons, the Hudson Bay Route had to lose much of its former terror. Members of the H.B.R. Association watched the progress of the *Manhattan* with the eagerness of shareholders.

The 1,005-foot long *Manhattan,* with a 155,000-ton displacement, was the biggest commercial ship to attempt the Northwest Passage and the first commercial ship to sail through those Arctic waters. It was not the first to attempt to go through those ice-infested channels, not by any means, and a few had succeeded. Captain Robert M'Clure, formerly of the Royal Navy, had gone through at the middle of last century but he had not been able to complete the journey by ship. He had entered the Arctic from the west in 1850, wintered at Prince of Wales Strait, and then had had his ship become so fast in the ice that he had been obliged to abandon it and complete the journey on foot.

The Norwegian explorer, Roald Amundsen, had entered from the Hudson Strait end with his good ship *Gjoa,* and after three years of minimal progress, had come into the Pacific in 1906. The next seaman to complete the Passage had been Henry Larson, in charge of the 104-foot motor schooner *St. Roch,* property of the Royal Canadian Mounted Police. The ship had left Vancouver on June 23, 1940, and after having struggled with the Arctic for two years, had reached Halifax on October 11, 1942. Nor had Larson stopped at that; on July 22, 1944, after having seen his boat fitted with a bigger motor, he had set out from the Nova Scotia port to more or less retrace his course through the North. Taking a slightly different route through the Arctic, he had completed the return trip to Vancouver in eighty-six days, to become the first skipper to have made a two-way journey over the old Passage.

There had been more records to be broken and "firsts" to be established in the North. The Canadian Navy ship *Labrador,* in 1954, had traveled from east to west via the in-shore route taken by Amundsen and after having reached the Pacific, the return to Halifax had been made through the Panama Canal, to become the first boat to completely circum-navigate the continent. United States Coast Guard cutters *Storis, Spar,* and *Bramble* had made the northern Passage in an easterly direction in 1957, and the Canadian Coast Guard ice-breaker *John A. Macdonald,* under Captain Robert Fournier, had done it from the east in 1967.

But in cost and publicity, those expeditions were completely overshadowed by the now-famous *Manhattan* project of 1969. This huge floating laboratory, property of Humble Oil and Refining Company, expressed the oil industry's curiosity in and hope for water transportation as a means of solving the problem of moving Prudhoe Bay oil. Industry leaders wondered if all-year shipping by boat was within the realm of possibility.

It was a late-summer undertaking, with the big tanker sailing from Chester, Pennsylvania, on August 24, 1969, pausing briefly at Halifax, and arriving at Point Barrow, Alaska, at the end of a 5,000-mile trip, on September 24.

As would be expected, the big ship encountered many difficulties. Again and again it was stuck in ice, requiring to be extricated by the Canadian icebreaker *John A. Macdonald*.

Prairie people who had pioneered in promoting the Hudson Bay Route were both keenly interested and hopeful. If a commercial ship could get through the extremely heavy ice in places like M'Clure Strait where the ice was said to reach as high as twelve feet in thickness, it should be a comparatively simple matter to extend shipping seasons for Churchill and Hudson Strait. Moreover, it would help the cause of Hudson Bay traffic if a politically strong group like that of the oil industry were to share a working interest in the fuller use of Hudson Strait.

Speaking at a press conference when the *Manhattan's* success in getting through seemed assured, the ship's project manager, Stanley Haas, said he was more confident than ever that the obstacles to all-year shipping through the Arctic waters could be overcome. It was exactly what those Canadians who had been pleading for a longer shipping season for Churchill wanted to hear. Here was the assurance they desired, that with the aid of technology and the support of governments, ways could be found to overcome ice in the Churchill harbor and ice in the Strait for a substantially longer shipping season.

But the *Manhattan* project brought fresh issues of concern as well as comfort. One of these involved sovereignty and Canadians were brought to wonder about the validity of their claim to those northern waters. Although there was excellent co-operation between Canada and United States in the conduct of the *Manhattan* project, it was disturbing to Canadians that the big tanker, when in what Canadians regarded as their offshore water, did not fly the Canadian flag. Traditionally, a ship would fly the flag of the country in whose waters it was sailing but the *Manhattan's* foremast did not carry the Canadian flag until reaching Sachs Harbour. The Captain, it seemed, chose to believe he was navigating in international water. Steps would have to be taken to establish firmly Canada's sovereignty over the waters concerned and supporters of the Hudson Bay Route were quick to point out that Churchill and Bay shipping was already one of Canada's best evidences of claim, another reason for its use.

It was expected that the United States representatives would challenge the Canadian claim to so much of the Arctic area as territorial water and take the matter, if necessary, to the International Court of Justice. Government Ministers in Ottawa explained that ships of all nations would be invited to use the Arctic shipping lanes for peaceful purposes but Canadian sovereignty would have to be recognized. It meant among other things that Canada would define and enforce regulations to protect the very vulnerable area against pollution, also that mineral and other resources on those Arctic Islands and in adjacent sea beds belonged entirely to Canada.

To long-time members of the Hudson Bay Route Association, the challenges and problems emerging from the *Manhattan* voyage were really old ones appearing in a new light. The many aids brought to this shipping experiment on the old Northwest Passage, could be extremely useful in extending Hudson Bay shipping. If oil could be carried from Prudhoe Bay throughout a long shipping season, wheat could probably be carried from Churchill with just a fraction of the risk and difficulty. Moreover, public interest in shipping to and from Prudhoe Bay helped to make Canadians more aware of one of their own northern shipping facilities, one still struggling to fulfill its purpose.

There was no doubt about it; what the *Manhattan* went through helped to place shipping conditions on the Hudson Bay Route in a very much more favorable light. "After a man has won in a fight with a wildcat," a Northerner observed, "an encounter with the neighbor's Collie dog is not so frightening."

A FRESH ASSESSMENT

After scores of studies and investigations, millions of words in House of Commons debates, numerous disappointments, and thirty-five years of varied experience, there were still many unanswered questions. "Why isn't traffic increasing more rapidly?" Western friends of the Route were asking, and "What is needed to make northern shipping a more viable force in the nation?"

Wheat shipments reached 21 million bushels in 1959 and were still at that level eight years later — about 5 per cent of the total annual grain exports from Canada. The shipments via the Bay had not increased fast enough, especially when there were shipping savings of some cents per bushel compared to shipping costs on similar cargo moving from Pacific and St. Lawrence ports. Why were annual exports from the Bay not reaching more closely to the 35 or 40 million bushels farmers had been led to expect? Something was holding the traffic back. How much of the trouble was due to old prejudices which refused to die? When would people stop talking about the *Bright Fan* and *Kastela* and recognize Churchill maturity and a good safety record, becoming more impressive with each passing year? Of course there had been some shipping losses but the Route should now be viewed in the light of its thirty-five-year record.

Conscious of some public impatience in the slow growth of traffic, the government of Manitoba acted in 1967 with a "Royal Commission Enquiry Into Northern Transportation," to be conducted by Commissioner Arthur V. Mauro, Q.C. The completed report was tabled in September, 1969, precisely when the much-publicized tanker *Manhattan* was inching its way through the Arctic ice fields, towards Alaska's northern coast. The report was far-reaching and one of the best summaries might have been found in a speech presented by the Commissioner to the 27th Annual Convention of the Hudson Bay Route Association held in Winnipeg in April, 1970.[1]

[1]Mauro, Arthur V., Speech delivered at 27th Annual Convention of the Hudson Bay Route Assoc., Winnipeg, April 20, 1970

Swiss, Russian and Norwegian grain freighters occupying berths at the Port of Churchill. — G. Saunders, Churchill, Man.

The Commissioner saw the struggle between the long east-west traffic axis and the more economical route to Hudson Bay as the survival of historic forces born in the years of the fur trade. Today it was more: the very problems confronting members of the Hudson Bay Route Association were the counterparts of national difficulties in gaining northern expansion and development. Canadians were slow in accepting and developing their vast North. It was not technology nor traffic which was lacking in the Canadian North, nor shortage of resources, but rather, a Canadian conviction and determination in meeting the northern challenges. It was with regret that the Commissioner saw the Hudson Bay Route up to that time functioning almost entirely for the movement of a single commodity, namely wheat. Wheat was of prime importance but the traffic should embrace more. Import and coastal shipments were of small consequence. Between 1958 and 1966, the outbound traffic from Churchill accounted for 93 per cent of the total tonnage, almost all wheat.

Stated another way, the imports via Churchill represented less than 1 per cent of the dollar value of exports, but the Commissioner saw clear indication "that with revised rail rates reflecting Churchill's distance advantage over eastern ports and extension of the shipping season, import traffic could be increased." As an example, the growth of mining in the North and the importation of heavy machinery and building materials not required on a continuous basis, could add substantially to incoming traffic.

Mauro saw total port freight handlings increasing from 710,000 tons at the time of the study to 997,000 tons by 1985 — a 40 per cent increase. But if port facilities were expanded adequately and the shipping season lengthened to twelve months per year, "the 1985 traffic moving through the port could increase by 1.9 million tons or 170 percent over current traffic volumes." Most of the increase would be in exports; wheat would, no doubt, continue to be the principal item of cargo.

The study showed the savings in forwarding costs for wheat going from Churchill to Europe to range from 5 cents per bushel over Pacific coast ports to 9.5 cents per bushel over St. Lawrence ports. These savings by themselves were substantial but the trade could include much more than wheat; there could be other grains, products from northern mines, wood pulp, potash from Saskatchewan's extensive resources, and even petroleum products. In the case of pulp and paper, the potential for export from Churchill could range from 50,000 to 100,000 tons annually. And since Western Europe took a big percentage of the copper, nickel, and zinc from Canadian mines, these materials as mineral concentrates could furnish major tonnage for the port.

The real key to traffic expansion on the Route, as the Commissioner saw it, was in lengthening the shipping season. Not only would a longer season allow more boats to load and return for second and third cargoes but it would, as the Commissioner noted, prove more acceptable to overseas buyers who, for practical reasons of storage and inventory, would not choose to buy their year's supply or a big proportion of the year's supply for delivery in a comparatively short space of eighty-two days. "The short season is unattractive to those who desire a steady source of supply throughout the year. In addition, the navigation season at Churchill coincides with the harvest season in Europe, a time when storage facilities are required for domestic crop."

During what has been regarded as the normal period of navigation, the principal physical obstacles and reasons for worry were ice and fog in Hudson Strait and high winds at Churchill. "Growth of ice in the Bay begins in early November," the Commissioner noted, "but the shipping lanes remain open until the second week of November. Ice cover grows rapidly during late November and early December with the effective coverage of winter ice over the entire Bay and Strait by the end of December. A maximum thickness of five feet is reached in May. With the exception of ice fixed to the shores, the continual movement of ice results in leads and weaknesses which can be exploited by icebreakers. Thawing and breakup begin early in May and significant areas of open water appear by the end of the month."

The report recommended extending the season from the 82 days at the time the report was written to a 107-day period between July 23 and November 7, and advised that the neces-

Proof that vessels can enter Hudson Bay well into the winter season — the icebreaker "Louis St. Laurent" three miles out from the port of Churchill on December 3, 1970. — Jim Gray.

sary steps be taken to make it practical to extend the shipping time still more, to 130 days or even, possibly, to 214 days which would embrace the seven months from May 15 to December 15. This latter period, as noted, would fit well with the winter season on the St. Lawrence, insuring opportunity for more complete utilization of strengthened ships and icebreakers on the two routes.

For many years the supporters of the Hudson Bay Route were unhappy about apparent discrepancies between length of season in which shipping seemed practical and the shorter season dictated by the underwriters of marine insurance. As Commissioner Mauro found it, July 23 was the earliest date on which a conventional, unstrengthened vessel carrying insurance could pass Cape Chidley at the eastern entrance to the Strait. And October 15 was the latest date for such ships to leave Churchill, unless an extension of up to five days was purchased at a 25 per cent surcharge. Russian ships subject to other insurance regulations had operated outside this limited shipping period without evidence of trouble, leading officials of the Hudson Bay Route Association to believe that insurance as administered had a restraining effect upon Hudson Bay trade.

Unfortunately, river ice in the harbor and Arctic ice in the Strait did not reach problem proportions at the same time. River ice, along with the strong current near the wharf at Churchill, made it difficult to maintain ships at their moorings at certain times in November and could restrict loading when the Strait was still open for traffic. The opposite was true in the spring; the breakup of the river began in June and the harbor was likely to be free of ice in the latter part of the month, several weeks before the time when the Strait was expected to be sufficiently clear for safe passage by unstrengthened ships. Thus, Mauro said, the beginning of the shipping season was determined by ice conditions in the Strait and the closing by ice in the harbor.

Ice could form and would form on the perimeter of the Bay quite early and gradually extend inward but it was not the shore ice which was likely to limit shipping. "The earliest and latest dates when Hudson Bay at Churchill was packed with ice to the horizon were October 31 and November 30," Mauro explained and added that only when it was possible to control the slush ice at the harbor would the ice in the Bay become a factor in limiting shipping seasons.

Actually, the Commissioner could see something better than fixed dates for opening and closing the shipping season. Ice conditions varied from year to year and with improvements in navigational aids, including daily broadcasts of ice conditions and suggested "shipping tracks," sailing rule could and should be flexible. When long-range forecasts — up to two months — could be made with reasonable accuracy, the opening and closing dates for shipping could be adjusted to fit the circumstances. "This procedure," the author of the Commission report wrote, "would be preferable to fixed dates which result in lost opportunities during favorable seasons and delays when conditions are unusually bad. General severity or mildness of ice conditions can be forecast six to eight weeks in advance based on recent measurements of ice thickness, air and water temperatures, etc." Unfortunately, the strength and direction of the winds "cannot be predicted with certainty more than a week in advance."

In recruiting aids for a longer shipping season, therefore, there would be need for an efficient icebreaker service for the Strait in the early part of the season and some effective means of diverting or controlling the river ice or slush ice in the autumn. If the trouble imposed by that river ice could be overcome, Commissioner Mauro concluded, the close of the shipping season could be set back by at least thirteen days and perhaps as much as twenty-eight days. And if the early-season ice problem in the Strait could be solved, the season could be extended by the thirty-five summer days in which the harbor was commonly open ahead of the Strait. If both were achieved, it would make a major difference to the length of the season and the Route's usefulness.

One of the early steps, according to the Mauro recommendations, should be the construction of a tidal barrier at the point where Churchill River entered Churchill harbor, thereby eliminating the slush ice and strong currents which blocked shipping in the autumn while the rest of the Route was still navigable. Such an improvement would be self-liquidating because it would reduce the cost of shipping and handling wheat at the port end by 3.2 cents per bushel. An alternative to such a barrier would be in the diversion of the Churchill River, giving the harbor a totally salt-water character.

Coupled with the common complaint about the approved shipping season being needlessly short was the allegation that insurance rates were too high. Commissioner Mauro noted: "In the initial stages of the operation of the Bay route, insurance rates established by Lloyds in 1931 resulted in forwarding costs for grain carried aboard the Farnworth of 14.35 cents per bushel compared to 10.15 cents via the Lakehead. The hull insurance rates were lowered the following year but the underwriters resisted all attempts to bring about an extension of the insurable season of navigation which at that point extended from August 10 to September 30. The premium for vessels fitted with gyro compass has been substantially reduced since that time but the minimum additional premium fixed in 1956 still applies applicable to vessels not over 15 years old. . . .

"In addition to hull insurance, cargo insurance rates can have an impact on the utilization of port facilities. For example, the rate per $100 of cargo to the United Kingdom from Montreal is between nine and 10 cents, the rate from Vancouver 17 to 19 cents, and from Churchill approximately 55 cents per $100 of cargo. In fact, the additional hull and cargo insurance costs on grain through Churchill represent approximately five percent of the total cost in forwarding grain from the prairies to the United Kingdom. It is my view that the insurance rates on general cargo are excessive. The higher rate on grain can be absorbed due to the lower rail charges for the movement of this commodity but these insurance rates have tended to reduce the attractiveness of the Route for other commodities. There are indications that the insurers would be receptive to extending insurance coverage to a later date provided the ice problem in the harbor were solved and up-to-date information regarding ice conditions were provided. It was the view of the Commission that the revision of insurance rates was essential if the Port's potential is to be realized. The Government of Manitoba in consultation with the Department of Transport should in our opinion make representation to the London insurers to obtain an immediate revision of existing insurance scales.''

The historic journey of the tanker *Manhattan* was a little too late for the Mauro Commission's report but the Commissioner, when facing the Hudson Bay Route Association in convention some months later, presented some pertinent observations. "The recent trips of the Manhattan," he said, "have surely convinced the most confirmed doubters that navigation is possible in our northern waters. In fact, it was our view that current technology permitted the utilization of the Port of Churchill on a year-round basis. . . . Currently, we have seen intense activity related to oil exploration on the Arctic Shelf. The resources are there — the problem now is to move the oil to markets in the southern part of the continent. The voyages of the Manhattan represent one method." After reviewing other proposals for the transportation of that Arctic oil, the speaker offered something new:

"It is my view that serious consideration should be given to the movement of oil from the Arctic by pipeline to Churchill for trans-shipment from that point by water or rail. To begin with, the pipeline construction cost would obviously be less than a similar line stretching an additional 600 miles to the U.S. Border. Secondly, excellent port facilities already exist at Churchill which would eliminate the necessity of constructing new facilities of limited use in the High Arctic. It is clear from the operation of the Manhattan that such a ship could operate into the Bay area for at least eight months out of the year and navigation and support facilities would be less than that required through the Northwest Passage."

Most pipeline proposals were made with the idea of taking the northern oil to the nearest point on the United States boundary. A pipeline to Churchill, as Mauro suggested, would have the advantage of bringing Canadian crude closer to the Montreal and Eastern market which had long depended upon imported oil. Moreover, there was the thought that the pipeline to Churchill would present the least in pollution dangers.

Inasmuch as the Commissioner's appearance before the Hudson Bay Route Association followed closely upon the *Manhattan's* penetration of the Canadian Arctic, he would feel compelled to say something about Canadian sovereignty in those Far Northern waters. Canada would have to expand its presence in those northern areas and when there was a decision to establish reconnaissance or military bases, "Churchill should receive serious consideration due to the excellent facilities that are already in place."

His role in the exhaustive investigation appeared to reinforce the Commissioner's convictions about the future importance of the Hudson Bay Route. It would be more than a shortcut to European markets; it would be a major aid in integration of the South and North of Canada. Canadians, in their first hundred years, occupied the southern perimeter of their vast land and guaranteed its independence, "but the real challenge of nationhood remains — can we occupy and conquer the vast land itself?"

TOMORROW

Members attending the 30th Annual Convention of the Hudson Bay Route Association in 1973 looked backward with mixed emotions and forward with fresh hope. They recalled the presidential address of two years before in which S. N. MacEachern confessed that "for those of us who have been associated with the Hudson Bay Route Association almost since its inception, progress at the Port of Churchill has been exceedingly slow. The use of the Port to date has fallen far short of fulfilling the hopes of those who half a century ago fought for the construction of a railway to Hudson Bay and the establishment there of an ocean port."[1]

If progress had been disappointing at times, it was not from lack of patience and determination on the part of Association officers. The Presidential leadership had been marked consistently by perseverance and dedication. Deserving to be remembered were Presidents Walter G. Streeton who served from 1945 to 1959; J. S. Woodward from 1959 to 1968; S. N. MacEachern from 1968 to 1971, and Willis A. Richford from 1971. In the same period, the office of Secretary was served by Frank Eliason from 1945 to 1956; Mrs. Irma Eliason from 1956 to 1957; and James F. Gray from 1957.

Many times these officers and others working with them wondered if the effort was worth while. Their enthusiasm, no doubt, made progress seem slower than it was in reality. Probably they underestimated their own efforts. The accumulation of pioneer experience — even though it is unspectacular — may represent progress. The record of the years was growing impressive.

A report published by the Government of Canada in 1908[2] told that in the course of the preceding century and a half, 750

---

[1]Hudson Bay Route Assoc., *Report of Annual Meeting*, June 7 and 8, 1971
[2]McKenna, J. A. J., *The Hudson Bay Route*, Gov. of Canada Printing Bureau, 1908

Tourists returning to Churchill from an excursion to Fort Prince of Wales, c. 1965. Grain terminal can be seen in background. — Saskatchewan Government Photo.

ships in the service of the Hudson's Bay Company had crossed the Atlantic and had passed through Hudson Strait with only two losses, "a marvellous record when it is remembered that all the craft were sailors and most of them small and rude in construction."

To this could be added over a thousand ocean-going vessels coming to Churchill — most of them for wheat — in the forty years, 1931 to 1971, with only a couple of sinkings. The grand total of almost 2,000 ships and an extremely small number of disasters were sufficient in themselves to demonstrate a degree of mastery over northern waters and justify a new confidence.

Admiral A. H. G. Storrs, representing the Minister of Transport at the 1971 annual meeting, could say with significance that "the last 10 years have seen more progress in our understanding of northern ice-covered water and the behavior of ships in it than has taken place in the last 1,000 years."[1] Here was progress which nobody could dispute.

The experience of the years gave reason to conclude, also, that Hudson Bay Route growth and progress were likely to continue to be slow and steady rather than spectacular. "But that's all right," an Association director observed; "we've waited a long time and we can wait some more." Time was working to the northern route's advantage. The resource wealth and the growing importance of the Canadian North were being recognized and development in that direction was assured. All forms of transportation and communication were becoming more vital. Indeed, Canadians in 1972 were hearing about an ambitious proposal for another seaport on Hudson Bay, this one to be at Chesterfield, some 400 miles north of Churchill. This Far North port with name of Northport, as envisioned by the Great Plains Group, would offer deep-water facilities, rail, air, and pipeline communications, and fresh incentives in that part of the North.

Northport would also be costly. It would become a Far Northern hub or metropolis, it was suggested, one which would "eliminate Western Canada's dependence on the St. Lawrence

[1]Hudson Bay Route Assoc., *Report of Annual Meeting*, June 7 and 8, 1971

route." In the plan it was described as a new "land bridge" between North American and European markets. Reported widely, it won much editorial approval. Even loyal friends of the Hudson Bay Route via Churchill agreed that Canada needed a northern hub and an alternative to the St. Lawrence. It was encouraging to see added interest in northern communication. But didn't Canada already have water, rail and air facilities at Churchill, acquired at a fairly high investment cost? Rejecting a suggestion that "Churchill would never be much more than what it is now," supporters of the pioneer Hudson Bay Route Association insisted that Churchill could, at a fraction of the cost, be expanded to meet the new needs. Churchill could receive a trainload of wheat per day — as it did in 1971 — and load out a total of more than 25,000,000 bushels on forty ships in a season of eighty-eight days. As shown in the same year, ships could and would load for many parts of the world, including India and Iraq. And by keeping the Churchill harbor open for a longer spell in the autumn, improving the icebreaker service in the Strait in the spring, and effecting certain improvements at the port, the Churchill traffic and service could be doubled. Members of the Association knew what was needed. As they saw the situation in 1972, the harbor should be deepened near the wharf; grain loading galleries should be lengthened to accommodate the longer ships; grain storage should be increased to 20,000,000 bushels, and there should be a concerted drive for more traffic, both import and export. The long-standing demand for a longer shipping season and more moderate marine insurance was not being relaxed and to the list of requests supporters had added that of an all-weather highway to Churchill. Certainly, public funds would be required but what representatives of the Hudson Bay Route Association were trying to impress upon governments was that an expenditure for improved facilities on the Churchill connection with overseas market points would pay surer and bigger dividends than any similar sum spent on a new terminal on the Bay. "Let's have one efficient and flourishing port on the Bay before we try for two."

In saying that Churchill would never be "much more than it is now," the promoters of another port on the Bay were giving members of the old Association some new incentive and a clearer purpose. Faith was something in which the Association people were rich but they knew that the Churchill capacity for versatility would have to be demonstrated more clearly for public benefit. Too many Canadians were thinking of Churchill in terms of wheat alone, and on the port record they were almost right. For two centuries the only export goods passing through the Bay had been furs. Then wheat became the export commodity — practically the only one — and the loadings reached a peak at 25,914,854 bushels taken in thirty-seven ships in 1971. But it had to be admitted that imports were still embarrassingly low. Only two of the incoming vessels in that year of record wheat exports carried cargo. If the ships coming for wheat had an average capacity of 20,000 tons, it meant that over a million tons of shipping capacity went unused and wasted. The imports might have been very much greater. Considering one import product in particular, liquor, two Midwestern provincial governments brought in a total of 27,000 cases, but this amount represented only about 4 per cent of the amount imported by the three Midwestern Provinces.

With improved shipping, both import and export roles were likely to change. It seemed likely that even the export of wheat would take a different shape. More students of Northern affairs were sensing a new shuttle service between the ports of Churchill and Halifax to insure supplies of Western grains at an all-year position for ocean-going vessels. It was shown that wheat could be shipped from Churchill to Halifax at five cents a bushel less than if it were forwarded over the St. Lawrence route.

And Churchill was already developing something more than wheat, a growing role in coastal shipping, mainly for the benefit of the far-flung communities on the northern islands and mainland coast. Those remote points could be serviced by water transport from Montreal or from Edmonton via the Mackenzie River route but many of them seemed to be logically within the Churchill orbit for reasons of distance. Rankin Inlet, for example, was shown to be 2,371 water miles from Montreal and 260 from Churchill; the difference spoke for itself. Chesterfield Inlet was 2,331 miles from Montreal and just a fraction of that distance from Churchill, placing the latter in a favored position for service. In the ten-year period, 1962 to 1971, inclusive, an average of thirty-five coastal ships called annually at Churchill and took on cargo. Averaging 900 tons, these coastal ships were also considerably bigger than those in service during the previous decade.

In a developing and changing North, the broadened and more diversified use of the seaport was inevitable. There could be the various products from northern mines to be moved, the wood and wood products from forested areas, the harvests from north country agriculture, the transportation of tourists, and as the investigations of very recent years suggested, the possibility of heavy traffic occasioned by oil and gas discoveries in offshore locations in Hudson Bay. A $20,000,000 oil and gas exploration program was expected to begin in 1973 and contentious questions about who owned the offshore minerals, federal or provincial governments, would be answered later.

Nobody argued that Churchill had all the port advantages or even most of them. It had some natural handicaps, to be sure, just as the West itself had handicaps in the years of settlement. But Churchill and the Hudson Bay Route on which it was situated like a linchpin had a few enduring advantages for the sake of which a price in small handicaps should not seem too high. One of the unchanging advantages was in distances. Montreal and Churchill remained about the same distance from United Kingdom ports. And Churchill was still within a thousand miles of many prairie loading points which were 2,000 miles from Montreal. The huge potential savings offered by shorter shipping distances should be easy to recognize and easy to translate into dollars. In its brief to the Marine Underwriters visiting Churchill in 1972, the Hudson Bay Route Association spokesmen placed the saving at 15 cents a bushel for wheat and said: "The Hudson Bay Route eliminates the Great Lakes-St. Lawrence movement for grain completely, saving about 15 cents a bushel, and so Churchill use should mean a substantial extra return through the Wheat Board to producers in all three western provinces and an incentive price to the buyers which should mean increased sales."[1]

[1] Hudson Bay Route Association, *Submission to Marine Underwriters visiting Churchill, 1972*

There was yet that other need if the dreams of the pioneers were to be fulfilled. There was nothing startlingly new about it. It was simply the need for an all-Canadian determination to embrace the North and support it with enthusiasm and the tangibles like rail and other communications. Commissioner Arthur V. Mauro, whose report on Northern Communication appeared in 1969, expressed it well: "It is in my opinion not technology nor traffic that is lacking in the North now, nor the shortage of resources both human and natural. On the contrary, what is lacking is commitment by the political leaders and the nation to meet the northern challenge, as we did in the West."

APPENDIX I

Speaking at Niagara Falls, Ontario, on September 18, 1908, Prime Minister Sir Wilfrid Laurier made the first public promise that the Government of Canada would build the Hudson Bay Railway, making it in these words:

"We have undertaken the construction of another railway, the Hudson Bay Railway. The Hudson Bay Railway, I am sure, does not appeal very much to the people of Welland county. It concerns more the people of the West. But I say to you, gentlemen of Ontario, and you will agree with me, that what concerns one part of the community concerns every part of the community. Now, we have come to the conclusion that this railway is a necessity, owing to the conditions in which our fellow-citizens of the West are placed. This railway will give an alternative or optional route. At the present time all the wheat, as soon as it is tracked, is sent out to Lake Superior. We want to provide another railway by Hudson Bay. There will then be the present route and the Hudson Bay route and the man who raises wheat and cattle will have two outlets for his production. We have been asked: 'Are you not going to hurt the trade of the St. Lawrence, if you do that?' Oh, ye of little faith! the trade of Canada is too great even for these two outlets. What we see coming will be more than sufficient for both the St. Lawrence and the Hudson Bay routes. We have come to the conclusion that the time to build this railway is now; not tomorrow, but now; and we have surveyors in the field looking at the conditions of the country and preparing plans for us, which we shall be prepared to put into execution as soon as we receive them. The Government will build the railway, or rather, somebody will be entrusted with building it for us, but whatever we do, all the terminals and all the elevators shall be built by the Government, and retained under all and every circumstance by the Government so as to ensure the largest measure of benefit possible to the Canadian people in the Northwest provinces."

APPENDIX 2

Extract from REPORT OF THE HUDSON'S BAY RAIL-WAY SURVEYS by John Armstrong, Chief Engineer, Hudson Bay Railway Surveys, September 8, 1909 (Sessional Papers No. 20d, 1910).

PORT CHURCHILL

General Description

Port Churchill is at the mouth of the Churchill river where the river passes through a large tidal flat or lagoon mostly dry at low tide except near the outlet to the sea. The lagoon is surrounded by hills consisting of rock at the sea outlet and of sand and gravel further up the river. The only available situation for docks at present is out near Cape Merry, with the railway terminals from two to three miles up stream, and the townsite from three to five miles up stream. Another townsite is available on the west side, but it would be somewhat difficult to get railway and dock sites.

There is no possibility of improving the Churchill river so as to give inland communication by water owing to its shallowness over its many and frequent rapids. The neighborhood of Port Churchill is practically destitute of all forest growth for miles in all directions, the vegetation being restricted to mosses and patches of coarse grasses along the edges of the water areas.

The main fresh water supply is obtained from the numerous small lakes in the neighborhood and is of excellent quality. The tidal flats are thickly strewn with boulders, some so large as to be visible above high water.

Tides and Currents

The main current in the harbour is along the indicated channel of the Churchill river, being approximately down the centre of the lagoon, but striking more against the eastern side towards the harbour mouth. With the ebb tide the current attains a velocity of from six to eight miles, creating a somewhat difficult entrance for low-powered ships. The local pilots prefer to bring in their ships with the incoming tides.

It is quite useless for anything but a steam vessel to attempt the entrance at any other time. The current with the incoming tide is much less, probably not exceeding 4 miles per hour. The highest tide observed was 13½ feet, and the lowest 8 feet, both probably being subject to modification with a longer series of observations. The water is always more or less salt near the entrance. At low tide fresh water may be obtained in the Churchill channel opposite the Hudson Bay Company's post; when the tide is in this cannot be done.

Ice Conditions

The harbour usually freezes over about November 15. The open sea also freezes over during the winter four or five miles out from Churchill. The usual date for the opening of the harbour is about June 19. This last spring the harbour opened on June 7, or about 10 days earlier than usual. The ice lay off the coast and harbour this year, preventing the return of the survey party until July 13, when a start was made for York.

Five days more were lost by the sea pack off Cape Churchill extending about 30 miles out to sea, the best crew declining to venture outside of this. The boat in use was only a small sailing coast boat not well adapted to ice work. Probably no serious difficulty would have been experienced by a steamer making Churchill within a few days of the opening up of the harbour on June 7. At intervals between June 7 and July 13, ice would be drifted back into the harbour by north winds. This ice floating up and down the harbour on the strong currents existing there constitutes a serious inconvenience and danger to ships at anchor and to docks and other works which may be constructed along the shore. The harbour has been reported on occasions to have been blocked by ice as late as August owing to long continued north winds. This liability of the harbour to being filled with loose heavy ice drifting up and down with the strong currents will need to be seriously considered in choosing the type of docks to be built here. As shown on the chart, the direction of the currents tends to throw the drifting ice against the east shore, the only available place for docks at the present time. The ice, however, does not jam here very much but is swept on out by the strong current. Jams more frequently occur on the west side between the police barracks and Cockrill's Point.

Anchorage

At the present time very little shelter can be had at low tide by any ship drawing over 18 or 20 feet of water. Space to accommodate two or three ships of this size might be had, but anything larger would have to anchor almost in front of the entrance, which being about three-quarters of a mile allows the full force of the seas to be felt. The seas enter the harbour with sufficient force to cause a heavy swell to be felt throughout the harbour; in fact it is reported that at times it is impossible for the smaller boats to cross the harbour for two or three days at a time. The bottom, consisting of mud, affords a fairly good holding ground for anchors.

Material

The material forming the harbour bottom is mud, thickly strewn with boulders of all sizes, and is probably a deposit from the Churchill river. Excavating for ships berths close inshore to avoid the heavy drift ice will probably encounter solid rock as the solid rock in several places runs to the water edge.

Materials For Construction

Stones for construction purposes are very plentiful. Marble if you like to use it. All timber will have to be brought in either by rail or ship.

Defence

Fort Churchill being practically upon the open sea can only be defended by strong forts and batteries placed in the immediate neighborhood of the port itself.

PORT NELSON

General Description

Port Nelson is at the mouth of the Nelson river, while York Factory is situated at the mouth of the Hayes river, about 15 or 18 miles from Port Nelson. The site at the mouth of the Hayes was chosen by the Hudson Bay Company on account of the better communication with a greater number of inland posts, and also being a much smaller stream was· not so difficult to navigate.

A great deal of tracking had to be done on both rivers, and the Hayes being much smaller, offered less trouble in crossing and re-crossing to take advantage of paths to tow from. The Nelson river is known locally as the North river, and Port Nelson is named by the British Admiralty as York Roads. Hudson Bay vessels crossing to York Factory with supplies anchor about 15 or 20 miles from the post in York Roads. The site of York Factory was not chosen on account of its accessibility from the sea, but entirely on account of the easier communication with inland posts. The Nelson river proper may be said to end at Flamboro Head, which is the approximate limit to which the tide reaches. The estuary is a wide tidal flat with the main channel running approximately down the centre, finally discharging into an open sea abreast of Beacon Point, some 25 miles from Flamboro Head. At Flamboro Head the banks rise shear from the water edge to a height of 100 to 125 feet. From this point they gradually diminish in height on both sides of the river, until at Sam's Creek on the north, and Beacon Point on the south, they are about 10 feet above the water. The north shore is of clay with a sufficient fall for drainage, and covered with a fair growth of spruce.

A good site for terminals and town may be had in the vicinity of the point marked on the chart. About this point the banks become higher and much more abrupt.

The south shore is also of clay with a good slope for drainage, but at the present time is covered with heavy growth of moss, rendering it very wet. An abundant supply of fresh water may be had either from the Nelson river itself or from various smaller streams and lakes in the vicinity.

Tides and Currents

The main current when the tide is ebbing is along the main channel, the current over the flats running approximately parallel to it. As the water lowers the currents over the flats converge more and more upon the main current till at low tide they are approximately at right angles to, and approaching it. At the ebb tide, the current flows at the rate of about 3½ miles per hour, being strongest at the mouth abreast of Beacon Point. Under favorable conditions the current here might rise as high as 4 miles per hour. So great is the discharge of the Nelson river that a perceptible current may be noticed several miles out to sea. With the incoming tide a current of about 2½ miles is obtained.

During the observations, extending from March 20 to June 10, the lowest tide observed was 6.9 feet and the highest 10.9. A longer series of observations will probably establish greater extremes.

The Admiralty charts give ordinary spring tides as ranging from 10 to 14 feet. It is probable, however, that any rise greater than 12 feet may be classed as an occurance [sic] out of the ordinary, and due probably to some particular combination of wind and tides. The tides were found to be very variable, due no doubt, to the comparative shallowness of the water. This will require a long series of observations before accurate tables can be prepared. This condition is not peculiar to Port Nelson, but applies generally to the tides in Hudson bay.

Salt water is never found above Beacon Point except when a very strong easterly gale is blowing with the incoming tide, when a slight brackish taste may be detected two or three miles above Beacon Point. When the tide is ebbing fresh water is obtained far out to sea. Salt water is never obtained within many miles of the point selected for the terminals.

Ice Conditions

About the 20th of December the river is usually frozen over at Seal Island or Flamboro Head. From this time on the ice gradually creeps down the estuary and out from the shore line until the first half of the month of April. About this date the weather moderated to such an extent that the thawing through the day counterbalanced the freezing at night and the ice began to recede towards Flamboro Head, the estuary being usually again clear of ice by May 15. The ice is broken up into large floes by the rising tide, and is borne off out to sea by the ebb tide. Owing to the appreciable current of the Nelson river being felt far out to sea very little of this ice ever drifts back again. Between May 15 and June 1, the upper Nelson ice breaks up and passes down the centre of the estuary in the main channel, usually occupying from 24 to 36 hours in passing out to sea. During last winter no ice jams occurred inside a line drawn from Beacon Point to Sam's creek and a careful scrutiny of the shore line after the snow and ice had disappeared failed to find any trace of its ever doing so.

During the freeze up in the fall, a considerable quantity of slush ice comes down from the upper Nelson.

Last winter at Seal Island and along the shore the ice attained a thickness of between 4½ and 5 feet. The average thickness at York Factory, where a record has been kept for many years, seems to be about 4 ft. 8 inches. During the winter more or less ice floats up and down the open channel with the tides, but being very scattered no jams ever occur.

Anchorage

The anchorage being some 9 or 10 miles in from the mouth of the channel no serious sea is ever experienced which may cause trouble to anything larger than canoes or row boats. The condition of the seas at Port Nelson will probably be found to resemble those experienced at Quebec on the St. Lawrence. The bottom is of sufficient stiffness to furnish a secure holding ground for anchors.

Material

The material in the flats consists of blue clay with an occasional pocket of coarse sand and gravel with boulders scattered thinly around. In the channel the material is a very stiff blue clay, affording excellent holding ground for anchors. Probably all of the material can be handled by dredges at a very low cost and may be used for reclamation works around the docks. The bottom of the channel is swept clean and bare by the current of the Nelson, and is of so stiff a nature that the small anchor used by the Survey, probably weighing about 200 lbs. would frequently drag for some distance before taking hold. The material on the flats is not so hard on top, but becomes harder as depth is obtained.

Material For Construction

Stone for the construction of breakwaters and other works may be cheaply obtained. About 75,000 or 100,000 cubic yards may be picked up along the tidal flats in the shape of scattered boulders. Up the Nelson river, about 40 miles from Flamboro Head is a splendid quarry where any required quantity can be had, and landed cheaply at the works by means of the Nelson river.

Piles in large quantities will be obtainable from various streams entering Nelson river and Hudson bay. Cement and other materials, being brought in by water, should be comparatively cheap.

Defence

The defence of Nelson from hostile fleets will be comparatively easy, the long comparatively narrow channel approach being easily rendered impregnable by means of sea mines, and rendered otherwise dangerous by removal or changing of buoys and other channel marks. Battleships which carry the extreme long range guns are of such a draft as to render it somewhat dangerous to manoeuvre in less than 45 feet of water, thus preventing their closer approach than 15 or 18 miles, a distance considerably greater than the effective range of even the heaviest guns. The lighter ships which might approach closer carry correspondingly lighter guns. The establishment of strong batteries and forts at Sam's creek would seem to be all that is necessary to render Port Nelson absolutely unassailable.

It might be mentioned here in passing, the greatly increased difficulty a hostile fleet would have on blockading the Atlantic coast of Canada were the Hudson bay route opened. The fact that ships may enter and leave Port Nelson all the year round is a fact worth remembering when the possibilities of war are considered.

(Sgd.) John Armstrong,
Chief Engineer Hudson Bay Railway Surveys.
Winnipeg, Sept. 8, 1909.

APPENDIX 3

Grain Shipments from the Port of Churchill
1931-1972

Year	No. of Ships Taking Grain	Bushels Shipped
1931	2	545,000
1932	10	2,736,000
1933	10	2,708,000
1934	15	4,054,000
1935	8	2,407,000
1936	15	4,294,000
1937	2	604,000
1938	3	917,000
1939	6	1,772,000
1940	War Years	—
1941	'' ''	—
1942	'' ''	—
1943	'' ''	—
1944	'' ''	—
1945	'' ''	—
1946	9	2,929,000
1947	16	4,976,000
1948	15	5,314,000
1949	16	5,528,000
1950	20	6,768,000
1951	21	7,278,443
1952	26	8,585,000
1953	31	10,784,000
1954	36	12,485,000
1955	38	13,078,000
1956	48	16,250,000
1957	46	16,565,000
1958	55	19,598,749
1959	58	21,787,126
1960	48	19,582,490
1961	48	19,351,021
1962	49	21,525,205
1963	48	22,864,411
1964	41	21,644,774
1965	45	24,707,016
1966	40	21,817,320
1967	33	20,639,119

1968..........................	34	22,516,493
1969..........................	28	21,872,957
1970..........................	35	24,613,656
1971..........................	37	25,488,866
1972..........................	31	25,272,046

APPENDIX 4

Mileage Favors Churchill

Distances from Selected Western Canadian Points to Churchill & Montreal

From	To		
	Churchill (all rail)	Montreal (all rail)	Montreal (Great Lakes Route)
Regina	843 miles	1,713 miles	1,990 miles
Saskatoon..................	814	1,828	2,105
Prince Albert	760	1,871	2,148
Moose Jaw	885	1,756	2,032
Winnipeg...................	977	1,357	1,633
Brandon	937	1,492	1,767
Calgary.....................	1,214	2,220	2,497
Edmonton..................	1,137	2,147	2,424

Distances from Canadian Ports to Liverpool

Churchill..	2,936 miles
Montreal — via Belle Isle Strait.......................	2,760
— via Cabot Strait............................	3,007
Halifax...	2,490
Saint John, N.B..	2,756
Vancouver...	8,547

Distances from Selected Western Points to Liverpool

	Via Great Lakes & Montreal	Via Churchill & Hudson Bay	Mileage Saving in Favor of Churchill
Regina	4,750 miles	3,770 miles	980 miles
Saskatoon	4,878	3,750	1,128
Prince Albert	4,911	3,696	1,215
Winnipeg	4,393	3,913	480
Brandon	4,527	3,873	654
Calgary	5,226	4,182	1,044
Edmonton	5,224	4,082	1,142

INDEX

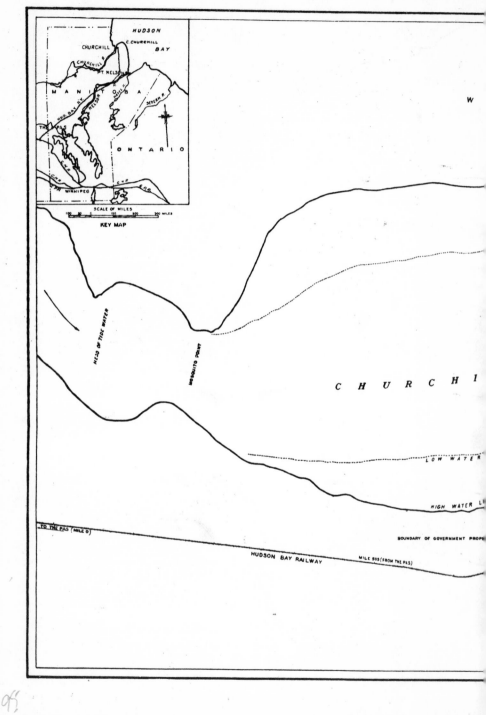

KEY MAP